MY CITY, MY NEW YORK

Famous New Yorkers Share Their Favorite Places

Jeryl Brunner

gpp®

Guilford, Connecticut

Editor: Amy Lyons
Project Editor: Kristen Mellitt
Cover Design: Bret Kerr
Text Design: Lisa Reneson, Two Sisters Design

Library of Congress Cataloging-in-Publication Data is available on file.

ISBN 978-0-7627-7139-4

Printed in the United States of America

10 9 8 7 6

In celebration of my mother, Elinor Sara Drachman Helfman, who taught me the joy of possessing both passion and compassion and so much more

And when [she] shall die
cut [her] out in little stars,
And [she] will make the face of heaven so fine
That all the world will be in love with night
And pay no worship to the garish sun.

—William Shakespeare

* I have books on all the great New York skyscrapers, and I like to take my kids to see all of them. There has never been anything like New York on the face of planet Earth. They can say what they want about ancient Rome, but it wasn't like this.

Wynton Marsalis
Pulitzer Prize- and Grammy-winning composer and musician

CONTENTS

Gloria Steinem • John Cameron Mitchell • Philip Seymour Hoffman • Evan Handler • Brad Farmerie • Tamara Tunie • Chris Boneau • J. Robert Spencer • Anthony Mackie • Tom Otterness • Rick Guidotti • Luanne Rice • Hoji Fortuna • Bill Pullman • Daniel Radcliffe • Charles Busch • George Whipple • Rick Newman

Jessica Lange • Francesco Antonucci • Tina Fey • Bill Ritter • Kevin McKenzie • Meredith Vieira • Deborah Koenigsberger • Barbara Corcoran • Jonathan Groff • Al Roker • Charlotte St. Martin • Geoffrey Nauffts • Dayle Reyfel • Glenn Close • Donna Murphy • Julie Alexandria • Rob Thomas • Daniel Humm • Kelli O'Hara • Padma Lakshmi • Jay Jay French • Alex Rodriguez • Liev Schreiber • Kerry Butler • Tony Roberts • Bob Balaban • Bette Midler • Hugh Jackman • Douglas Blonsky • Liza Minnelli • Shane Krige • Susan Stroman • Michael McKean • Aaron Tveit • Calvin Wiley • Gretchen Rubin • Judy Gold • Kelly Ripa

New York Eats **45**

Vera Wang • Anthony Bourdain • Mario Batali • Paul Haggis • Julianna Margulies • Harvey Wang • James Caan • Andrew Goldberg • Jessica Hecht • Anthony Malkin • Salman Rushdie • Gayle King • Parker Posey • Hal Rubenstein • Nanette Lepore • Steve Lance • Liz Smith • Heiko Kuenstle • Pam Nelson • Chaske Spencer • Maria Sharapova • Chris Noth • Blanche Baker • Marlo Thomas • Gretchen Mol • Raquel Bruno • Kristen Schaal • Chazz Palminteri • James Oseland • Scott Bond • Terence Winter • Janet Carroll • Karen Schaler • Kevin Spacey • Josh Fox • Tom McCarthy • Kyle MacLachlan • Cady Huffman • Bruce Morrow • Fred Armisen • Ruth Reichl • Cat Greenleaf • Elisabeth Moss • Rachel Dratch • Kelly Cutrone • Molly Shannon • Michael Stern • Sherri Shepherd • Katrina Bowden • John Legend • Christine Teigen • Mario Cantone • Jason Sudeikis • Mayor Michael Bloomberg • Amar'e Stoudemire • Harry Shum Jr. • Will Ferrell • Arianna Huffington • Bethenny Frankel • A.J. Calloway • Paul Dano • Zoe Kazan • Brooke Lyons • Nina Garcia • Robert Lopez • Henrik Lundqvist • Eddie Kaye Thomas • Mike Birbiglia • Petra Nemcova • Russell Jantzen • Jon Stewart • Megan Sikora • Nick Adams • Sutton Foster • Karen Olivo • Rick Newman • Hannah Yelland • Joy Behar • Bonnie Hammer • Jeanne Adlon • Jonathan Cheban • Marci Klein • Kelsey Grammer • Joe "Joey Pants" Pantoliano • Jean-Georges Vongerichten • Edward Norton

Nocturnal New York **101**

Sarah Jessica Parker • Woody Allen • David O. Russell • Joan Rivers • Will Shortz • Jason Sudeikis • Will Forte • Derek Cianfrance • Janet Carroll • Patrick McMullan • Lee Zalben • Matthew Settle • Bill Ayers • Amy Sacco • Les Marshak • David Wright • James Braly • Elizabeth Berkley • Zach Braff • Kate Shindle • Jim Caruso • Muriel "Mickie" Siebert • Michael Urie • Colin Donnell • Ken Davenport • Kathleen Marshall • Danny "Kootch" Kortchmar • Ron Delsener • Paul Shaffer

Superstar Structures, Sexy Spaces, Beatific Bridges & Arty Pockets 185

Keanu Reeves • Kenneth Cole • Peg Breen • Judy Collins • Douglas Carter Beane • Soledad O'Brien • Sidney Offit • Anthony Malkin • Rudy Tauscher • Dennis O'Hare • David Ippolito • Mehmet C. Oz, MD (Dr. Oz) • Brad Anderson • Fisher Stevens • Bryan Bantry • Richard Kirshenbaum • Spike Lee • Neal Shapiro • David Cross • Keith Olbermann • Angelo Vivolo • Paul Gunther • Malcolm Gets • John Patrick Shanley • Sir Clive Gillinson • David Hyde Pierce • John Leguizamo • Tom Seaver • Nancy Novogrod • Dick Cavett • Jon Robin Baitz • Jay Jay French • Maguy Le Coze • Lidia Bastianich • Joanne LaMarca Mathisen • Elise Finch • Ana Gasteyer • Lillias White • Cynthia Rowley • Yigal Azrouël • Amy E. Goodman • Alex Von Bidder • Sarah Jones • Karen Mason • Jenny Lumet • Stone Phillips • Sally Jessy Raphael • Justin Gimelstob • Debi Mazar • Lainie Munro • David Parsons • J. Elaine Marcos • Juliette Jeffers • Joy Behar • Michael Moore • Jane Stern • Michael Urie

ACKNOWLEDGMENTS

I love Edith Wharton's quote, "There are two ways of spreading light: to be the candle or the mirror that reflects it." And when I think of all the people who guided, inspired, and supported me on this journey, I imagine a hall of mirrors of Versailles-sized proportions. (Actually, make that several halls!)

Countless thanks to Wendy Morris, Rick Newman, Cindy Helfman, Nick Steele, Tammy Peters, Holly Cara Price, F-stop Fitzgerald, Cynthia Parsons McDaniel, Louis Pearlman, CarolLee Kidd, Louisa Ermelino, Greta Peters, Nancy Marshak, Aik Wye Ng, Simon Halls, Julie Safer, Alex Dubee, Rima Suqi, Carol VanderKloot, Paula Conway, Jill Heymann, Helene Crystal, Lee Alexander, Heidi Christenson, Jennifer Niederhoffer, and Bryan Bantry—aka rock stars!

To my patient editors over the years who were my teachers and comprise one of the coolest virtual J-schools around: Alison Gwinn, Jason Oliver Nixon, Ariel Foxman, Lisa Arbetter, Rich Beattie, Robin Sayers, Eleni Gage, David "Hutch" Hutchings, Susan Breslow, Barbara Stepko, Stephanie Tuck, Debra Michals, Patti Adcroft, Lisa Gabor, Donna Bulseco, Laura Manske, Hilary Sterne, Rob Medich, Dawn Baskerville, Martha Nelson, and Tim Allis.

Special thanks to Susan O'Keefe, my dynamite *National Geographic Traveler* editor, who inspired this book and challenges me to be a better wordsmith.

To Rick Guidotti, a Picasso with a camera. I am convinced that the dazzle in his photos begins with him.

To my fiercely fantastic friends who simply make the world a better place: Ilene Angel, Abbie Kozolchyk, Wendy Paris, Lainie Munro, Elaine Gilbert, Heather Gary, Lisa Gilbar, Shandana Durrani, Alyssa Morganlander Reiss, Christy Walker, Julie Besonen, and Kathleen Beckett.

To Karen Jones for your compassion, genius book publishing 101 guidance, and the constant reminder to stay the course.

Merci mille fois to my Belgian family, who helped ignite my extreme wanderlust and joy for travel: Simon, Anne Marie and Pascale Paradowski, Philippe and Simon Dauvister, and Loïc Evrard.

To Eugene Pack and Dayle Reyfel for finding the right words to lift my spirits, for your unwavering belief in me, and for laughing at my jokes.

To Jodie and Bruce Morrow who seem to live their lives as if everything is a miracle and with so much love, inspire me to discover my own miracles.

To Tina "Sparkle" Reine for her divine wisdom, giant loving heart, curious nature, brilliant cheerleading finesse, and for always seeing my sparkle.

To the Zuckerbergs—Barbara, Lloyd, Charlotte, Hillary, and Roy for embracing me like family. Hillary, Lloyd, and Barbara, I will never forget how you reached out to so many people on my behalf. Where would I be without you?

A gargantuan, super-sized thank you to Dina Zuckerberg for her intrepid passion, fearlessness, colossal caring, beautiful friendship, endless pep talks, and truly mind-blowing commitment to this book. You are a superstar!

To the extraordinary and magnificently insightful Nancy Winston who saw all the possibilities in my "Jeryl-ness," long before I ever could and in her immutable way, uncovered my wings to fly.

To my uncompromisingly stupendous agent, Jessica Regel, who never gave up on me and to Tara Hart and the Jean V. Naggar Literary Agency. And to the amazingly talented wonderful Karen Schaler who, with such astounding generosity, led me to them!

To my fabulous and stellar editor, Amy Lyons, who saw magic in *My City, My New York*, nurtured it with such care, loves it as much as I, and is such a treasure! And to Kristen Mellitt, John Spalding, Bret Kerr, and the entire intrepid and seriously cool staff at Globe Pequot.

To my loving, caring, and phenomenal sister, Bonnie Brodner (I'm always happy to play Robin to your Batman), her terrific wife, Sherry Brodner, my father, Charles Brunner (who, early on, helped inspire my love for New York City), and my awesome nephews, Curt Brodner and Eli Brodner. And to my extended family and their loved ones.

To the many people who generously shared their stories, passion, and love for New York City. What a gift to feature you in this book!

I owe you all a tremendous debt and am astonished by your generosity.

I can only dance in your light.

INTRODUCTION

Most New Yorkers have rituals that connect them to their city in unique and personal ways. Matthew Broderick loves riding his bike along a majestic path beside the Hudson River to upper Manhattan, making stops along the way. John Legend does brunch at Frank Restaurant and has to order the baked eggs ragu. "The best tastes in one dish," says the musician, "parmesan cheese, eggs, tomato sauce, and meatballs." For director Nora Ephron, it's buying seriously discounted knock-your-socks-off roses in rainbows of color at the wholesale flower district at 6 a.m. A trip to Gino's Pastry Shop in the Bronx for perfect cannolis is Chazz Palminteri's idea of paradise. These activities are as diverse and eclectic as the city itself. Just thinking about them is exciting and satisfying, like visiting an old friend or reading a favorite sentence from a cherished book.

So what's my New York fix? It was inspired by the day my mother "kidnapped" my sister.

Well, sort of.

It was the kind of October day that was a holdover from an endless summer in September. The sky was that perfect powdery shade of bright blue. The sun glowed a bright golden hue. It was the kind of day that spoke to my mother so clearly: go outside. Nature was her salvation. And there was no better salve than a very long, long walk.

The day held promise for my mother, but she was not supposed to be outside. On this day, she was admitted to Memorial Sloan-Kettering Cancer Center to begin treatment for a bone marrow transplant. After many months, she finally got clearance for the procedure. And should it take, she had a 50 percent chance of survival. Without the transplant, doctors said there was no hope.

But her cure was punishing. It first involved several days of high-octane super-charged chemotherapy that would completely ravage my mother's immune system and destroy the cancer cells. Then my mother needed to embrace an unknown donor's cancer-free bone marrow as her own.

That meant that for about six weeks, she would be quarantined to a completely sterile tiny bubble of a hospital bunker and tethered to a dizzying number of tubes. She was to have no tactile human contact. Everything that touched her would have to be sterilized. And perhaps most unthinkable, she was to be completely divorced from outside air. It was verboten in any form, even through an open window.

Forms and more forms were signed. The chemo was to begin early the next morning and my mother was taken to her room. Bags were unpacked and when she was just about settled in, she told my sister and stepfather that she needed to go outside and get some air one last time before the transplant.

She bolted to the elevator, zipped out of the lobby, and was outside the main entrance—my sister and stepfather trailing behind. "Where should we go?" asked my sister. "Around the block? Across the street? To the East River?" My mother surveyed York Avenue and suddenly her hand shot up. The woman was hailing a cab. Despite my sister and stepfather's protests, she jumped into a taxi and advised that she was going—with or without them. "Central Park please," she told the driver. "Fifty-ninth Street and 5th Avenue."

In medical terms, my mother was neutropenic—her blood count so low that it was miraculous that she had the strength to walk. Yet she strode into the park at a strong, respectable clip in utter bliss. They walked north through the zoo, under the elaborate Delacorte Music Clock and along winding passageways amid valleys of green and red blooming trees and purply foliage. They lingered at the boat pond, visited the Alice in Wonderland statue, and marveled at the cathedral of elm trees lining the Mall.

My mother, in a most tranquil, blissful, beaming state, took it all in. She grew more agile and more energetic with each step—inhaling everything in her wake. The hospital, the chemo, the transplant all but disappeared. My mother was in Central Park on a magical fall day and that's all that mattered. The park was a gift and she felt so joyful to be alive and experience it all.

Everyone returned to the hospital renewed. My mother survived the debilitating chemo, transplant, and the quarantine. And that following May when she was regaining her strength my mother, my sister, her wife, and I were in Central Park to celebrate. It was Mother's Day and my birthday. We sat on the grassy slope overlooking the glassy boat pond eating sandwiches, watching wobbling toddlers on blankets. My mother's hair had returned. She was beatific, grinning like a Cheshire cat. My sister-in-law was newly pregnant. There was so much beauty and hope all around us in Central Park.

Although the transplant gave my mother more than an extra year of life, sadly, that was to be her last Mother's Day. She passed away that following December. But nearly every Mother's Day, I follow my mother's route. I walk through Central Park and linger at the boat pond—watching parents and children maneuver their model sailboats along the water. When it's windy, the milky white sails seem to ice skate along the pond. I add to her jaunt by walking north along the East Drive, stopping to peek into the giant windows of the Metropolitan Museum of Art and meditate on the sun-filled sculpture court. I cross the ornamental cast-iron bridge and stroll around the Reservoir and make sure to idle at the 90th Street entrance by 5th Avenue where the skyline seems to gracefully bolt and dance into the clouds.

As I retrace my mother's footsteps, I feel more of a peaceful gratitude than sadness. And I give thanks to my beloved park—the park that rescued my mother.

SECRET GARDENS
& HIDDEN SPACES

 In New York, you don't have to drive a hundred miles to see different people. You can go 2 blocks, and there's a whole new neighborhood, a whole new group of people, and that's the joy of it. I remember when I first came to the city from the Midwest—I was petrified. Everybody was rushing around, and they all seemed to know where they were going except me. I was intrigued and frightened, but it was clear to me that I definitely wanted to live here. It was this huge village that was intimate and friendly. New Yorkers are fast, and maybe that's mistaken for rudeness. But unlike what people say, they're really friendly and smart and funny and authentic and I can't imagine living anyplace else.

Gloria Steinem, journalist, author, and activist

Liz Christy was a painter and passionate gardening activist who lived in the East Village. It was 1973, a time when the city was filled with garbage-strewn abandoned lots. But when Christy walked past the junk-filled spaces, she saw potential for magic. She and her friends, who dubbed themselves the Green Guerillas, would stand before the lots' fences and hurl "bombs" or "grenades" filled with seed, fertilizer, and water to help ignite a garden amid the chaos. They ultimately gained access inside, doing all they could to transform the places— removing trash, installing fences, adding topsoil. By 1974, the city determined that all would benefit if the community officially tended these ramshackle locales. They approved a $1 lease to create the "Bowery Houston Community Farm and Garden," the city's first community garden. Sixty vegetable beds were added,

The Church of St. Luke in the Field
COURTESY OF HANNAH FRANK

and eventually trees were planted. And soon other communities followed suit, building their own gardens from the rubble.

Over 600 community gardens now exist throughout the city, and best yet, they're all open to the public a minimum of 10 hours a week (see www .greenthumbnyc.org/gardensearch.html for listings and more information). And the Bowery garden? After Christy died in 1985, it was renamed the Liz Christy Community Garden. Today it contains a pond stocked with red-eared turtles, rare plants, the tallest dawn redwood tree in Manhattan, weeping birch trees, and hundreds of different flowering perennials.

In addition to community gardens, the city is bursting with a plethora of hidden pockets. These people found refuge in them. They managed to carve out their own public escape and find tranquility. They discovered their own slice of magic and didn't even need to hurl seed bombs.

....
John Cameron Mitchell, Golden Globe–nominated actor, director, and writer

I have a very strong connection with the Church of St. Luke in the Fields in the village. The church has a very beautiful garden. It's filled with flowers and is a peaceful oasis. The place is very important to me because I used to rehearse for *Hedwig and the Angry Inch* there. I would lie in a patch of grass under a certain tree. And I would go though the whole show over and over in my head—that was my rehearsal place. I always liked the 1950s statue of Our Lady there. It looks like she's clutching her hand to her chest saying, "I couldn't eat another thing."

When I came to New York in 1985, the city was full of sex. It was kind of dangerous and I lived in a sublet on 14th Street. I was understudying for Huck Finn in *Big River* on Broadway. I was only on for a week and then I got an action movie.

I had just come out that year. Coming out was filled with excitement and immortality. And New York was punk rock, and I wasn't ready for it. I would go to the Pyramid in the village and hang out with the drag queens. AIDS had just hit. It was very powerful and scary. I'm not scared of it anymore.

I had to move away for five years. But when I came back, I was ready. And I was more accepted here as an actor. I felt wanted.

The Church of St. Luke in the Fields, 487 Hudson Street; (212) 924-0562; www.stlukeinthefields.org

....

Philip Seymour Hoffman, Academy Award–winning actor, director, and co-artistic director, the LAByrinth Theater Company

I came to New York for college when I was 18 years old, and I think a lot of my first kind of creative instincts and juices started flowing here. One of my favorite things to do is meet up with a bunch of friends at about 2 o'clock in the afternoon. We'll go to a favorite outdoor haunt when you can be outside, eat lunch and drink a lot of coffee for the next three hours, and be incredibly stupid. That is the good time to be had. You sit for a long time and say stupid stuff. I like to do that.

....

Evan Handler, actor and writer

It's nice to have relief from Manhattan sometimes. And there's a public garden on 89th Street, between Columbus and Amsterdam Avenues. It's a really beautiful, quiet, and peaceful spot. It's a community garden where people do their gardening but it's open to the public. And when I lived in New York, I would visit a couple of times a week and I would read scripts there. It was so calming.

West Side Community Garden, 123 West 89th Street, between Columbus and Amsterdam Avenues; www.westsidecommunitygarden.org

....

Brad Farmerie, executive chef at the Michelin-starred Public, Double Down, and Madam Geneva

I have two children. My son is two and a half and my daughter is only three months old. We live right on the water by Columbia Street in Brooklyn and so we're just north of Red Hook.

Red Hook is a very unique neighborhood in Brooklyn along the water that is only about 3 or 4 miles from Manhattan. I've actually walked from there to work in Manhattan and it takes me a little under an hour. The largest buildings are 3 to 4 stories. So you just get this feeling that you aren't in the middle of a big city. It's kind of cut off physically from the rest of Brooklyn. But there are buses that go to Red Hook and there's a water taxi from Manhattan. And they've revamped a lot of the bike paths so during the warmer months, you see a lot more bicyclists.

Every Saturday during the summer, we love to drive down Van Brunt and basically make our way toward two destinations. One is Valentino Pier, which kind of juts off the tip of Brooklyn toward the Statue of Liberty. It's such an unusual, interesting, very non–New York, very non-Brooklyn, tucked away place. It's surrounded by an industrial area with really cool old warehouses that are 150, 200 years old.

On the way, we almost always stop at Baked, a little coffee and pastry place on Van Brunt, which is a great way to charge up and get ready for the day. I get the pain au chocolat. And we'll get cakes there for special occasions. They do this crazy chocolate salted caramel cake. It's really addicting. I think I've gotten it for my son's birthday, my birthday, my wife's birthday. It's one of our go-to cakes.

At Valentino Pier, people lay blankets out. And it feels as if you can reach out and grab the Statue of Liberty—it's so close. I love the amazing graffiti murals there. And it's never crowded because it's unknown. Visiting Valentino Pier is such a very un–New York experience. There's just a tiny, tiny little beach. And so my son almost always wants to go in the water. He's got his little swimsuit on and he'll go hang out right on the edge of the water. There's also a kayak club there. They take trips out to Governor's Island. And not only that, you can spot people standing up on surfboards and paddling with really long oars. You see beautiful tugboats go by. You see sailboats. It fills me with joy. And if it's a beautiful day, you can put your feet in the water.

Valentino Pier has a very unique feel in different parts of the year. During the summer it's very plush with beautiful wild grasses blowing in the wind. In the fall, there's more of a seaside town feel. When it's cold, you see the wind breaking off the water. You're bundled up but it's still a lot of fun.

Also what I think is really interesting is there's always people fishing off the end of the pier, which you don't really catch in New York that often. They pull up striped bass or eel—which are on the rocks right in that area. And there are usually four or five guys at that end all enjoying themselves making a day of it. For my son that's really very interesting, and it's a way to capture a lot of cool stuff that is not the normal thing that happens in New York or even Brooklyn.

Steve's Key Lime Pie is right next to Valentino Pier and they are famous in Brooklyn. My son loves this little treat called a Swingle. Basically it's a really small key lime pie put on a stick and then dipped in chocolate. They've got a 1941 Ford delivery truck, parked out front.

There are so many beautiful parts of this ritual, which makes it multilayer amazingness. A man named Ian Marvy (who founded Added Value, a nonprofit organization that promotes sustainable development of Red Hook) was very despondent because of the lack of fresh fruit and vegetables available in Red Hook. So through grants and funding he raised money and basically tore off a huge concrete slab that was a really horrible playground. And he brought in topsoil and he created a farm that is incredible.

Red Hook Community Farm is self-reliant. It works on volunteer power. And they do composting right there. And they don't only grow corn and peppers, which a lot of people grow, but they have jalapeños and grow really interesting things. They grow fresher stuff I've never even used before as a chef. It's kind of like a CSA [Community Supported Agriculture] times ten but also the general public can go there and buy vegetables.

From June through October, there's a farmer's market. The farm lasts a lot longer than most CSAs. It runs from the spring right up to Thanksgiving. They have tunnels so they can continue to grow stuff when it's just a little bit cold. Close to October, they start doing their harvest and pumpkin festivals. And you can pre-order turkeys when Thanksgiving's coming up. They sell organic eggs, pork, chicken, turkeys. I actually tried to get the pork in the restaurant because I was that impressed with it. During corn season, my son eats it raw off the cob. It doesn't get much better than that. They do a lot of the summer berries—blackberries and raspberries, strawberries, wonderful gooseberries. It's like heaven.

There's something about going to Valentino Park and eating the berries that were grown right around the corner while watching kayaks go out into the water in this tucked-away little place. It's very special.

Baked, 359 Van Brunt Street, Brooklyn; (718) 222-0345; www.bakednyc.com

Steve's Authentic Key Lime Pie, 204 Van Dyke Street, Brooklyn; (718) 858-5333; www.stevesauthentic.com

Valentino Pier, Ferris Street between Coffey Street and Van Dyke Street, Brooklyn; www.nycgovparks.org/parks/B418/

Red Hook Farmer's Market, Red Hook Community Farm at Columbia and Bay Streets, Brooklyn; (718) 855-5531; www.added-value.org/the-farmers-market

....

Tamara Tunie, actress

I'm from Pittsburgh, but my mother says I was born a New Yorker who just happened to be born in Pittsburgh, because as soon as I could get to New York I did. When I finished drama school at Carnegie Mellon University, I packed my car and drove to New York and pretty much haven't looked back.

My first trip to New York was when I was a freshman in college. When my feet hit the pavement, I knew this was my city. And what's special about it is what Mayor Dinkins called a mosaic—I love that when I walk out my door pretty much every country of the world is represented in a block in New York City. You can hear languages from all over the world and I think it's poetic.

If the weather is beautiful, I love to go to the New York Botanical Garden in the Bronx. It's the most glorious beautiful green place within the five boroughs. I mean, I haven't been to every place in the five boroughs, but the last time I was up there, there were these amazing massive sculptures. There's always a treasure to find. You can take a picnic or grab a sandwich and sit on the lawn and it's like you're in another country. You wouldn't think that a couple miles away is Interstate 87. It's an amazing retreat.

My first visit to the Botanical Garden was five years ago. I didn't realize how close or easily accessible it was. And when we walked in, it was like walking into the Emerald City. It was that kind of overwhelmingly beautiful. My favorite time to go is in the spring when everything is just blooming and bursting forth. And also in the autumn, because that time of year, the colors of the foliage and flowers are just so vibrant and gorgeous.

....

Chris Boneau, co-founder of Boneau/Bryan-Brown, leading theater press representatives for Broadway and off-Broadway productions

When you are a busy New Yorker, you literally don't take the time to smell the roses. But I was kind of forced to do this when a friend hosted a birthday party at the Peggy Rockefeller Rose Garden at the New York Botanical Garden in the Bronx. There were about 40 of us. And I think many of us thought, oh, that's a nice outing, but it's in the Bronx and then we have to go back to Manhattan and there's a dinner. It seemed like a lot. But it doesn't take very long to get to the gardens on the train.

I didn't realize how special the experience would be. The Botanical Garden itself is magical. You could spend an entire day there walking or touring on a tram that takes you around. There are so many spots to get lost in. But the Peggy Rockefeller Rose Garden is like a zen chapel. Peggy Rockefeller endowed this garden and there are species of roses that are not found anywhere else. First of all you're outside and in a garden devoted to rare species of roses. There are so many variations. It's amazing.

If you go at the right time and they're all in bloom, you can only imagine the sensory overload. The colors, the smells, just the beauty of it. And to think that there's this oasis right outside Manhattan that allows you to literally walk through and really experience them. You can't cut them, you can't take any with you, and there are no flower shops on the way out, which I love. You go in and then leave the beauty alone. But there are benches and you can take pictures.

Sometimes I find myself falling asleep thinking about that experience. I have a whole photo album devoted to my time there. Afterward, we went back to Manhattan and had a party at a restaurant and it was my bright idea for us to all drink rosé. It was a celebration of the roses.

Some people get a little put off by museums because they feel overwhelmed, but these gardens are not overwhelming at all. The only thing that is overwhelming about it is how gorgeous it is because you are surrounded by all this amazing natural beauty.

And I confess, I'm not a rose lover. It's not something that comes naturally to me. I don't pick roses and bring them home. I remember before I went thinking, "Oh roses, that's boring." And they are not boring, they are anything but boring. Curiously, some of the roses don't even look like roses but resemble other kinds of flowers. And they have tons of plaques that explain what they are and how they grow. And it just was an eye-opener to me.

My first visit to the Peggy Rockefeller Rose Garden turned out to be one of the most amazing days of my life. And I don't get out there enough. So if I had an hour, I would go back and start at the gate and spend the entire hour literally smelling the roses.

The New York Botanical Garden, 200th Street and Kazimiroff Boulevard, Bronx; (718) 817-8700; www.nybg.org

....

J. Robert Spencer, Tony-nominated actor

Around 14 years ago I was living in midtown on 47th Street between 10th and 11th Avenue. I had gotten my first Broadway show. But I was tired of constantly hearing ambulances and police cars. The inner city life was keeping me awake. And one day, I took the A train uptown and got off at 181st Street, and when I stepped out, all I heard was birds chirping.

I thought, where am I? What is this place? Then I walked further and discovered Fort Tryon Park and the Cloisters. I found a magnificent garden at the entrance. I'm a nature guy to begin with so I was in heaven. There's the most beautiful view overlooking the Hudson River with New Jersey on the other side and the George Washington Bridge.

Then my wife and I moved close by, around 187th Street. And we had a Labrador and it was so wonderful to be able to experience that environment four seasons out of the year. We go to the New Leaf Restaurant, a stone structure right in the middle of the park. Whenever my wife's parents come to town, we have brunch there and they have great Bloody Marys. It's so unbelievable that after a quick train trip you can be in the heart of big hills, rocks, and trees, walking through a beautiful garden beside the river.

I particularly love visiting in the fall—walking as the leaves are just starting to change and it's not too cold, not too hot. And when you go further on the trail, there's a castle where Al Pacino filmed *Looking for Richard*. You really feel as if you've gone back in time.

Sometimes I like to go into the park and sit on my favorite hill where my dog and I used to play. Instead of making a right to go to the New Leaf Restaurant & Bar, you go up the hill and to a bridge with a huge grassy section where you can see the rocks and have a gorgeous view of the Hudson River. It's nature, zen, quiet, and a beautiful gift to New Yorkers.

Fort Tryon Park, Riverside Drive to Broadway, West 192nd to Dyckman Streets; www.nycgovparks.org/parks/forttryonpark

New Leaf Restaurant & Bar, Fort Tryon Park; One Margaret Corbin Drive; (212) 568-5323; www.newleafrestaurant.com

The Cloisters, Fort Tryon Park, 99 Margaret Corbin Drive; (212) 923-3700; www.metmuseum.org/cloisters

....

Anthony Mackie, actor

I love when me and my friends get together and play flag football in Prospect Park. It's a bunch of out-of-shape 30- and 40-year-old dudes fumbling over each other and trying to play football. Prospect Park is fantastic. Sometimes Central Park can feel saturated, but Brooklyn is the true quintessential New York. A lot of true New Yorkers live in Brooklyn now—like Crown Heights, Bed Stuy, Prospect Park, and Fort Greene. Those areas are where my friends are. It's green and it's beautiful and quiet. And while there may be a lot of people, there's a lot of space. I just love living in Brooklyn.

Prospect Park, Prospect Park West, Flatbush, Parkside, Ocean Avenues, Brooklyn; (718) 965-8999; www.prospectpark.org

....

Tom Otterness, sculptor

My friend, [artist] Justen Ladda, and I have lived on Stanton Street for thirty years and on Sunday mornings, we have breakfast at El Castillo. They have a special for $3, which is two fried eggs, potatoes, and toast. We've eaten at the place since we first moved in the neighborhood and it's probably the same price. El Castillo is a Dominican restaurant and a lot of the local people who have been here for years and years hang out there. It's a really sweet place—a place we kind of grew up at. I also recommend the octopus salad. The Cuban sandwich is really good too.

Then, we go see Justen's park on Allen Street [the Allen Street Mall] between Delancey and Broome. There's a garden area in between two lanes of traffic. He's done this beautiful design with scholar rocks with a kind of Chinese landscape. Scholar rocks are formed by water. They are perforated rocks imported from China. I don't know how many centuries it takes for water to weave its way through. But the rocks look like Swiss cheese in different configurations and are really beautiful. He has done custom plantings all around them so they are like little landscapes.

The rocks are part of Chinese culture. They meditate on them and a lot of old Chinese paintings are based on these bizarre rocks. The landscape Justen created makes these lower bushes and small plantings seem like a bonsai; like an enormous landscape that has been miniaturized in some way. We just look and sit and hang out. I like to fantasize about the rocks having little figures running around in them.

The next stop is a few short blocks away. On Delancey Street, we go two blocks to Forsyth Street to Sara D. Roosevelt Park. On Sundays, groups of Chinese men take their songbirds in cages. They keep them in their homes and bring them out in nice weather to sing to each other. You can listen to their songbirds and it's just amazing. They've got exotic Southeast Asian songbirds, nightingales, finches. It's such a scene, but it is only in the morning on Sundays. It will start early and go until about noon. It's a part of New York nobody ever sees. They have these bizarre really finely made kind of ornamental bamboo cages and these beautiful birds. And then you hear this singing mixed in with the traffic sounds on Delancey Street.

Finally, for a little pick-me-up, we go to Lucky King Bakery on Grand Street, just two blocks south. It's just like walking into a modern Taiwan bakery. It's not old, it's new. It's modern in this very Taiwanese way. It's like walking into a different country. I think that's what's really wonderful about New York. You walk through the door and literally the people hanging out there are all Taiwanese or Chinese. And you just get the scene. You're transported. Save the ten-hour flight and there you are. They have great desserts and all kinds of bizarre sweet things everywhere. Justen has his addiction, but I have to stay away from it. So I get a cup of tea, but I might get a pork bun . . . maybe.

El Castillo de Jagua, 113 Rivington Street; (212) 982-6412

Allen Street Mall, between Delancy and Broome Streets

Lucky King Bakery, 280 Grand Street; (212) 219-8434

. . . .

Rick Guidotti, photographer and director and co-founder of the non-profit organization, Positive Exposure

Gramercy Park is so beautiful and one of my favorite sections of New York. I have lived in this neighborhood since 1983. The townhouses and mansions have such great history and date back to the 1800s. You get a good sense of the way New York was when you're here. And the park is one of the last private parks in the city. Its gates are locked and you need a key to get inside. Margaret Hamilton, the wicked witch from *The Wizard Of Oz,* lived on Gramercy Park South. Theodore Roosevelt's birthplace is nearby. I'm a member of the National Arts Club, which is just across from the park in a mansion built in the 1840s and is now a National Historic Landmark.

You can find a major dog culture around the section just outside Gramercy Park. Most people don't have keys to get access inside the park. And besides, you're not allowed to bring dogs. So many people walk on the sidewalk along the perimeter just outside the park. Unlike the inside, that area is absolutely public.

It's so incredible wandering with your dog. You run into billions of other dogs, and everybody knows everybody by their dogs' names.

My dog, Buster, does a very peculiar thing. It's very cute. I may sound like a really proud father, but I am. Buster lives for the day that he can eat a squirrel. They come right to the edge of the park by the cast iron gate, and just taunt him. You can practically hear the squirrels saying nah-nah-nah-nah-nah. But Buster can't get into the park to get them.

So Buster developed this walk around the park where he runs with his front legs on the elevated ledge surrounding the park and his back legs on the street. And like a ballerina, he kind of does a two-step around the circumference of the park over and over for hours and hours and hours. It's just hysterical. People just start laughing. Truck drivers toot their horns and little old ladies will just sit and watch. One time when Buster was doing his shuffle, he ran right towards Jimmy Fallon. Jimmy looked at me and looked at Buster and said "Now *that's* funny!'

Gramercy Park, between East 20th Street (Gramercy Park South) and East 21st Street (Gramercy Park North); and between Park Avenue South and 3rd Avenue (Gramercy Park West and Gramercy Park East)

....

Luanne Rice, best-selling author

I love small parks. Every neighborhood in New York City has its own character and rhythms and they all have little vest pocket parks. My neighborhood is Chelsea and I'm really lucky because there are a couple of really wonderful ones that I visit and they're just a respite from the city itself.

There is so much nature in just a small space; for example, I'm thinking of two little parks. One is the seminary garden—it's called General Theological Seminary. But the garden is really on 20th Street, which is known as the seminary block. It's the most magical place. In June it's just blooming with roses. And not only does it have an incredible rose garden, there are enormous old trees there. They may be some of the oldest trees in New York City. It's built on what used to be a farm.

Long ago, this park was Clement Clarke Moore's farm. He was thought to have written *'Twas the Night Before Christmas*. Some of the trees that remain from that time are towering. You can't put your arms around the trunk they're so large. There are little benches hidden throughout. It's very small; it's just a part of a city block. But, you just have this feeling of refuge there.

So I'll just sit there and look up in the canopy at these tremendous old trees and see warblers: the pine warbler, palm warbler, hermit thrushes. You can see them right here in my neighborhood. And then, when I feel like a slightly different kind of park, I go just a couple of blocks away to Clement Clarke Moore Park.

One thing about both parks is that inside both are trees and gardens and it's very beautiful. When you're sitting there, you look through wrought iron fences and see the neighborhood houses, which are landmarked homes from the early 1800s. The ones on seminary block are especially beautiful small federal brick houses. Those seen from Clement Clarke Moore Park are called the Fitzroy Houses. They are brownstones that were also built at the same time that Chelsea was first developed, long ago in the 1800s. You feel like you've stepped back in time.

Clement Clarke Moore Park is open all the time, The seminary is only open at certain hours. I like to go as a break from writing. So I'll just take a walk around the neighborhood. I usually go a couple of times a day. I leave my desk and take a walk around the block, go down the Hudson River a few blocks and then cut back up through the city streets on 10th Avenue and choose one of those places to go.

I'll sit on a bench and get lost. I always have a book with me—I usually have a little notebook for taking notes. I'll either think that I'm going to read or think that I'll write in my notebook, yet so often, I'll just get really lost in the rustle of the leaves overhead and the birds singing. I'll follow a bird and really watch it until I can't see it. Time flies by.

In between the parks is a little bookstore called 192 Books. It's a singular bookstore in the city; I don't know any other like it. It's owned by one of the gallery owners in Chelsea, Paula Cooper, and it has a very art slant so there are a lot of art books, but also a lot of literary fiction, poetry, and memoirs. But it's very tiny in keeping with the size of these parks. Usually on my stroll, I'll stop in there and browse a little bit. Some of my great finds there were *Take Care of Yourself* by

Sophie Calle, *The Night Watch* by Sarah Waters, and Colm Toibin's *Mothers and Sons*. Sometimes I'll buy a book and take it to the park.

I'm a big believer of the neighborhood in New York. It physically can seem so overwhelming, as if it's just one big entity, but it's actually made up of little, tiny towns or villages. Most of my life has been spent in Chelsea, but all neighborhoods have their own character. I laugh about how I very rarely leave the neighborhood. It's true. So, all of these places are just really beloved to me.

I came to New York as a young writer when I was 19. I feel as if my roots are here. As a kid, I had visited the city often. From the time I was able to take the train from Connecticut and go to the theater. When I was a teenager, I was writing and always submitting my short stories to the *New Yorker* magazine. In doing that, I connected with Brendan Gill who was the drama critic.

Brendan is also originally from Connecticut and he read my stories. He invited me to lunch at the Algonquin. We sat right next to William Shawn, the editor of the *New Yorker*. Brendan pointed out Dorothy Parker's round table. He said to me, "If you want to have a literary life, you have to live in New York." I took him at his word, and I moved into just a room really, in Chelsea. Brendan would take me to incredible *New Yorker* parties where I'd meet John Updike, George Plimpton, William Styron, artists like Charles Adams, William Stevenson. And then I'd go home to my little room.

Chelsea was very different at that time in the late 1970s. It was very rugged, very gritty—a rough neighborhood. The writer Alice Hoffman and I are close friends, and she lived in New York at that same time. We often talk about how we'd walk down the street holding our keys to the apartment. Our hands would almost be shaking because we'd need to get inside really fast. It was all scary and threatening. But that was the only place that I could afford. I fell in love with it, even back then.

I've watched many, many changes take place over the years in Chelsea. Recently the art galleries came and then the High Line opened as a park and then development followed that. So, it is in a time of transition. That's the thing about New York. It is sort of a living and breathing entity that never stands still. There is a lot of the old left, but it is always changing.

The General Theological Seminary, 440 West 21st Street; www.gts.edu

Clement Clarke Moore Park, West 22nd Street and 10th Avenue; www.nycgovparks.org/parks/M257

192 Books, 190 10th Avenue; (212) 255-4022; www.192books.com

. . . .

Hoji Fortuna, actor

In 2007 when I first came to the United States from Portugal (after living away from my home country, Angola, for fourteen years), I came to Fort Greene, Brooklyn. I loved the energy and the fact that everyone I came across was smiling and greeting me. My wife Anja kept asking me why everyone was smiling at me and nodding their heads in recognition. I remember joking that maybe those people were recognizing the aura of the African king in me. The fact is, I inhaled the air and thought: "I could live here."

Not much has changed since that first revelatory inhalation. I'm still in love with Fort Greene. My favorite spot is Fort Greene Park. That's my refuge when I need to escape from the world and reconnect with myself.

I love watching the squirrels jump around. (This was, in fact, where I saw my first squirrel ever!) I think they put me in touch with my child spirit. I love taking in the smell of the grass and the plants in the spring and the peaceful energy that the park exudes. I like going there and sitting by my favorite tree above the hill, facing the soccer players on late afternoons or just contemplating the people: the parents with their kids and dogs, the man sitting on a bench with his two parrots, or the middle-aged man carrying his stereo around with Motown tunes blasting from it, or even the eagle that stops by every summer watching the squirrels' every move and trying to catch one of them.

I love watching the tennis players and attending Sunday afternoon parties, called Soul Summits, that take place during summer. Soul Summits are summer parties where people of all ages and backgrounds gather in Fort Greene Park to jam or dance. At these Soul Summits, one can see the old school people from the Brooklyn neighborhoods, break-dancers performing their crazy moves and competing in a circle, Asian Capoeiristas doing Capoeira with such grace that one wonders if Capoeira really came from Brazil or Angola, DJs and drummers. It's pretty cool and one can't resist joining the dance floor. People basically dance and interact through dancing. One can bring food or go to one of the neighboring restaurants and cafes, grab a bite, and come back to the dance floor. I think of it as a very liberating experience that sets people in a great mood for the coming working week. And it certainly embodies well the spirit of the block parties.

Or I love just looking at the sky and watching the planes pass by, admiring the beauty of the trees, or the fireflies flying around when the night falls. I achieve such moments of joy on these outings that I literally feel like crying from happiness.

Fort Greene Park, Myrtle Avenue, Cumberland Street, DeKalb Avenue, Brooklyn; www.fortgreenepark.org or www .nycgovparks.org/parks/FortGreenePark

. . . .

Bill Pullman, actor

New York is the place that probably excites me the most for getting out and mixing with people. I love to talk with people in the street. You can watch and observe. As soon as you go outside your door, you're in this big river of humanity, and it's mesmerizing. Also, I feel like I connect to anonymous humanity in a way here that is different than when you're in your car driving around. I have none of those same sensations, only because I'm on foot and everybody else is on foot, and they're revealed in a different way.

I'm in the Village. And lately, I've really been enjoying St. Luke in the Fields. It's an enclave of buildings that was built in the early part of the 1800s. I think the church, St. Luke in the Fields, is from 1822. They have a connection of gardens that are laid out almost 18th-century style in formal geometric squares, but they're planted in kind of a more informal garden. It is very gentle in there. The scale of the buildings, maybe because of the small size of them, reminds me of being in Manhattan two hundred years ago. I like that feeling of kind of being off the grid there.

Lots of times, if I have a free morning then I'll have a picnic there. On the way over, I will go to Murray's Cheese and I'll pick up a little bread from Amy's Bread right next door. And I'll have coffee, cheese, and bread and read there. It feels like a kind of a place where there's other people, and you sense other people, but you don't really see them clearly because of plantings and things. It's a very private place.

The Church of St. Luke in the Fields, 487 Hudson Street; (212) 924-0562; www.stlukeinthefields.org/web

Murray's Cheese Shop, 254 Bleecker Street; (212) 243-3289; www.murrayscheese.com

Amy's Bread, 250 Bleecker Street; (212) 675-7802; www.amysbread.com

....
Daniel Radcliffe, actor

I love the city. I love the people. I've got a lot of friends over here. I love London and I miss home, but New York is a wonderful place to work.

My favorite thing to do in New York? Sleep. But outside of that? I mean, I just walk around the West Village really and go down and sit on the piers and go around there. That's just a nice way to relax really.

Hudson River Park, www.nycgovparks.org/facilities/kayak/5 or www.hudsonriverpark.org

....
Charles Busch, Tony Award–nominated playwright, actor, novelist, screenwriter, and drag legend

I feel that I live in the most beautiful part of the world, which is Abington Square in the West Village. The little park at Abingdon square is just . . . well, I feel like I'm in an MGM musical. It's the flowers and trees and it's all groomed perfectly with a beautiful fountain and a statue. The park is really just like a beautiful set from a studio back lot. Sometimes when I'm a little moody, I just go and sit.

Everybody has a dog except for me. I think that's going to be rectified shortly. So, I just like watching all the little doggies. Don't I sound sappy? I don't sound like the edgy female impersonator. I'm kind of like an old Yiddish lady. Actually, I don't leave my neighborhood. A friend of mine was going to Eastern Europe and somebody else said, "Are you going to go with him?" I said, "If I won't go to 15th Street, I'm not going to Poland."

Abington Square, at Hudson Street, 8th Avenue, and West 12th Street

....

George Whipple, television reporter, NY1

I love going to see the walk of extraordinarily beautiful cherry blossoms in the Brooklyn Botanic Garden in the spring. I believe that the cherry trees brought into the garden are older than the ones in Washington DC that were a gift from the Japanese government.

The trees have a huge tragic history because they brought in a disease that killed all of the chestnuts. They carried this incredible blight that ruined the most important hardwood in America. So, there's a bitter sweetness to it. The Japanese write about the cherry blossoms in every stage: as it buds, it blooms, and then as it fades—and the whole process is beautiful. So, any day that you visit will be different. And to hit it is like trying to hit the peak of the fall leaves—although you can't lose.

Seeing the daffodils and the tulips at Wave Hill in the Bronx is also amazing. These are very old and traditional, New York things. And you get to see when the Bronx was in the country. I remember when there were dirt roads in the Bronx.

Wave Hill is a preserved old estate along the water from the 1840s and they have beautifully planted gardens, as does Madison Square Park, which used to be a junkie park. In fact, Madison Square Park is one of the oldest parks in New York, from pre-Civil War. What they have planted is just unbelievable. It's like Holland today with all of the thousands of tulips and daffodils and all of the other blooming plants and trees that they have in there. That's a more recent phenomenon in the last decade—that's it's gone from Needle Park to Tulip Park. You almost couldn't walk in Madison Square Park because of all of the junkies 10 or 15 years ago.

Wave Hill, West 249th Street and Independence Avenue; (718) 549-3200; wavehill.org

Madison Square Park, between Fifth & Madison Avenues, 23rd & 26th Streets; www.madisonsquarepark.org

Brooklyn Botanic Garden, 1000 Washington Avenue, Brooklyn; (718) 623-7200; www.bbg.org

Rick Newman, founder of Catch A Rising Star and producer

Since I was born in the Bronx, I feel most comfortable living in concrete. However now that I'm living on the Upper West Side, my wife, Krys, and I have a great escape from the city. Early Sunday mornings we walk down to the river to Pier i on 68th Street with the Sunday papers. And we'll spend a few hours reading the *New York Times* with pitchers of Bloody Marys, coffee, and muffins. It's our mini-vacation! You really feel like you're away from everything.

And there's a cafe at the pier with about a hundred tables and umbrellas. And it's really cool because you're underneath the West Side Highway. Actually, it's kind of weird and interesting because you don't see any cars. You just hear them and you're looking out at the river. You don't see any tall buildings, so you can be anywhere. Or if you don't want to go to the cafe, there are loads of beautiful places to sit or even lounge along the water. And I make great Bloody Marys.

Pier i Café, Riverside Park, Riverside Boulevard and 68th Street; (212) 362-4450; www.piericafe.com

CENTRAL PARK: ACRES OF GREEN

 There's nothing like walking in Central Park. It's a brilliant piece of landscaping. I love the gardens there. Frederick Law Olmsted, who designed the park, was an absolute genius. I love the Poets' Walk between the elms. It's so rare to see those aged elms. You look at them and they have such presence and such power. You can walk around hundreds of times, thousands of times and it's always a new experience.

—Jessica Lange, Academy Award–winning actress

Landscape architect Frederick Law Olmsted was 36, in debt, and lacking in substantial planning experience when, in 1858, he won the competition to design Central Park with architect Calvert Vaux. Talk about making lemonade out of lemons; at the time, the space was swampy and rocky—anything but manicured. But Olmsted's insight and pure genius made up for his shortcomings. "The time will come when New York will be built up, when all the grading and filling will be done," he once said. "And when the picturesquely varied, rocky formations of the Island will have been converted into foundations for rows of monotonous straight streets, and piles of erect, angular buildings, there will be no suggestion left of its present varied surface, with the single exception of the Park." How could he possibly have known?

Yet, more than 150 years later, this 843-acre oasis of uber prime real estate remains untouched. Imagine 26,000 trees, 9,000 benches, 21 playgrounds, 36 bridges and arches, 48 monuments and sculptures, 7 bodies of water, labyrinths of walkways, and 126,000 bulbs' worth of blooming flower beds teeming with daffodils, hyacinths, tulips. All this smack in the center of Manhattan. Somehow Olmsted understood the priceless gift that the park would have upon the city. "The enjoyment of scenery employs the mind without fatigue and yet exercises it; tranquilizes it and enlivens it," he said. And many of us couldn't imagine a better playground.

....

Francesco Antonucci, acclaimed chef/owner, Antonucci Restaurant

I love to sit on a bench in Central Park and watch people tango. Many years ago, when I was walking in the park, I heard music playing and discovered people dancing around 7 p.m., at the Poet's Walk on 69th Street by the 5th Avenue entrance. On Saturday nights, there's a small community of tango dancers and they take this very seriously. You see everyone from six-year-old children to older people in their eighties. They dance with so much passion and so much zest and joie de vivre—you feel like you're in Argentina. And the women have beautiful high-heeled tango shoes. I don't ever join them. I'm much more interested in watching than I am in dancing. It is like a free party. Some people give lessons and charge $12 an hour and some people just dance. And many people dress in a very elegant style. You don't see many in sneakers and blue jeans.

Central Park Tango, Saturday from 6 to 9 p.m., June to September; Literary Walk in the Mall, Shakespeare Statue, off 66th Street; www.centralparknyc.gov

....

Tina Fey, Emmy- and Golden Globe–winning actress

My favorite spot in New York City is the middle of 48th Street, between 6th and . . . no. Actually, I like to go to the park. Central Park and Riverside Park are awesome playgrounds all year long. And what I like about New York is just being able to walk everywhere. I don't have a driver's license. I take the bus everywhere and walk.

....

Bill Ritter, ABC News correspondent and co-anchor, WABC Eyewitness News

I grew up in Los Angeles, where all the seasons are pretty much the same. You can get away with having a jacket that just goes to your waist. But that's the extent of seasonal change in Southern California. And when I first got here, at the end of November of 1992, a friend of mine at ABC said to me, "There will come a time sometime in the spring when everything will just be perfect. The blooms will be out. The sun will be shining. You go sleeveless. And all of a sudden it all makes sense why you're here."

And the first time I felt that was in the spring of 1993. I was walking in Central Park with my young daughter and that spring hit me. And so I have paid close attention to this ever since. Plus there's something about Central Park. And I know it's not the intellectual center of New York. I know it's not the theatrical center. I know it's not the educational center. But there's something about this giant park, this 840-acre park. It's the City's backyard—it's our backyard—both individually and collectively. It brings us together and in touch with nature in a way that no other place in New York can do.

So I use it all the time, and I live not far from the park. That spring of 1993, I took my daughter to the carousel and she was less than a year old. And I'm riding around it and she is having a blast. And something hit me: I thought, if I should die right now, I would be so happy. I was just so happy that I couldn't imagine life getting better than at that very moment.

I think that every spring I take that attitude and I can't wait for it to happen, especially after a brutal winter. The sun is finally out and you can just feel people's liberation after hibernation. I love either walking or biking as my kids get older. I have three children now. My kids are 18½, 15, and I have a 19-month-old and so I'm doing this whole thing again. I cannot wait for spring for my 19-month-old to experience it.

Central Park is so democratic. We're all there together, sharing nature's reawakening. And it's a reawakening for New Yorkers as well. And when you're biking in the park, there are so many places to stop and enjoy, especially if you experience it through the eyes of a child. We go to the Pinetum with the pine trees and the little swings in the grove. Then we head over to the Great Lawn where there's a potpourri of things going on. And there's this coagulation of all these interests—from bicyclists riding leisurely to speed cyclists trying to maneuver among the tricyclists and the skateboarders, rollerbladers, runners, walkers, and the little kids learning how to get up on their two-wheels for the first time. All this is happening in one place.

So from the Reservoir to the Pinetum to the Great Lawn and then over to Sheep Meadow and across the ball field, we get to the carousel. I think it is the most magical part of Central Park—more than Belvedere Castle, and the little pond there where you can feed the ducks, and more than the marionette theater.

The carousel is just so significant. And it embodies the spirit of New York. This thing almost died several times over the course of its 100 or so years. It was one of the original carousels made in Brooklyn. There have been all sorts of disputes over taking care of it and whether the vendor can make it and how much it's underwritten by the park and the city.

All that aside, you go back to something so purely innocent when you're on this ride. You go back to your own childhood. And through the eyes of your children, you can see how wonderfully simple and beautiful this ride is and how it reflects the wonderment of not just New York but of life. Life is like a carousel. All these people from so many decades have been on this ride. All these people who have sat on it, all the children who have grown up on it and now have children and grandchildren of their own. It's all there, on this little *farshtunkene* carousel in the middle of Central Park.

The Central Park Carousel, midpark at 64th Street; www.centralparknyc.org

....

Kevin McKenzie, artistic director, American Ballet Theatre

I work in many different neighborhoods. ABT performs at the Met in the spring, at BAM in the winter, and City Center in the fall, so I'm actually working in lots of different parts of the city. And I live on the Upper West Side. So I really enjoy being out and about in the city, but the thing is that with all the hustle and bustle of the city combined with the hustle and bustle of my job, I deal with people, people, people, people, people all the time. But when I have time in the city to really relax, I tend to want to go the parks and just fall in love with the age of the trees and the planning of the parks in general.

I have a ritual. Nearly every spring, I go to the Conservatory Garden, that beautiful park around 105th Street on the 5th Avenue side of the upper corner of Central Park. To walk through those blossoming apple trees and tulip gardens is breathtaking. It fills me with such energy and awe. The power of nature is just remarkable. And there it is, right in the middle of the city. It's the best-kept secret. I'll mention it to a lot of people I work with and they say, "Really, there's a garden up there?"

I also love walking on Riverside Park from the hundreds down to 72nd Street right along the river through all the different parts of the park. I like those big allees, community gardens, and walks along the river. There's such diversity. In certain parts there is grandeur and you feel as if you were dropped down into the middle of Paris.

And then you get to another part of those gardens, those community gardens at around 89th and Riverside, and you see how incredibly well tended and wild they are at the same time. There are outlandish choices that people make for their little square foot of earth. You gaze out to the other side of the Hudson and there's the majestic Palisades. And all of a sudden, I hear what sounds like rushing water. I can't see the cars but I realize, my God, that's the sound of the cars. And I become aware that the highway is right there. So I'm always aware that I'm in the busiest city in the world but there's all this incredible open space that is such a wonderful antidote to the hustle and bustle one has to deal with in living in New York.

Conservatory Garden, Central Park, 5th Avenue and 105th Street; www.centralparknyc.org

Riverside Park, Riverside Drive to Hudson River, West 59th Street to Clair Place; www.nycgovparks.org/parks/riversidepark, www.riversideparkfund.org

....

Meredith Vieira, Emmy-winning NBC News special correspondent and host of
Who Wants to Be a Millionaire

I love to be outside so walking in Central Park or Riverside Park is my favorite thing
to do. And I like to people watch. I like to sit in a cafe and look out and see people;
that's always fun to do. I don't live in the city. I live in a much quieter area. I'm sort
of a hermit by nature. I'm kind of shy and like to be by myself. But it's great to be in
the city sometimes and have a glass of wine and watch everybody.

One of my favorite spots in Central Park is Strawberry Fields. When I first
moved to New York, I lived right across from there. And after John Lennon was
murdered and they had the service to open it, it was just very special. It was very
sad, but it brings back a lot of memories. I was at Channel 2 News. It was my first
entree into New York.

....

Deborah Koenigsberger, founder and executive director of Hearts of Gold and
owner of Noir et Blanc

I basically fell in love with Strawberry Fields when both my sons were babies. My
oldest is 19 now, the younger one is 16. When you are raising children, live in New
York City and the weekend is here, you say, "What are we going to do?" I usually
needed a place for my kids that was outside. So I would make a picnic lunch and me
and my kids and my great friend and her two kids would meet at Strawberry Fields.
We'd all throw out picnic blankets, have lunch, watch them play and basically grow
up. In fact, I have this great picture of my sons holding on to each other's hands
beginning to walk.

When you enter Strawberry Fields, just on the left is an intimate open green
area that is beautifully protected by trees. And there's this big rock in the ground.
It's such a safe rock because it's round and it's smooth. I didn't have to worry about
them hurting themselves. No animals are allowed so it's very clean. The grass is
always green and perfectly manicured. It's such a cozy area enclosed by shrubs.
You feel like you are in your own mini park. I could see where the kids wandered off

and they couldn't get very far—so I didn't have to worry. I had this whole bird's-eye vision. We would bring toys to this beautiful and green piece of New York.

After my kids got older, we would still visit. They'd play ball games. And I would meet friends there. Their kids would bring other kids. So it grew into this little meeting spot. People used to always say to me, "Oh, are you going to move? Are you going to get a backyard for the kids?" and I just felt like we had our backyard. When I think of Strawberry Fields, I think of my kids and their happy childhood in the city.

Strawberry Fields, near Central Park West between 71st and 74th Streets; (212) 310-6600; www.centralparknyc.org

....

Barbara Corcoran, real estate mogul and author

I like to get on my sky blue ten-speed, a 50th-birthday gift from my five sisters. My son, Tom, jumps on his red mountain bike and we put our little shih tzu, Max, in the wicker basket on the front of my bike. And we pedal the full loop of Central Park. We'll start at East 96th Street and go up and across 110th Street, then down to Central Park South, and back up the east side. The whole trip takes us about 45 minutes. Depending on the season, we see a melody of incredible daffodils, tulips, and apple blossoms. We pedal past horseback riders, people on roller skates and skateboards. And everyone is smiling. Max sits motionless, except for his ears flopping back. Where else can you go and get a thousand smiles in less than an hour?

....

Jonathan Groff, Tony Award–nominated actor

Bethesda Fountain is the heart of Central Park. The minute you walk to the top of the stairs it takes your breath away. On summer afternoons I can sit there for hours and hours people watching, enjoying the view, and looking at the birds. It's unbelievable. Coming from Pennsylvania, we were told that Central Park was dangerous and scary. And the first time I saw the park was when I was on a high school field trip. And our teacher took us through Central Park and we were so scared. But then the park opened up and there was this beautiful statue in Bethesda Fountain. And it sort of was a revelation—about Central Park and about New York itself. Suddenly, it wasn't this scary place. I realized it can be very inviting, safe, and beautiful.

Bethesda Fountain, midpark at the 72nd Street Transverse; www.centralparknyc.org

....

Al Roker, co-host on *Today*

I like going for a run in Central Park. You can run with someone and have a great conversation or run by yourself and disconnect and not have to talk on the phone. The great thing about Central Park is its vast diversity. The southern end is more urban. Then you get to the northern end and feel like you could be in some primeval forest. You can hear rushing water from a brook. You get to run past the Harlem Meers, which is such a pastoral setting and the gardens that are there. It's a little bit of everything.

Also, the park is different depending on the time of day you go to it. At night, the lights are twinkling. There are beautiful shadows and pools of light. In the morning, the fog comes off the reservoir. It's almost like you're somewhere in England.

I grew up in Brooklyn and Queens. And to me, New York feels like the center of everything. It's home and where my job is. It's still a place where in the afternoon you can eat a hotdog and in the evening you can eat a five-star meal and everything in between. No matter what you want, you can get it here.

....

Charlotte St. Martin, executive director, The Broadway League

When I moved to New York from Texas in 1995, I arrived with an 80-pound golden retriever named Maggie. She was only three at the time and needed lots of exercise. So during one of my first Saturdays here on a particularly beautiful day when I was walking her, I discovered a whole group of people at this little outdoor cafe in Central Park by the boat pond where they have the little motorized tiny sailboat races.

They had all their dogs with them and were having a doggy birthday party. It was just the funniest thing I'd ever seen. Imagine all these dogs with hats on and birthday music playing from a little boom box. And they had doggy cupcakes. I never saw a party like that again, but I still see a lot of dogs there.

I still love going to this spot in Central Park and I visit every Saturday morning on a year-round basis as long as it is not raining, sleeting, or horrible weather. Nicole, my current dog, an Australian labradoodle, and I will start at 84th Street and 5th Avenue, head down Madison Avenue past all the wonderful stores to around Barneys on 61st Street. And we'll come back up and walk into the park to the place that I call the doggy cafe by the model boat pond.

It is such a pretty spot. The cafe has like 10 or 12 tables with chairs and some benches. And the pond has ducks flying in and out and trees going all the way around it. And just across the pond from the little cafe is the Hans Christian Andersen statue where regular storytelling takes place. In the mornings, the area is filled mostly with people who have dogs. And those who don't have a dog come to enjoy the other dogs. There's such a camaraderie, it's almost like you're having a family reunion. Golden retrievers have to be the most loved dogs on the face of the earth because when I had Maggie with me, so many visitors would come up and say, "Oh can I hug her? I miss mine at home."

Nicole is also pretty busy at the park. People want to know what she is because she's so unique looking. Most everybody there has an appreciation for dogs. So you're so welcomed. And nobody gets dressed up or wears makeup. Everybody's just there for the love of the park and their dogs.

The Kerbs Memorial Boathouse, east of Conservatory Water (or Central Park's famous model boat pond), just north of the East 72nd Street entrance; www.centralparknyc.org

....

Geoffrey Nauffts, actor and Tony Award–nominated playwright

One of my favorite things to do to relax in New York is to take a rowboat out in Central Park. It's so magical. I discovered it when I was younger. And I would go out there often when I needed to clear my head. It's also a great special place to take people, especially when they're new to the city. It's a real unexpected surprise.

Suddenly you're in the middle of this beautiful park on a pond. And it's great. There's no place like New York.

The Central Park rowboat rental, East 72nd Street and Park Drive North;www.thecentralparkboathouse.com/sections/boats.htm

....

Dayle Reyfel, Drama Desk winner, actress, playwright, and producer of *Celebrity Autobiography*

As I have returned to New York City, my hometown after being away for a few years, I find I have feelings of renewed romanticism—everything is fresh! And in the course of falling in love again with my city and especially Central Park, I also like the idea that you can actually be walking in the park and end up at Belvedere Castle or the Shakespeare Garden or the carousel. Here is this gorgeous park with all these beautiful bodies of water, trees and landscaping and there also happens to be a carousel.

So every once in a very blue moon, in the spur of the moment, you get a little ticket, it costs two dollars, and you just jump on. The little kids look so happy. And even if I don't go for the ride, I just like knowing that it's there.

....

Glenn Close, Tony- and Emmy-winning actress and Oscar nominee

I came to New York when I arrived from college in 1974. I came here to seek my fortune and become an actress. So this is where I began. New York is a very special place for me. I've always lived on the East Coast and I've always liked the energy of New York. It's a challenging place to live but it's also a creative place. There was a time in the eighties when everyone went west and crack came in and the city was not in great shape. But New York now is where it is. It has an incredible vibe, creative buzz, and creativity. And as far as the craft of acting, in America, this is where you have to be.

For me, New York is infinite, infinite. And I use Central Park a lot. I have two terrier mutts, Bill and Jake, and we go there and just love it. I love the light in the park and the people that you meet and all the different seasons. So I'm a park addict. My favorite spot? I love to stay near the entrance at West 81st Street. And what's nice is that between nine at night and nine in the morning, you can let your doggies off the leash so they can run. It's fun.

....

Donna Murphy, Tony Award–winning actress

I live close to Central Park and feel so lucky to have it in my backyard. If I have a decision to make, my husband and I will make a date. And he will pick up some sandwiches, maybe get a bottle of wine, and we will meet in Sheep Meadow. It has all that space and whatever decision I'm obsessing about, it helps to open my head. I can look at all the issues from the sky.

....

Julie Alexandria, star of MTV's *The Seven*

Going to Central Park is a moment of zen. In the midst of the hecticness of the city, you can just go to Central Park, sit on a bench, and zone out. During summer, I love going to Sheep Meadow. My friends and I will have a picnic there, bring a board game, and just lay out. It's so relaxing and you get the buzz of New York in a different way. Also, my father is a huge fan of Central Park. That's his favorite space. When I was about five, he introduced me to the Alice in Wonderland statue by the sailboat pond and it was the best. I grew up going to it and climbing all over it and for some reason I nicknamed it Mountain Bridge. And I would beg him to take me there all the time. It always looked so huge. And I went back to see it as an adult and wondered, how did I think it was insurmountable. It's just a little statue.

   Sheep Meadow, west side from 66th to 69th Streets; www.centralparknyc.org

   Alice in Wonderland statue, east side at 75th Street; www.centralparknyc.org

....

Rob Thomas, songwriter and lead singer of Matchbox Twenty

It's amazing how much fun you can have hanging out—taking a picnic basket into Central Park. Just spending time on a fall day is perfection. My wife and I love to picnic near the lake [Turtle Pond]. The one with the swans near Belvedere Castle. We've had some good memories there. We'll go to a great food store like Dean & DeLuca or stop by Magnolia Bakery, then get a little wine and we're good to go.

Turtle Pond, midpark between 79th and 80th Streets; www.centralparknyc.org

Dean & DeLuca, 1150 Madison Avenue; (212) 717-0800; www.deandeluca.com

Magnolia Bakery, 200 Columbus Avenue; (212) 724-8101; www.magnoliabakery.com

. . . .

Daniel Humm, Michelin-starred chef at Eleven Madison Park

New York is a very international place, but at times, it can be kinda rough to live here. It's expensive. The weather is not great. It can be dirty. Sometimes you hate it. But most people who live in New York are here because they want to achieve something special in their field. You meet people who have big dreams and they're here because they want to achieve them. It's an inspiring place.

I couldn't live in New York without Central Park. I grew up in Switzerland in a small town outside Zurich, and I love nature. Although I do love living in the city so much, I need a place to escape. That place for me is Central Park. And I run marathons so I love running there.

I'll start near the restaurant at 24th Street and run up 5th Avenue and enter the park and run the entire loop. Here you are in a quiet place with beautiful trees. But on the outside, the high-rises line all the way around. For me, there is no other place in the city where you're really feeling nature like this. So it's a very special place.

When you're by the reservoir, especially from the east side around 90th Street, the view is pretty amazing. You're on the reservoir and then you see the trees, and then the high-rises. And from that spot you can see a couple of buildings on the west side that are quintessential New York.

The Reservoir, 85th to 96th Streets, east and west; www.centralparknyc.org

....

Kelli O'Hara, Tony-nominated actress

I'm a quiet, peaceful person. I love to find things that give me peace and get away from it all. I love to walk in Riverside Park by the water. And in Central Park there's a place in the middle of the 80s called the Ramble. You would never know you're surrounded by the city. It's like a mountain somewhere. There's hiking trails that go up. And I like to get lost a little bit. In New York, you can get lost in the people, but I'd rather be lost among the nature.

....

Padma Lakshmi, cookbook author and host of *Top Chef*

I adore walking in Central Park. I love just about anywhere in the park. I grew up in the city. And I grew up roller-skating in the park. And I'm a big believer in all of New York City's parks. I think they bring a lot of joy to all of us.

....

Jay Jay French, Twisted Sister guitarist and founder of the Pinkburst Project

New York City is such an iconic place. And so many people have visions and ideas of it because of what entertainment has done to its walls. But it's not just Times Square; it's not just the Village. There's so much more of this city that is phenomenal. And anyplace you can go in New York City where you don't feel like you are in New York is a particularly magical experience. I believe that if you can live in this city and think it's a laid-back piece of real estate, then you've conquered civilization.

To that end, Central Park itself is a wonder to behold. But most people concentrate on Central Park south of 86th Street beginning at the reservoir and down. People don't understand that the geology and the geography of the Park starts above the reservoir. This is where the valleys of New York really start to show. We never think of New York as a valley, and yet we have huge valleys and these valleys become apparent when you see the formations as you go above the tennis courts. They border the northern part of the reservoir. It's utterly stunning.

The Conservatory Garden off of 5th Avenue and around 102nd Street is part of that beautiful stretch. It's not a touristy place and sort of off the beaten path. It's not overwhelmed with people, even in the middle of summertime. And it's so breathtakingly gorgeous and laid out and landscaped so beautifully.

The gardens were set up and carved out to be a presentation piece and a place of tranquility. Aesthetically, it's a place to go and appreciate the flowers and the shrubbery because it's on several steps and levels. You can see it from the 5th Avenue side. You can walk in halfway through the park and stand up on a higher plain and look down at it. So there's geometry, cultivated grasses, fountains, and molded lawn sections. You wouldn't expect it in New York City, or you don't expect it unless you see it. I get a cup of coffee and a doughnut, walk in there on a Saturday, and kind of let the world go by. It's a place to recharge your batteries.

On the west side of the park above 96th Street, there's a beautiful and intimate lake [the Pool]. It's in a wooded area. You can get so completely lost in it. You wouldn't know you are in New York City. You would think you were in Long Island or Upstate New York. It looks like something out of a French Impressionist painting with weeping willow trees reflecting off of the lake and pathways that lose the skyline.

For a truly magical perspective of the city—something out of a rom-com type movie—go to the Great Lawn which borders 79th to 85th Streets. If you stand on the northern border and stare south on a spring morning, the downtown skyline of Central Park South is breathtaking. Tourists who walk around Central Park almost always stop and take a photo of that skyline as it borders Central Park South with their friends standing in the foreground by the fence on the northern side of the Great Lawn. I've seen people running and all of sudden they stop and say, "Wow, that view is amazing! Amazing."

Conservatory Garden, Central Park, 5th Avenue and 105th Street; www.centralparknyc.org

The Pool, west side from 100th to 103rd Streets; www.centralparknyc.org

The Great Lawn, midpark from 79th to 85th Streets; www.centralparknyc.org

Alex Rodriguez, third baseman for the New York Yankees

One of my favorite things to do in New York is to spend time with my daughters. My daughters and I love Central Park. We love spending time at the zoo. We love walking in the park and exploring everything the park has to offer. New York is such a great place to be and I'm so fortunate to be here.

Liev Schreiber, Tony Award–winning actor and director

(My son) Sasha and I like to go to the Central Park Children's Zoo where you can pet the animals. The animals eat out of your hand.

Kerry Butler, Tony-nominated actress

I love to go to the Central Park Zoo. It's so relaxing. I bring my daughter there all the time. I love the children's petting zoo and the polar bears. And I love the rain forest and the monkeys. You can sit for a long time and watch the monkeys. One time they just had the best time playing with a cardboard box. They entertained us for an hour.

Central Park Zoo, Central Park; (212) 439-6500; www.centralparkzoo.com

Tony Roberts, Golden Globe– and Academy Award–nominated actor

I grew up in New York City. I remember visiting Belvedere Castle when I was ten years old with my nanny. It means different things to me at different points in my life. When I was a child, I was afraid of Central Park. It used to be a very threatening, foreboding place. It was like going into Sherwood Forest or *Peter and the Wolf.* There were bad gangs there. Now it's everybody's backyard and a place of great serenity. I feel very lucky that I can walk out of my apartment building in the middle of New York City and find myself in all that natural splendor. Anytime you have access to that kind of beauty and still live in New York City and can get anything you want, 24/7, it makes you feel rich.

Belvedere Castle, midpark at 79th Street; www.centralparknyc.org

. . . .

Bob Balaban, actor, director, writer

If I had a free hour in New York and it was a lovely spring, summer, or autumn day, I would go walking in Central Park now that the crime rate is down. I would stop first at the Shakespeare garden, which contains only growing things mentioned by Shakespeare in his plays and sonnets. Then I would take a look at the model boats in the boat basin, watching kids and parents navigate their incredibly cool remote-controlled ships and schooners. I'd watch ecstatic little kids climbing all over the statue of Alice on the mushroom and playing hide-and-seek. I would then stop by the zoo at the stroke of the hour and watch the animated clock as the animals parade around it. I've been making regular visits to this venerable old timepiece since I was eighteen years old. To me, it's the equivalent of a Proustian madeleine. That would be my idea of a lovely New York hour.

Shakespeare Garden, west side, between 79th and 80th Streets; www.centralparknyc.org

. . . .

Bette Midler, Grammy-, Emmy-, Golden Globe–winning and Oscar-nominated actress and singer

One of my favorite things in New York is to go to the park. I love the park. I go to parks all over town and I love the gardens and I love the Conservatory Garden. I love being in nature, and it can be hard to find nature in the city. That's really what our organization, the New York Restoration Project, does.

....

Hugh Jackman, Emmy- and Tony Award–winning, Golden Globe–nominated actor and singer

My son's idea of a great day in New York is to hike. He'll wake up and not have any breakfast and go to Central Park and then come back when it's dark, literally. He loads up his backpack and treats Central Park as a forest.

....

Douglas Blonsky, president, Central Park Conservancy

There's nothing better and more rewarding than being able to spend two or three hours walking though the park. Because I have a lot of staff working in the park, I like doing it in the evening, after I'm working, when people don't notice me. It's nice just to be able to be a park user and kind of blend in. I particularly enjoy visiting during winter, before it gets busy. At night, with none of the leaves on the trees, you can see every light in the park from the south to the north end. You really get to see the undulation and the grades and how the park really flows. You see the vision of what Frederick Law Olmsted and Calvert Vaux intended it to be.

My favorite walk is from my office, which is at 60th Street. I'll start at 5th Avenue and walk along the path by the east drive that goes through the zoo. At first, I'm in a low area with beautiful outcrops on either side. It's called the Dene. When you walk up the hill, there's the surprise of Balto, the statue of the dog. Then right next to Balto, I go under Willow Dale Arch. When you get on the other side of Willow Dale, that's where you really enter the Mall and can spot incredible American elm trees. They are some of the last great stands of American elms in the country.

This spot is what people refer to as the Literary Walk. And looking at this cathedral of elms, you can really understand what Olmsted and Vaux were doing. You're walking through a masterpiece of landscape architecture meant to draw you into the park. It was actually intentional for you to come in and say, "Wow. That looks really cool. Where do I go next?" And when you're standing at the south end of Literary Walk, you can just barely see the wings of the Bethesda Angel. But the water draws you to the angel. When you get down there, you think, "My God, look at this whole Bethesda terrace and this incredible sandstone structure."

From Bethesda Terrace, I go towards and over Bow Bridge into the Ramble. One of my favorite places in the park is the whole area around the Ramble. We've done a lot of work on it over the last five years, opening up some of the great caves and great vistas. Through the Ramble, I would go to Oak Bridge, which is actually a new bridge that we just built about two years ago. We brought back a historic bridge that was missing for about 80 years. It's actually one of the most beautiful bridges with the most amazing views looking south over the city skyline. It's just off of the west drive at around 77th Street.

Then, from Oak Bridge I go directly north and to the right, and I end up at the surprise of Belvedere Castle. The castle makes me think about the history of the park because you're in a castle in the middle of New York City. Historically, you didn't look over the Great Lawn. You looked over the original reservoir in Central Park. So, I like to sit there, close my eyes, and visualize what it historically was. Then, when I open them, I understand that instead of this incredible parry of water, now there's this beautiful, lush lawn.

From the castle, I look over the Great Lawn, down into Turtle Pond and see thousands of turtles. The Turtle Pond is one of my favorite picnic spots. That landscape is neat because when you're by the water, you've got the castle behind you and solitude. But then, when you look north onto the Great Lawn, you get to look at all the crazy activity going on at the same time. So, you kind of get the peace and quiet where you're actually picnicking and then you get to really experience everybody having fun on the Great Lawn too.

After the castle, I head down to the Delacorte Theater and up around the Great Lawn. One of the really cool places that many people don't get to is the Pinetum. It's a wonderful collection of pine trees. I like it because of the historical perspective. People don't realize that at one time, most of the park contained evergreens. But unfortunately the trees couldn't handle it because of the pollution. So, back in the 1970s, Arthur Ross, a great philanthropist, started planting these evergreens to actually show people what the park looked like back in the 1880s and 1890s. These trees are 40 or 50 years old and let you know that Central Park was a different place. A lot of these are great Himalayan pines and white pines, and they soar up into the sky. Actually, when you're in the middle of it, you feel like you're in kind of an alpine forest.

I love to picnic in the Shakespeare Garden. It's ideal when you want seclusion and to be alone. The garden is really a hidden jewel because it sits behind the Swedish Cottage, off the west drive of the park and 79th Street. It's tucked in between the Belvedere Castle and the Swedish Cottage. It's a small little cute garden with meandering pathways and flowering plants that you can enjoy 365 days a year. It's always spectacular and so quiet, you often have the place to yourself. You're surrounded by beautiful plants and looking up at the Belvedere Castle. And Shakespeare's lines are carved into a stone and little plaques throughout the garden.

Central Park, (212) 310-6600; www.centralparknyc.org

....

Liza Minnelli, Oscar-, Tony-, Golden Globe–, and Emmy-winning actress

Why do I live in New York? Where else would I go? I can't imagine! And there's nothing like walking through Central Park. No matter what season it is, it's always fascinating. It's always beautiful. It doesn't matter where I go in the park. I'll go anywhere. It's a haven in the midst of all this bustling and hustling.

....

Shane Krige, general manager, The Plaza Hotel

Running in Central Park has become one of my favorite pastimes over the years, particularly during our picturesque spring and fall days when all the leaves are changing with the colors of the season. I leave in the morning from the hotel, and run directly into Central Park through the Central Park South entrance. My normal route takes me around the reservoir twice, and then around the historic Central Park boathouse. While I am running I enjoy taking in all of the sights, people, and activities that surround me. It reminds me of all the possibilities and different people that come together to comprise this small island of Manhattan. The overwhelming feeling of pride I get when I'm leaving the park and approaching The Plaza is irreplaceable, and there are days I can't believe I have the pleasure to work in such an iconic landmark every day. With the flags proudly flying, representing different sections of the world, I begin the work day knowing I am living in the best city in the world. It's a city I have the pleasure to call home.

....

Susan Stroman, Tony Award–winning director and choreographer

My very favorite thing to do in New York City is to walk through Central Park. There are so many magical spots. But the Literary Walk is my favorite. Whenever I have down time, that's where I run to. I sit on a very special bench that was dedicated to my late husband. And I sit on that bench and think about life and how blessed and lucky I am.

Also that area is great for people-watching. There's always a street musician there and usually a different one each time. I love listening to the music, sitting on the bench. and watching the people go by. It's very creative and the most special place to me. Sometimes I get ideas for characters there. For those of us in the theater who are directors and choreographers, observing people is a big part of what we do, and a big part of what fuels us.

Literary Walk, midpark from 66th to 72nd Streets; www.centralparknyc.org

....

Michael McKean, actor, Academy Award–nominated composer, director, and writer

I was born here many years ago in October. And whenever October approaches, I think that's New York in its prime. And walking through Central Park when the leaves are turning and everyone is just starting to think about putting on a jacket and not putting it on yet, there's something about that that's not like anyplace else in the world. New York lights up in a special way then. Maybe it's because I'm an October baby, but I always have that feeling of rebirth here. New York really is an eternal city. I've never been to Rome, but it's close enough to eternal for me.

I love to watch the Broadway League softball game. It's one of my favorite things to do. If I am in town, I make it a point to go there on Thursday when they play. During the *Hairspray* run, I didn't play because I'm not a good player. But that was my team and I was the official scorekeeper. When you work in musicals, you are desperately trying not to get hurt. If your ankle goes out, you're not going to dance that night. No one wants to get hurt but everyone still plays hard.

....

Aaron Tveit, actor and singer

Playing softball at Heckscher Ballfields in Central Park with the Broadway Show League is one of my favorite things to do in the city. On Thursday afternoons, the casts and crews from Broadway and off-Broadway shows play each other in the middle of Central Park. We have fun on our team. We have a good team element. I play against people I know and we get very competitive. I've actually hit some home runs in the past. But I bat lead off so my job is really to get on base and not actually hit home runs.

I grew up playing baseball my whole life and I'm a huge Yankees fan. So I played a lot of sports when I was younger. It's the one outlet that I can still play and I don't have to worry about getting hurt. I can't play basketball anymore. I might blow a knee out or something. So baseball is a nice competitive outlet for me.

Also, Central Park is an amazing oasis in the middle of our city. And how great that you can be playing softball in the middle of Central Park with the world revolving around you. It's incredible to know that you are playing softball at noon on a Thursday when the rest of the world is working. I just love it so much.

The Broadway Show League, Heckscher Ballfields, inside Central Park near 63rd Street; info@broadwayshow league.com; www.broadwayshowleague.com

....

Calvin Wiley, creator of the dance brand Calvinography and world renowned fitness and dance professional

When I have free time in New York City, I like to get out of my neighborhood. Normally we travel in the same circle where we live. So I like to explore somewhere else.

One of the best things is to go to a Summer Stage concert. They have all kinds of concerts in Central Park, but they also do smaller concerts throughout the different parks in the City: at East River Park, Saint Mary's Park in the Bronx, and parks in Brooklyn and throughout the boroughs. And by going to all these concerts, I get a chance to see all these green spaces. Summer Stage goes from the end of June to the end of August, and it's free. People just don't realize all of the free stuff you can get in New York City.

Summer Stage has all these dance companies from around the world. I've seen Alvin Ailey in Central Park. I saw an Israeli dance company perform a show called PeepDance. They had these little tents with dancers inside. And you walk around the tents and look through these peepholes and see what the dance is in the show. So with Summer Stage, you experience a free art performance. You get a chance to see a different neighborhood. You sit on the lawn with a picnic, and enjoy a show.

Summer Stage, (212) 360-2777; www.summerstage.org

....

Gretchen Rubin, best-selling author, *The Happiness Project*

If I had a free afternoon in New York City, I'd walk through Central Park. As many times as I've visited it, I always find a new element to admire; it is inexhaustible. The statue of the heroic dog Balto—the turtles in the Lake—the dramatic view of Belvedere Castle—the ducks landing on the water—magnificent Bethesda Fountain—the blossoming trees—and on and on. Each season has its special delights, and each section of Central Park has its treasures. Last year, as a creative project, a friend and I wrote a story, and we illustrated it with photographs of our heavily costumed children in different parts of the park, and one of the many pleasures of working on that book was the opportunity to highlight the beauty of Central Park.

....

Judy Gold, Emmy-winning writer, actress, and comedian

The greatest thing about having a picnic in New York is that you can be isolated and have your little space, but you can also stare at people and watch them the entire time. I get inspired by all the characters I see for work. But then everyone I'm with gets mad at me, "Can't you just enjoy yourself and stop criticizing everyone who walks by?"

Picnicking in New York is also great because you can get the best food in the world. You get a picnic basket. You go to Zabar's. You get a baguette. You go to the cheese department. You get salami. And you cut up the cheese, and you just finger food eat it. I think my best times have been with my kids and their friends and their friends' parents, picnicking in the park. Great bottle of wine and just a potpourri of food from Zabar's. And God, their rugelach . . .

Zabar's, 2245 Broadway; (212) 787-2000; www.zabars.com

....

Kelly Ripa, Emmy-winning co-host of *LIVE! With Regis and Kelly,* producer, and actress

I love that New York is not a one-industry town. I have never actually done this, but I've heard that you can go to a dinner party and sit next to an artist, politician, athlete, and schoolteacher. Everyone does something different.

I love running through Central Park. It's my number one favorite thing to do. The trees are beautiful. The lawns are beautiful. It's great people watching. I just love everything about it. And I love Victorian Gardens in the summer. It's this quaint little amusement park and a hidden oasis in the spot where Wollman Rink is. Victorian Gardens sort of looks like an Alice in Wonderland fantasy village that pops up in the middle of Central Park. And most people don't know it's there. To me, I always know it's summer when you see those vans moving in and setting up shop. They have a little tiny Superman ride [Kite Flyer] where you lay down like Superman and fly around. It's just charming.

Victorian Gardens at Wollman Rink in Central Park, enter Central Park from 59th Street and 6th Avenue and walk north; (212) 982-2229; www.victoriangardensnyc.com

NEW YORK
EATS

 Restaurants in New York are like entertaining. Like nightclubs.
God, I love restaurants. I love the Waverly Inn, Morimoto,
the Lion, the Mark, Bar Masa. I sort of sound like a Zagats.

—*Vera Wang, designer*

No matter how many cooking shows are TIVO-ed from the Food Network or PBS, many New York City stoves remain cold. In fact, studies show that the average New Yorker will dine out at least four times a week. Why? As Ruth Reichl, former *Gourmet* editor in chief and author, once explained, "This is a city of strangers, a place where people yearn both to be left alone and to connect. And nowhere do public and private come together so completely as they do in restaurants. That is why New York is—and always will be—a city devoted to the joy of eating out."

At last count, the town had over 20,000 eateries. Yet, despite the bewildering variety of offerings, many gravitate toward a favorite few haunts and stay loyal. There's comfort in nesting there. Case in point: In nearly every *Seinfeld* episode, Jerry and his pals convened at Monk's Cafe (aka Tom's Restaurant). The place was practically a fifth character with a starring role in the series. How comforting for Jerry, George, Elaine, and Kramer to park themselves at their booth and banter about life's joys, travails, and utter quirkiness. How reassuring for us to find them there week after week. It was home. So when it comes right down to it, maybe each of us simply craves our very own Monk's Cafe.

Balthazar Restaurant
Courtesy of Sylvia Paret

....

Anthony Bourdain, chef, author, and host of *No Reservations*

I've often said that cooking is a dominant act. It's an alpha act. But eating should be a submissive act. And chefs are at their happiest when they go to a restaurant and know someone in charge is cooking well. When that happens, I can completely switch over to the other side and experience it washing over me. I know I'm in good hands. And great meals are simple things. That explains why so many chefs are kooky for sushi. There's no disguising it. It's either great or it isn't. There's no artifice. No cute puddles of sauce. So when I want to reward myself with sheer self-indulgence, I will go alone to Masa's sushi bar and say "give me whatever's good."

Masa, 10 Columbus Circle; (212) 823-9800; www.masanyc.com

....

Mario Batali, chef, restaurateur, author, and television personality

My favorite thing to do in the city on a warm weekend day is to take my kids to the Houston Street basketball court and play some ball with them and a bunch of their pals. Later, we head to Da Silvano around the corner and eat lunch al fresco and catch up with some of our friends. We are usually a table of 10 to 15, everyone orders and the kids head back to the courts that we can watch from our table outside. When the antipasto comes, we call them in, they wash their hands, eat, and then head back to the game. Same when the main courses arrive. We are usually there for three or four hours and just totally love the scene and the people watching.

    We love Da Silvano for Silvano (Marchetto) himself and because the place is totally relaxed, the food is excellent, and the menu usually has some special very seasonal items, like baby eels or white truffles or crazy Scottish langoustines. And we love Houston ball field because it is the closest one to our house and we have always played there. After that, around 5 we head home in time to watch the sunset over the river from our terrace and chill NYC style.

Da Silvano, 260 6th Avenue; (212) 982-2343; www.dasilvano.com

....

Paul Haggis, Academy Award–winning screenwriter, director, and producer

New York is the best city in the world. What is not to love? I love that I can be completely alone. But if I'm cutting a movie or walking to my office, just walking to my editing suite and back, I feel like I'm part of humanity.

I love to write in public. I get to fool myself into thinking that I'm doing a social activity when I'm actually just alone. I fool myself that I'm still part of life. I can rewrite in my office, but first, I have to feel that life is around me.

I'll circulate between four or five places. But if I go to one place too often, I start to feel a little pathetic. I think people must feel sorry for me that I don't have an office. But I do have an office. The Tea Spot on MacDougal is quiet. There's a plug so I can write there. And no one knows about it. But actually now they will. But that's OK. It's not a scene.

I found the Tea Spot five or six years ago. They have fabulous teas and I'll have one pot after another. They don't mind if I sit there for hours. Ten hours is the longest. I tip them very well and I always go alone. I actually wrote *In the Valley of Elah* and *Next Three Days* there.

Tea Spot NYC, 127 MacDougal Street; (212) 505-0969; www.teaspotnyc.com

....

Julianna Margulies, Golden Globe– and Emmy-winning actress

The thing I love about New York is wherever you meet someone for lunch, there's always something to do there. Whenever I meet my girlfriend who lives on the Upper East Side, we always start at Fred's at Barneys and have the Mark's Madison Avenue Salad. It's my favorite salad in the whole world. It's a garden in a bowl. Then I'll go to the Whitney or the Met because there's always something to see. And the Guggenheim is phenomenal. My dad used to live on 89th and Madison and I grew up thinking that they closed the Guggenheim on Mondays so that the skateboarders could skate down it. He had me believing that until I got to college. I thought, of course they do!

My friends make fun of me because if we plan to meet at, let's say 107th Street, I'll leave an hour and a half early and walk from SoHo. There's the world right in front of you. I'll put on my iPod and walk the 75 or so blocks uptown. It's fantastic walking though town listening to the Glenn Gould Sonatas, especially on a rainy day. He's one of the most genius pianists of all time. And then I suddenly hit the 40s or 50s, I'll think that I need to put a step in my gait and switch to Aretha Franklin, Black Eyed Peas, or Everlast.

Fred's At Barneys, 660 Madison Avenue; (212) 833-2200; www.barneys.com

. . . .

Harvey Wang, photographer, acclaimed documentary filmmaker, and commercial director

I grew up in Queens and have lived in various places in Manhattan (Chinatown, the East Village) and Brooklyn (Ditmas Park, Carroll Gardens). And I have photographed all over New York. But one of my favorite places has always been Brighton Beach, down the boardwalk from Coney Island.

I've shot short films and portraits in that area for a long time. I photographed Eddie Day, the Cyclone roller coaster brakeman, and social dancers and mah-jongg players at the Brighton Beach baths for my book about the city. Many of those people and places are long gone, but I always enjoy going back to Brighton Beach.

I love to get a table on the boardwalk at one of the Russian restaurants. One in particular is Tatiana. They have two locations on the boardwalk and an extensive menu. For lunch and dinner, weather permitting, you can dine outside, and they also have a mind-blowing, over-the-top Las Vegas–style dinner/show at night, with singing, skimpily attired dancers, fire, water, the works. The expansive menu includes incredible smoked, pickled, broiled, and raw fish dishes, Ukrainian and spinach borscht, and my favorite, pelmeni—tasty boiled dumplings filled with meat.

The food is good, but the parade of humanity strolling along the boardwalk beats any show and is worth more than the price of the food. You can listen to the conversations in Russian, feel the breeze, hear the seagulls and the sounds of the waves in the distance, smell the ocean, and the delicious food. You can close your eyes and have no idea you are a subway ride away from Manhattan.

There are people who escape the heat of the city by going to their upstate country house, beach house, the Hamptons, whatever. But for me, when I want a quick getaway to another world, nothing beats Brighton Beach.

Tatiana, 3152 Brighton 6th Street, Brooklyn; (718) 891-5151; www.tatianarestaurant.com

....

James Caan, Academy Award–nominated actor

I was born and raised in Queens. I love the life here. But mostly, I like the moral code about loyalty and friends that somehow is embedded in you when you are from New York.

New York has a lot of good eats. We go to Rao's a lot. It's been there for a hundred and something years. I like all the characters who go there and the owner, Frankie No. We call him "Frankie No" because you can't make a reservation. You say, "Hey, can I have a table?" Frankie says, "No."

Rao's, 455 East 114th Street; (212) 722-6709; www.raos.com

....

Andrew Goldberg, Emmy-winning documentary film producer, director, and founder of Two Cats Productions

My wife—who is pregnant at the time of this writing—and I and our cat live in a quiet apartment that faces an empty courtyard in the West Village. This allows us to be in New York without having to deal with New York coming through our front windows. On late weekend nights, the front of our building gets a regular helping of loud, strung-out prostitutes who've wandered away from the Path Station on Christopher Street. New York can be so colorful!

When it is light out, most of what we do is within a mile or two from our apartment. We regularly go to about four restaurants and an ice cream parlor. We had our wedding at the Rubin Museum of Art, which is devoted to Himalayan art and occupies the beautiful old Barneys building on 17th Street. Our reception was held at Fig & Olive on 13th Street—which has the best penne in New York City. And Stogo did the ice cream. Their chocolate chip cookie ice cream is fantastic. In our neighborhood we love the fried artichokes, ravioli, and sautéed mushrooms from Meme Mediterranean restaurant on Hudson. For Indian food it's Junoon on 24th Street. For baked goods, especially red velvet cupcakes, go to Baby Cakes on the Lower East Side. For yoga there is only Jivamukti.

Rubin Museum of Art, 150 West 17th Street; (212) 620-5000; www.rmanyc.org

Fig & Olive Restaurant, 416 West 13th Street; (212) 924-1200; www.figandolive.com

Stogo, 159 East 2nd Avenue; (212) 677-2301; www.stogonyc.com

Meme Mediterranean Restaurant, 581 Hudson Street; (646) 692-8450

Junoon, 27 West 24th Street; (212) 490-2100; www.junoon.com

Jivamukti Yoga School, 841 Broadway; (212) 353-0214; www.jivamuktiyoga.com

....

Jessica Hecht, Tony-nominated actress

When I'm downtown, I do a little crawl right by NYU (New York University), where I went to college. I'll visit a diner called Cozy Soup 'n' Burger and go to the Strand (828 Broadway; 212-473-1452; www.strandbooks.com), a giant bookstore specializing in used and out-of-print books.

I've been going to Cozy for the pea soup for more than twenty years. And I have such profound memories of that place in a very specific time in my life. I sat at that table at Cozy Soup 'n' Burger for years having discussions with friends about projects. And the pea soup has the best croutons. Actually, the croutons are really what give it credence. On a bad day I'll ask for double croutons. They are completely saturated with butter. They're perfect. The inside is slightly chewy because there's so much butter in them.

Adam Sandler, who was also an NYU student, went to Cozy when we were at school. Adam is the just about the only person to have a picture of himself on the wall.

One day my mother, who is the consummate New Yorker from the Bronx, was with me at Cozy. It was the day before the Tony Awards. I was nominated for *View from a Bridge,* was feeling very anxious, and I had absolutely no desire to go to the ceremony. I really felt the tension and didn't want to go through all this. You can feel on display and so small and in the midst of it. And there are these big stars around you and it can make you feel very empty. So I really was not in the mood to go.

And my daughter had a little performance by NYU with a theater company that she works with. My mom, my daughter, and I decided to go to Cozy before the performance because it's such a comfort place for me. And we sat down and I ordered the pea soup. And my mother ordered these eggs, which she orders in a very complicated way: "like over, not too hard, not too soft." She describes it "like a medium, like just set, like really just set. And I want just a few potatoes or I'm gonna eat them all." She says this in a charming but an assertive way. And she goes on and on. And the waiter just looked at her completely stone faced.

And so he brings everybody's food and walks away. And as he's walking by two minutes later, he says, "Is everything okay?" My mother says, "No, it's not. Do you want to know the truth? It's not. I spent a lot of time describing the eggs. It's not exactly the way . . . you know I wouldn't have said anything, but you asked." I mean he asks everybody in the same manner.

But we ended up having this fantastic conversation with the waiter who's served me pea soup for like twenty years. My mother said, "Look, when I describe something, I feel like I've described this kind of eggs for so long so that you know I get to expect that. If you want me to tell you again, it's just . . ." and she goes through the description. The guy is so stone faced again, but he proceeds to get the eggs, returns to the chef, and comes back like five minutes later with these absolutely perfect cooked eggs.

It was very charming and then for the rest of the meal my mother was in heaven with her eggs. She told me why she didn't think it was likely that I was going to win the Tony Award but she was very proud of me. It was classic. It just made me want to be back at NYU. It made me want to be younger and not tense and not thinking. At NYU, all I wanted was to be in the world getting a Tony nomination. And here I did not want to go to the Tonys. And there was something about the simplicity of being in that environment at Cozy. I just wanted to eat my soup and maybe teach a class. And of course twenty-four hours later I was in my beautiful Carolina Herrera dress. I was at the dance and it was lovely.

Cozy Soup 'n' Burger, 739 Broadway; (212) 477-5566; www.cozysoupnburger.com

. . . .

Anthony Malkin, president, Malkin Holdings and an owner of the Empire State Building

As a kid, meaning in my late teens and early 20s, I was all over New York City. I had a lot more spare time. I used to love going to places which are now considered quite commonplace—like the East Village. I'd go to restaurants on Avenue A. Back in the late '80s and early '90s, that was a real feature of the edge if you will. There was the Pyramid Club, Hawaii Five-O, and U Bar. El Mundo was a big old dance hall and performance theater which had been transformed into a disco. But those were the olden days. And I must say, my affinity with the corners of New York really began when I was at Choate and I would come to New York on weekends and visit with friends. We were always looking at the corners because we had grown up with exposure to what was in the middle of the field so to speak.

But now that I'm older and I have less time and it's so insanely programmed, I like to slip in these special moments if you will. So for me there are a couple of things that are just quintessentially New York. There's nothing to me like having dinner at Raoul's during a blizzard. Raoul's is this wonderful restaurant, which has been in New York forever. It's really maintained its bona fides. While the crowd may be a new group of people, it's got the same feel over all these decades. It's a wonderful, warm, just-crowded-enough place where the food is terrific.

The oysters are wonderful. The artichoke is wonderful. The steak au poivre is fantastic. They have terrific wine. I'll never forget, for our anniversary, my wife and I took our boys to dinner there when they were young. We figured they were old enough. We sat there in a banquette and it's so comfortable and nice and there's some pretty risqué photos on the walls. And the kids were sitting there looking around saying, "Wow, this is really cool" and then I heard, "Yo! What is that!?"

Raoul's is one of those great establishments where the people are part of the fabric of the place. And I mean this literally. It's almost like upholstery. I love going places where you can people watch but not where everyone is craning their necks around. It's an intimate environment. And when it's snowing it's the best. My wife and I used to live on 11th and 5th and we'd walk in the snow down to Raoul's and it was magical. You walk right down 5th through Washington Square. You're no longer in New York City so to speak. You're in the Village.

Raoul's, 180 Prince Street; (212) 966-3518; www.raouls.com

....

Salman Rushdie, novelist and essayist

I go to the Shake Shack. I have a fourteen-year-old son and it's his favorite place in the city. I have to take him there and I like the caramel milkshakes.

....

Gayle King, O magazine editor-at-large, host of the *Gayle King Show* on OWN

Everyone has their own special cheeseburger, but I love going to Shake Shack on the Upper West Side. They have the best cheeseburger and really good fries. And then they don't call it Shake Shack for nothing. You've gotta have a caramel shake. There's always a line but it's always worth the wait.

And I really love the Lobby Lounge at the Mandarin Oriental hotel. I normally go after work. I live on the Upper West Side so it's also very convenient. The Lobby Lounge is one of my favorite places because it's great if you want to have a business meeting. It's great if you want to be on a blind date. It's great if you are dating. I mean it just fits so many different situations.

The Lobby Lounge is intimate and yet it's also a very public place. You can have a private conversation. You can have a little noshing if you want to. I don't drink so they've got really great white hot chocolate. They have another thing called The Half Circle, which is pomegranate and pineapple juice and Sprite that I love. And the other day I was there, they were telling me about a new drink called The Palm Royale, which is some kind of citrusy something with apple cider and pear nectar, which was really good. And the view! I always like to sit by the window to look out. You can see the cars going around Columbus Circle. It's such a pretty place with those giant windows.

I'm fairly new to the city. And I didn't come to New York when I was a girl. I lived in Turkey when I was a kid. My first time coming here was really as an adult. I've lived in Connecticut since 1981 and moved to New York after commuting from Connecticut for over ten years after my kids were out of college and all that good stuff.

There's such vibrancy to the city that you don't find anywhere else in America. In the world. And I love that. And I know it's clichéd, but I love that song "if you can make it here, you can make it anywhere" because New York is tough.

I don't think New York is for the faint of heart. When you travel around the country and go to the South, there is that Southern hospitality, no joke, it's very true. The Midwest, West, and California have a very laid-back, casual kind of vibe. But New York takes no prisoners. But that said, there are a lot of wonderful stories in the naked city of New York where people open their hearts to you too. Generally speaking I think it's tough. But I love this city.

And you know what I really love? When I see a movie that features anything in New York and I think, I know that place. I've been there. I know that street. I've seen that building. That doesn't get old. Before I was here, I had no point of reference, and never really paid attention to it, but now that's always cool to me. That doesn't get old. Our offices are here in the Hearst building so it's very exciting. And the building has been in a couple of movies. I love seeing our escalators, or the exterior of the building. It's just cool to be part of the fabric of the city. Or when someone makes a reference to a specific restaurant or to a particular street or a building, I get a big kick out of that.

Mandarin Oriental, New York, 80 Columbus Circle; (212) 805-8800; www.mandarinoriental.com/newyork

Shake Shack, 366 Columbus Avenue; (646) 747-8770; www.shakeshack.com

....

Parker Posey, Golden Globe–nominated actress

I live in the West Village and I love walking down to Chinatown and eating at Joe's Shanghai or New York Noodle Town. I like that people from all over the world come to live here. So when I go to Chinatown, I feel that there's a whole other country in New York. It just reminds me of how exotic this place is. And it's not everywhere you can see a pig hanging from hooks in a kitchen in the background. I actually once saw Martha Stewart at New York Noodle Town. They have good dumplings and wonton soup.

New York Noodle Town, 28 Bowery Street (at Bayard Street); (212) 349-0923

Joe's Shanghai, 9 Pell Street; (212) 233-8888; www.joeshanghairestaurants.com

....

Hal Rubenstein, fashion director, *In Style* magazine

Anything and everything in New York is within an arm's reach. There's something very equalizing about a walking city. All classes have to mingle. It's a mix of wealth and race, and you never end up in an ivory tower. Some of the most interesting and ambitious people in the world live here. I have great friends in New York and find them fascinating, especially since they don't do what I do. And I have never ever looked at the New York skyline and taken it for granted. Whenever I drive over the Triborough Bridge, every time I see it, I think, "How cool is that."

I love spending time at Bar Pitti downtown because it's the only restaurant in the city with an outdoor cafe with a wide enough sidewalk. You can actually watch the world go by and still not be disturbed by the people who pass. I love the crowd who goes to Bar Pitti because it's a great mix of Village people, artists, and designers like Calvin Klein and Francesco Clemente. But nobody ever calls attention to anybody there. There are never any photographers. It's real New York. It's not a tourist place. They also have great food for the money. I always order off the blackboard. I know it by heart. I could recite everything on the blackboard right now from memory, and I wouldn't make one mistake.

Bar Pitti has quite a few of my favorite things. There's the veal meatballs, pasta with rabbit sauce, the puntarelle salad, with celery, mixed greens, and anchovy dressing. They make the best veal Milanese in the city. The food is authentically Italian in the sense that it's hearty but it's clean. You feel full, but it's never overbearing like Italian-American food, which is usually heavier, but precious. There are so many Italian restaurants that feel so precious. They're precious and overpriced, and full of people who are very proud of themselves. Whereas, Giovanni (Tognozzi) who runs the Bar Pitti is just absolutely charming.

He doesn't take reservations. But basically, there's a very egalitarian feeling when you eat there.

My favorite time to visit is either around two in the afternoon for lunch, or we usually go around eight at night when the weather is nice. We just watch the city go by. It's everything from people who live in the Village to kids who just finished playing basketball on 4th Street, to lovers walking up, arguing, to guys on the prowl. There are loads of people hanging around waiting for a table. There's just a great energy there. It's a place that always fills up and is happy.

....

Nanette Lepore, designer

I love shopping in New York—walking through the West Village and discovering little shops that I never knew were there. But if I had an hour, on a sunny day, I would sit outside at my favorite restaurant, Bar Pitti, and have lunch and sit in the sun. They have the best waiters, the best food, like spaghetti and meatballs. There's a nice relaxed feeling about the place. It feels very European to me.

Bar Pitti, 268 Avenue of the Americas; (212) 982-3300

....

Steve Lance, author and lecturer

When my two sons were young, about six and eight years old, they loved the subway. And on Sunday mornings I would get up early with them, around seven or eight o'clock, and I'd let my wife sleep in. And depending on the weather, I would bundle them up, head out, pick up a Sunday *New York Times*. And as we'd walk to the subway I would say to them, "What country do you want to visit?"

They were playing "Where in the World is Carmen Sandiego" so they knew countries. They asked what country I suggested. I said, "Do you want to go to Greece? Would you like to go to Russia? Where would you like to go?" And they would pick the country and we would jump on the subway in the front car and ride the subway to that country.

In the front car, you could see out the window and watch the train going into the tunnels and stations. It was a very dramatic ride. And I would sit in the front seat and read my *New York Times* while they called off the stations.

And when we finally got to the country that we were going to visit, we would explore. We would spend a couple of hours there. And the joke was they were not adventuresome when it came to food. We ended up at the pizza parlor. I'm a fan of ethnic food so I remember them looking for a pizza parlor while I was just drooling at souvlaki. In every country there would be some native food that I would be dying to try. And the best I could do would be to grab something to go.

We went to you name the country. Little Odessa out in Brighton Beach, Poland in Greenpoint, Greece in Astoria, and Israel in the East Village. And now that my sons are 24 and 26, when they come to New York they travel all over the city. They don't restrict themselves to one neighborhood. They roam the entire city.

I remember visiting "Italy" on Arthur Avenue in the Bronx. Arthur Avenue is what Little Italy used to be. There are still many small shops where you can get fresh homemade cheeses, meats, and delicacies. And there's family-style dining in a lot of the restaurants. It feels far more authentic than Little Italy in many ways. There is no shortage of all sorts of Italian foods on Arthur Avenue.

The Arthur Avenue Retail Market is the closest you get to a real Italian market in New York City. There are many individual franchised shops so you can pick up pasta, meats, pizzas, pastries. And they're all separate shop owners. You can eat there or walk down the block to a little park at the end.

In New York, every block holds a surprise, an adventure, something new to see, something happening. The city has a certain magical edge to it that surprises you in ways that you never thought you could be surprised. It's sort of like living the old Dr. Seuss book, *And to Think That I Saw it on Mulberry Street*. A boy is walking home from school and he sees a guy with a horse and a cart going down Mulberry Street and he thinks to himself, "Well, I can't tell my parents that I saw a horse and a cart on Mulberry Street. There's nothing extraordinary about that. Maybe I'll give the horse a fancy bandwagon." And he keeps building in his imagination what he saw on Mulberry Street until it's finally this massive parade, a circus parade of performers and jugglers and animals. To me, that's New York City.

Arthur Avenue Retail Market, 2344 Arthur Avenue, Belmont, Bronx; (347)590-6710; www.arthuravenue.com

....

Liz Smith, gossip columnist and author

I have been living in Manhattan since September 1949. The minute I stepped foot in the station I knew that I was here to stay. Back then, the old Penn Station was one of the most beautiful buildings in the world. I'm told that the windows were copies of Diocletian ones. I lined up to buy tickets to *South Pacific* and *Gentlemen Prefer Blondes*. The tickets cost $2.50. I had seen shows on the road in Fort Worth, Texas, but precious few of them.

So, I am a real Manhattanite. While everything changes in New York, essentially nothing changes. Just the names in Times Square change and big buildings keep being built bigger and bigger. But what I really like is when somebody comes along with a car and they just let me sit in the front seat while they drive around, up the East River and down the Hudson. I just love being driven around the city. I love seeing the Riverside Church and the little red lighthouse under the George Washington Bridge.

Then, I have a tossup of where the actual center of New York is. You see, there is a there there. It's either Radio City or it's 57th and 5th by Bergdorf Goodman. The buildings change around it like the Trump Tower, but it seems like the center of things to me. The park is just a stone's throw away; these great hotels like The Plaza and the Pierre are there. The windows at Bergdorf are so fabulous and artistic.

I also like the crazy stuff that's in Barneys from Simon Doonan. I was once the subject of one of his windows. I was in the window with a horse—to show from the horse's mouth. He's very clever. Though I haven't been to the Statue of Liberty in years, and I haven't been on the Staten Island ferry in a long time, I love to go down there and walk around. The Irish park down in Battery Park has stone from every county in Ireland. It's a very unpretentious little place, but it's a dazzling example of the many things Manhattan has to offer. I just can't get enough of it.

I can never go to the theater enough. And I'll go to Joe Allen's afterward. It's clubby. It has posters on the wall of all the shows that failed. The food is all-American. They make great hamburgers and buffalo wings and I always see somebody I know from the theater. Then I see Joe [Allen] occasionally. I've known him for many, many years. Barbetta's nearby is also wonderful. I believe it's the oldest continuously operating restaurant in Manhattan. It's been there more than 100 years. It's elegant, has a beautiful garden and owned by one family all this time. They have a champagne risotto there that is just great.

Joe Allen, 326 West 46th; (212) 581-6464; joeallenrestaurant.com

Barbetta, 321 West 46th; (212) 246-9171; www.barbettarestaurant.com

....

Heiko Kuenstle, general manager, the Pierre

I live in Harlem and there's a little French bistro nearby on 104th Street called Cafe du Soleil. There's nothing better than Sunday brunch there with great French food done very well and a wonderful atmosphere and a comfortable place. There's a very mixed crowd—young, old, out-of-towners. You get a lot of Columbia students. There is outdoor seating. They make a great eggs Benedict dish and a delicious Cobb salad, salad nicoise, or you can have brunch food like omelets and French toast.

Afterwards, I visit the Metropolitan Museum. I love the neoclassical architecture and how it lies next to a beautiful spot in Central Park. You see great art in many museums, but the Metropolitan has a beautiful physical frame for it. When you walk up the steps you're kind of humbled already. Then there are those gigantic pillars and rotunda and you have a good feeling of what to expect. The permanent collection, which includes Egyptian, Chinese, European art, photography, master drawings—you name it, is phenomenal.

And their temporary exhibits are quite amazing too. You never really run out of anything interesting there. I learn something new every time I go. And what I really like about the Metropolitan Museum of Art is while they suggest a certain donation, it's ultimately up to you what you can pay. To make that available to people, especially in a time like now where people are struggling—it's important to know that you don't have to pay the full fee but you can pay what works for you. So it's a great opportunity to get a bit of culture and do something beautiful and fun for the family.

Cafe du Soleil, 2723 Broadway; (212) 316-5000; www.cafedusoleilny.com

....

Pam Nelson, co-founder, Butter Lane Bakery

I once heard someone say, "You live more life in one day in New York City than you do somewhere else in a year." I thought, that sums it up. If you are greedy for life, that's what New York is all about. If you're trying to get as much as you can every day, this city is the place to be. I especially think that's true in your working years. There are other places that I want to see, or maybe spend more time in when I retire—like the South of France. But if you are making a living, New York is where you can get the most of life just walking down the street.

The real misconception about New York is that it's not intimate. But New York is one of the most intimate places in the country. You know your dry cleaner. You know the guy who runs the coffee shop. I mean, I have the same bus driver twice a week. You're not going to get that in a lot of other cities where you're driving all the time. It's a very cozy place to live and I think a lot of people who haven't lived in a walking city sometimes don't understand that. I would really miss that. It's a giant city with these really small moments that make it worth it.

The West Village in April is so spectacular. The trees start to bloom. And every day, it seems, a new block goes from green to white. It's glorious. On a perfect day, I would ride my bike up Hudson Street (which begins around Chambers Street in Tribeca) to West 12th Street. Bike lanes are everywhere.

Then I would make a right on West 12th Street and make my way through the West Village. I'd cut down to 11th Street. Eleventh Street is probably the prettiest block during that tree blooming time in April. The blooming trees and brownstones are gorgeous. Tartine there is my favorite brunch place in the whole city because you can sit outside and the wait isn't too long. And they have a fantastic brunch menu with great eggs Benedict and good hearty potatoes. It's fun people watching and you're in the middle of where all the trees have bloomed.

Afterward, I would head toward SoHo by going across on Spring Street all the way to McNally Jackson, my favorite bookstore. It's one of those bookstores where everybody who works there loves books and knows them. So, if you walk in and say, "What was that book about the lady on a ship that was in the *New York Times* Book Review last weekend?" they know exactly what it is and get it for you. It's inviting. It's just large enough to have just about everything you want, but it's cozy enough to feel like your local neighborhood bookstore. There's a little cafe so you can indulge in a brownie and a cup of coffee.

And from there, I would go to Balthazar. It's the place to meet a friend and talk about all the books you bought. What's so great about Balthazar is that it's always crowded, but you can always find a spot at the bar. So it's one of those bustling places where somehow, you can fit in. The bartender is always going to find some little nook for you and your friend to sit down. So you feel like you're in the middle of something really special that's happening. But you're not overwhelmed.

The food at Balthazar is always consistently great. The perfect dish there is beef stroganoff—think of a meaty and creamy sauce with big wide ribbons of pasta. I'd have that and a great glass of red wine, like a côte du rhône. And I love that the bartenders are always just so thoughtful. I have my own bakery and believe that Balthazar has great customer service. It's a bistro that finds a way to welcome everybody.

That's a good Sunday.

Tartine, 253 West 11th Street; (212) 229-2611

McNally Jackson Books, 52 Prince Street; (212) 274-1160; mcnallyjackson.com

Balthazar, 80 Spring Street; (212) 965-1414; www.balthazarny.com

. . . .

Chaske Spencer, *actor*

I came to New York with a hundred bucks and a one-way ticket. I landed at LaGuardia so $50 of that went to the taxi driver. And the other $50 was for scrounging around. I ate pizza and McDonald's french fries for a long time. I found a bartending job and like every struggling actor, struggled with acting. But then I started finding a little work here and there. And I fell in love with New York.

I've been all over the world and it's the best place in the world. There are a lot of creative people here. I like that I can meet artists but also meet interesting people who work on Wall Street. I love that we all get along and we're all growing together in this one big city.

A great day is when I can start it having breakfast at the Lodge, a restaurant in Williamsburg, Brooklyn. I love their steak and eggs, which melts in your mouth. I like to mix my steak and eggs together. It's just so good. And I just love the music there. One morning, they played nothing but early Rolling Stones from 1962 to 1965. I can relax, drink my coffee, and the waitstaff is really cool and nice. There's a really cool chill vibe there.

And then I love to head to Union Square. Back in the day when I was broke and could only afford to do free stuff, I would first go to Virgin Records before it closed and listen to music. Then I'd walk over to Barnes & Noble. And I would just browse and pick up a book and read the whole thing for free. I spent hours there. And I still love going there. I am a photographer too. So I'll take my camera and go all over downtown. I'll take lots of pictures of skyscrapers.

Lodge Restaurant, 318 Grand at Havemeyer, Brooklyn; www.lodgenyc.com

....

Maria Sharapova, tennis champion and winner of several Grand Slam singles titles

When I was younger, I thought the city was a bit overwhelming and a little too much for me. I appreciate it so much more now that I'm older and have visited different parts of the city and explored them. There's such a mix of eclectic people here and crazy energy. It's so much fun. You might see someone wearing high rainbow-colored socks. Just by walking I get inspired. I've met people who have taken me to their favorite places, which is always great.

I love SoHo. I just love browsing around and going to Aroma Espresso Bar and getting a halumi sandwich (with grilled halumi cheese, cream cheese, pickles, lettuce, and tomatoes) and drinking a cappuccino and watching the people go by. Then I'd go to Isabel Marant and the Cole Haan store. That's my perfect afternoon.

Aroma Espresso Bar, 145 Greene Street; (212) 533-1094; www.aroma.us

....

Chris Noth, Golden Globe–nominated actor

What makes New York unique is its history, tradition, culture, architecture, and people. There's the diversity of character of the people—that's the spirit of New York. I like places that represent what New York has been for decades and hasn't been rolled over and turned into another ubiquitous death by trendy restaurant.

When I first came to New York, I went to a small and intimate place called Trax where late at night you could hear a fantastic jam session. The music was spontaneous. Joni Mitchell and James Taylor jammed there. They came out and played and nobody knew what was going to happen. Anyone could show up, whether it was a scheduled band or artist, or somebody who was in town doing a big show and just wanted to relax and jam in a loose and unpressured environment. I love a place where serious music lovers can pop in to relax, hear new stuff and great music.

One of my favorite restaurants is Da Marino, right in the heart of the theater district and very much old New York. It's a neighborhood of friends and artists who come in to taste Pasquale Marino's southern Italian food. His mussels are incredible. Or sometimes he'll say, "I'm inspired, let me just make this dish for you." Pasquale is from Calabria, very spirited and truly the captain of his ship. Yet, sometimes someone will get on the guitar and just start singing.

Knickerbocker Bar and Grill also represents the spirit of New York. The place has an incredible wine list and a great old bar and some of the best steak in the city. And then there's Elaine's. I had been going there for years before it closed down. They should name a street after Elaine. It was a place where adults could go and have a conversation. It was a real social habitat.

Da Marino, 220 West 49th Street; (212) 549-6601

Knickerbocker Bar and Grill, 33 University Place; (212) 228-9490; www.knickerbockerbarandgrill.com

....

Blanche Baker, Emmy-winning actress

I like that Manhattan is an island. I live in Riverdale right over the Hudson River. And I love living right on the water all year around. Right outside my window during winter there are these plates of ice and you can hear the sound as they sort of clank together. I think it's quite romantic. And it's beautiful to look out to the Palisades here.

I used to live way downtown. My husband actually belongs to the Sailing Club of Manhattan by Battery Park City. In the summers we go sailing and I love visiting all these beautiful walkways down there. Even during winter, I bundle up and love going to look at the water.

There's this little cove where the boats go out, by my husband's sailing club. And there's a bunch of restaurants tucked away in the enclave. It's called North Cove. Take the subway nearby to the World Trade Center site and you will be close by.

I love sitting outside at one of the restaurants or on a bench and just gazing at the water. There's a wonderful old clock across the river and you can see lower parts of Manhattan. And when we go out on the water, we go around the end of Manhattan. It's so beautiful, like a mini vacation. And I think that sometimes we forget that we live on an island.

Southwest NY is a Southwestern restaurant right at North Cove, which overlooks the marina. If we have our kids with us, we always go there because they have great hamburgers and the best french fries—the kind that come in a cone. They have really good margaritas there too. But it tends to be a little noisy. So if it's just the adults, we tend to walk down a little ways along the water to an Italian restaurant called Gigino. And as you walk down the new pathway there are the most beautiful parks and places to sit. Gigino is along right on the water and you can linger there. And the spaghetti a la vongole, made with real clams, is unbelievable.

Southwest NY, 225 Liberty Street; (212) 945-0528; www.southwestny.com

Gigino's at Wagner Park, 20 Battery Place; (212) 528-2228; www.gigino-wagnerpark.com

....

Marlo Thomas, Emmy- and Golden Globe–winning actress, producer, author, activist, and founder of Marlothomas.com

I love to jog in Central Park every morning. I know every twig, rock, and leaf in that gorgeous, giant plot of green. Like most New Yorkers, I consider Central Park my very own. I even dedicated a bench in honor of Phil's and my anniversary, which I surprised him with!

A perfect afternoon for me is riding my bike to The Boathouse—especially in spring—and meeting friends for lunch. I love a table near the rail, so I can see the boats on the lake, and the gondoliers in their striped shirts. It's such a gentle, pastoral scene and then just beyond is one of the world's most famous skylines. I think that's what makes it so magical. If I'm there for brunch, I'll have the very decadent eggs Benedict, or a lobster salad for a later lunch. All the food is fabulous.

And nighttime? Well, that's my favorite New York time of day. The west side of my apartment has large windows, and the moment those first beautiful, orange streaks of sunset break over the park, I've got a front row seat. This always makes for an enchanting cocktail hour, and sets the perfect mood for having guests over for a cozy dinner, or heading out to Phil's and my favorite Italian restaurant, just down the avenue.

The Boathouse, Central Park, East 72nd Street and Park Drive North; (212) 517-2233; www.thecentralpark boathouse.com

. . . .

Gretchen Mol, actress

One thing I adore about New York is that you can walk around without any kind of agenda. You can be spontaneous. Or I love getting in the car and driving out to some part of Brooklyn that you never have visited before and discovering a good pizza place. It's like finding a treasure. There are all these cool little secrets. There's a place in Bushwick called Roberta's that has really delicious pizza. It's sort of hidden behind a door and you would never know what's behind it.

Roberta's, 261 Moore Street; (718) 417-1118; www.robertaspizza.com

. . . .

Raquel Bruno, producer, Drive Entertainment Group

In my rock & roll life, I used to love and still love seeing a show and afterward, late at night, I'd find myself at Odessa down on the Lower East Side. It's like walking into Telly Savalas's New York bar in 1978 and getting kielbasa and pierogis.

Another place that is a dying breed in New York City is the New York Jewish deli, which basically is like going to Mom's kitchen and getting things like chicken in the pot soup—which is just this massive thing of matzoth balls and kreplach. There aren't a lot of places that still serve those dishes. But my fiancé, my aunt, and I love heading to Sarge's to grab kasha or chicken in a pot or any kind of sandwich that is overstuffed. There's the bowl of pickles that's on the table, the side of coleslaw, which is a meal by itself, and that delicious soft challah. Thank God there's still Sarge's, which is family-run and one of the best places in the city.

Odessa, 119 Avenue A; (212) 253-1470

Sarge's Delicatessen, 548 3rd Avenue; (212) 679-0442; www.sargesdeli.com

....

Kristen Schaal, actress, writer, and comedian

My favorite thing in New York is to go to Keens Steakhouse and eat steak and drink really good fancy scotch. It's the oldest steak house in New York. The steak is brilliant and the atmosphere is like a Chuck E. Cheese for historians. It's full of history. It dates back to the 1800s and you can find a pipe that Ulysses S. Grant used to smoke. I like to get the porterhouse steak and ask for it to be cooked medium because honestly, they'll cook it medium rare anyways. I love the creamed spinach, mashed potatoes, and au poivre sauce on the side.

Keens Steakhouse, 72 West 36th Street; (212) 947-3636; www.keens.com

....

Chazz Palminteri, Academy Award–nominated actor, writer, and restaurateur

I love visiting my old neighborhood in the Bronx. I'm there about once a month. I wrote the movie *Bronx Tale* about the place. The neighborhood is still part of my life. It just makes me feel like when I was younger, when I was a kid, again.

The Bronx sometimes gets a bad rap, but there's one area which really is the original Little Italy. The food is unbelievable. There's Jerome who's called the Cannoli King. His father originally had the bakery, and he passed away. He was making cannolis for fifty years there. Now Jerome has it. The place is called Gino's on East 187th Street. They have the greatest cannolis I've ever tasted. And I've been eating their cannolis all my life, since I was a little boy. They're just perfect. The cream is perfect. The spicing is perfect. The seasoning . . . perfect.

I go to Mike's Deli, which has great cold cuts. For ravioli, I head to Borgatti's Ravioli & Egg Noodles, which has been there for almost a hundred years and he never franchised. He makes just enough and when he runs out, that's it. He closes up. The best mozzarella is at Casa Mozzarella. I can't even tell you how good it is. It's pretty phenomenal. You can watch him make it—stretching it in every direction.

And there are great restaurants. The fettucini alfredo at Rigoletto's is just so delicious, I can't explain it. Roberto's is great too. The porcini risotto there is the best. I'm so enamored with my neighborhood that I'm opening up a restaurant in Baltimore right on the water. It's called Chazz, a Bronx original. And they're actually going to open up a little theater in the Bronx and want to name it after me. The Chazz Palminteri Theater.

They say you can't go home again but when I go to that part of the Bronx, I do.

Gino's Pastry Shop, 580 East 187th Street, Bronx; (718) 584-3558

Mike's Deli, 2344 Arthur Avenue, Bronx; (718) 295-5033; www.arthuravenue.com

Borgatti's Ravioli & Egg Noodles, 632 East 187th Street, Bronx; (718) 367-3799; www.borgattis.com

Casa Della Mozzarella, 604 East 187th Street, Bronx; (718) 364-3867

Pasquale's Rigoletto, 2311 Arthur Avenue, Bronx; (718) 365-6644

Roberto Restaurant, 603 Crescent Avenue, Bronx; (718) 733-9503; www.roberto089.com

....

James Oseland, editor in chief, *Saveur*

For many decades, I have been doing this great centering activity. And that is taking a trip to Chinatown, usually on foot—from wherever I'm coming from. I just moved back to Manhattan from Williamsburg, Brooklyn, and even from Brooklyn I would walk across the Williamsburg Bridge and into Chinatown. Walking is part of this journey. It gives the experience of a take-you-someplace-else quality.

I head to Mulberry Meat Market to get a takeout lunch. In Chinatown it's known as a takeaway rice plate lunch. It's rice and a few other dishes served alongside. Mulberry Meat Market is not only a restaurant; it's a butcher and a place for one-stop shopping. It's actually one of my favorite shops in all of New York and it's old timey in the most wonderful way. They've got really wonderful meats, tofu products, eggs, and a small assortment of some of the most impeccable vegetables you'll find anywhere in Chinatown.

And in the middle of this great mix of things for sale is prepared food. There's just a tiny little counter. And at any given time they've got about 25 prepared foods. I don't know how they manage to squeeze it in. They have everything from stir-fries to red cooked dishes to rice porridge, roast duck, and roast pork. It's a gorgeous array of food.

The menu changes incessantly so you're never going to find any of the same things there. They almost always have a stir-fry in season. I'll get bok choy or Chinese mustard greens simply stir-fried with garlic and a pinch of salt.

I'll get a takeout container with rice and two or three of these wonderful prepared foods and walk a block and a quarter south to Chatham Square to eat my food. There's something about the whole activity—sitting down in Chatham Square under the trees with the Chinese opera singers and the gambling men and ladies—that's just a really, really deeply satisfying New York moment. Chatham Square is very special. It's the center of old Chinatown and has been for over 100 years. The vibe is like nowhere else in New York. A lot of New York shifts and transforms, but there's something very constant about Chatham Square and how it looks and sounds. It's very otherworldly. It grounds me. It nourishes me in the most terrific way.

I work very intensely and have one of those seven-day-a-week jobs that's with me day in and day out. But this particular activity takes me away from all of that in a very clean, succinct way. I don't have to take a four-week trip to Southeast Asia. I can take a brief trip to Chinatown. Granted, it's not the same experience that a four-week trip to Southeast Asia would deliver, but somehow it affects me in a similar way and pushes the same buttons.

Mulberry Meat Market, Inc., 89 Mulberry Street; (212) 267-0350

....

Scott Bond, celebrity hair stylist and owner with George Wilman of Hair in the City and Know! Hair & Body

On a gorgeous New York City day, my partner George Wilman and I love to hit Bleecker Street between Cornelia and Leroy Streets in Greenwich Village. Bleecker Street is such a treasure of a street that has been immortalized in songs from Led Zeppelin to Joni Mitchell to Iggy Pop. It's lined with little boutique shops and eateries and even a couple of trees. We stock up on tasty items at four of our favorite mom-and-pop specialty food stores and have a picnic in the park at Father Demo Square that's about a block and a half east of the stores.

First we hit Faicco's Pork Store. Talk about a spotless old-school butcher shop! Even though they have fantastic meats and unbelievable sandwiches, we usually grab a tartuffo or two and then move on. We go here first so the tartuffo has time to get soft and gooey.

Next door is Murray's Cheese Shop. The minute you walk inside, the mouthwatering aroma of cured meats overtakes you, which is only to be overtaken by the smell of wonderful cheese. The choices here are a bit overwhelming. So we stick with our favorite—parmiggano Reggiano Bonati. This cheese is made on a farm with less than a hundred cows that are fed a vegetarian diet. Due to the small herd, they are only able to produce four wheels a day. And a small piece of the Montgomery cheddar is also always a must. This cheese is to die for! With all that dairy one needs a little protein, so we add some sliced chorizo (for the cheddar) and some prosciutto di Parma (for the parmiggano), and we're off to our next store.

Lobster Place is right next to Murray's and a stop not to be missed. In fact, it's like the seafood version of Faicco's. This is where we order up a quarter pound of lobster salad to lighten up the meal. On the corner next to the seafood joint is Amy's Bread, where we find hands down the best baguettes in the city. Our usual order is, "One baguette and two coffees to go please."

Once we're armed with our extraordinary snack, we walk one minute to the park to eat. A favorite place to relax and enjoy our gourmet goodies is by the beautifully landscaped fountain, Father Demo Square at Bleecker and Carmine

Streets, where we sit amid the flower beds and swaying trees. And we marvel at our delicious finds.

George and I have been doing this too many years to count. Every visit we enjoy our snacks and take time out of our hectic lives to just relax and rejuvenate, and that's why this New York experience will always hold a special place in our hearts.

Faicco's Pork Store, 260 Bleecker Street; (212) 243-1974

Murray's Cheese Shop, 254 Bleecker Street; (212) 243-3289; www.murrayscheese.com

Lobster Place Seafood Market, 252 Bleecker Street; (212) 352-8063; www.lobsterplace.com

Amy's Bread, 250 Bleecker Street; (212) 675-7802; www.amysbread.com

....

Terence Winter, Emmy-winning writer, executive producer, and creator of *Boardwalk Empire*

I love the diversity of New York. My wife and I spend a lot of time in Los Angeles and have little kids. And I always say that my kids see more walking down a block in New York City than they would in a month in LA. You see everything here and are exposed to all kinds of people—all kinds of cultures, all kinds of entertainment from highbrow to low to everything in between. It's just so vibrant and 24 hours a day, there's something to do.

You can walk into any pizzeria in New York and it's great. But my number one place is Spumoni Gardens in Brooklyn. It's near and dear to my heart because I grew up in Brooklyn and used to hang out there. I've been going to Spumoni since I was a kid. But they also serve amazing pizza. And I love just their plain cheese pizza. You cannot beat Spumoni Gardens Sicilian pizza. Also you can buy it and freeze it and have it at home. So whenever I'm there I buy a couple and bring it home.

Spumoni Gardens, 2725 86th Street, Brooklyn; (718) 449-1230; www.spumonigardens.com

....

Janet Carroll, film, television, recording, and stage actress

Ever since I came to town in the 1960s, I have always been drawn to the Upper West Side. I loved all the other world-famous sights—the Broadway houses, Carnegie Hall, and the Met. But when I have any free time, I walk up the West Side—on Broadway, Amsterdam, Columbus, or Central Park West. I can never get enough of it. Now that I live here I am happily snuggled into my lovely Upper West Side apartment.

The minute you walk in the door at the restaurant Vince & Eddie's on West 68th Street, all heads turn to see who is coming in. It's that small. The conversation is subdued. It's not a noisy place. It's like you're walking into an intimate, very personal, cozy spot where people nod and say hi and you feel welcome. And the staff acts like they've known you forever. And no matter where they seat you, you're going to be comfortable and you'll be able to hear yourself having a conversation. It's an incredibly refreshing place to go—whether you have a little bit of time or want to spend a more leisurely evening dining.

The food is really scrumptious and delectable. Their fish dishes are great. I love the melt-in-your-mouth beef liver and onions. (Yeah, I know.) And their European-style roast duckling is so delicious. They have great salads, and my son has enjoyed the pork chops and meatloaf. They always bring roasted garlic oil and bread that you can dip into it. You can have as much as you can stand and I love it.

Vince & Eddie's Restaurant, 70 West 68th Street; (212) 721-0068; www.vinceandeddiesnewyork.com

....

Karen Schaler, Emmy-winning television travel host and author of *Travel Therapy: Where Do You Need to Go?*

I'm one of those New Yorkers who loves my own neighborhood. It takes a lot to get me away from the Upper West Side. I literally groan every time I have to go cross-town. So the fact that one of my favorite places in the city is all the way in the Bronx is a testament to how incredible Madonia Brothers Bakery is. My mouth is already watering just thinking about it!

As a travel correspondent, I'm always searching for unique places to explore. So after moving to the city, I stumbled across a small blurb about how New York's "true" Little Italy is in the Bronx—covering 4 blocks along Arthur Avenue. When I asked some longtime New Yorkers about Arthur Avenue, many had never heard of it, except for a few foodie friends who seemed surprised I was asking. They call it one of New York's best-kept secrets.

Intrigued and hungry, I jumped on the D train, heading uptown, and twenty minutes later got off at Fordham Road and then walked about 15 minutes to Arthur Avenue. As soon as I hit the street, I felt like I had just stepped out of a time machine and was transported back 50 years.

Lined up one after another are tiny, quaint mom-and-pop Italian and seafood restaurants, cheese, meat, and pasta shops, and old-fashioned bakeries. Most of the businesses have been in the same family for generations, so there's a sense of history and authenticity and a small-town friendly atmosphere. Each time you pass a store or restaurant new delicious aromas beckon you inside and it's almost impossible not to fill a shopping bag full of goodies.

Still, my ultimate favorite find is Madonia Brothers Bakery and its phenomenal olive bread, which costs five dollars. From the moment I first sank my teeth into the thin crunchy crust and savored the warm, soft, chewy middle that's packed with plump, juicy, black, salty olives, I knew I had found something spectacular—olive bread worth the hour trek to the Bronx and every single sinful calorie.

From the outside, Madonia Brothers looks like any other traditional bakery with a blue awning shadowing large windows showcasing everything from fresh baked bread to cookies. Inside the bakery is small and can get crowded on the weekends, so better to go during the week if you can. You also need cash; they don't take credit cards. Be prepared to be in awe the first time you walk in. Cannolis are filled fresh while you wait, and biscottis will tempt, but head straight for the bread; that's the real star here.

Besides the heavenly olive bread, other traditional favorites include the prosciutto or jalapeno-cheddar. No matter what loaf you pick you really can't go wrong. For three generations Madonia has been making its bread fresh daily, on the premises. Just be sure to pick up at least two loaves because there's a good chance you'll polish off the first one before you get home.

Madonia Brothers Bakery, 2348 Arthur Avenue, Bronx; (718) 295-5573

....

Kevin Spacey, Academy Award–winning actor, director, producer, and artistic director of the Old Vic

The best thing that is going to happen later tonight is that I'll get to Joe's Pizza. It's the best pizza in town.

....

Josh Fox, Academy Award–nominated documentary filmmaker, playwright, screenwriter, and director

Joe's Pizza serves the best pizza in the world. I like to get the plain and fresh mozzarella slices. You just cannot describe the best pizza in the world. And there's always something happening there. There are all these people crowded around there. But visit about four o'clock in the morning, when the bars are letting out—and there is a line around the block. This really is the greatest city in the world. I mean you've got the best pizza in the world and they're open at *four in the morning*.

Joe's Pizza, 7 Carmine Street; (212) 366-1182; www.joespizzanyc.com

....

Tom McCarthy, Oscar-nominated writer, actor, and director

I love going to the matinees at the Film Forum. Then I'll have lunch somewhere right in the area. Westville on 10th Street and Bleecker is awesome. This great guy opened it, and it's a little place and usually packed. And there are a lot of celebrities in there. They have the most amazing hot dogs, and they've also got a great complete menu. I'll get the hot dogs with the works: chili, relish, ketchup, and mustard.

Westville Restaurant, 210 West 10th Street; (212) 741-7971; www.westvillenyc.com

....

Kyle MacLachlan, Emmy- and Golden Globe–nominated actor

New York is a lot about restaurants, and going to a great place to eat is always wonderful. I have many friends who are in that business. John Macdonald recently opened Burger & Barrel on Houston Street and it's fantastic. It's so cozy and beautifully decorated and the food is really satisfying. I can't eat there all the time because if I do, I'll get fat. Not only is the food great, John is a great and friendly host. They do a special caramelized onion burger there that's amazing that I always order. It's very, very good. Also, I love just driving past Times Square. Whenever my wife and I have a chance and we're coming from uptown to downtown, we always try to go through Times Square. It's life and it's fun. The atmosphere of New York is the best in the world.

Burger & Barrel, 25 West Houston Street; (212) 334-7320; www.burgerandbarrel.com

....

Cady Huffman, Tony Award–winning actress, dancer and singer

I love Broadway! It's the reason I live in New York City. And I love just walking around the theater district, especially 44th Street. It's the home of the St. James, where I performed in *The Producers.* The St. James has an incredible history. Carol Channing starred in *Hello Dolly* there. Carol Burnett played there in *Once upon a Mattress*.

In addition to the St. James, the street also has the Shubert, another very famous theater. The Shubert is where *A Chorus Line* played for all those years. It's one of those magical theaters. I'm from Santa Barbara, California. And when I was a little kid, I saw *A Chorus Line* in Los Angeles. That completely changed my life and inspired me to become a performer. My brother and I played the album for three months straight. Then when I was 16 and in New York on a ballet scholarship, I remember walking by the theater. It always made me feel elevated. It's amazing. I still get that same feeling walking past there.

When I was in *The Producers*, after I performed, I loved going to Angus McIndoe to check out all the Broadway people out of costume. Right after the shows, at 11 p.m., it's a big theater hangout. If you want to see Broadway folks, head to the third floor. And they have great desserts, but I try not to get any of them. Angus has fantastic pie, which comes hot with a big scoop of ice cream on it. Sometimes he sends it over, and I'm forced to eat it under duress. I just love every single bite.

Angus McIndoe Restaurant, 258 West 44th Street; (212) 221-9222; www.angusmcindoe.com

. . . .

Bruce Morrow (aka "Cousin Brucie"), legendary broadcaster, photographer, and author

If I ever want to show New York to out-of-towners, I have to bring them to Little Italy, especially Mulberry Street. That's the real New York and it hasn't changed. And each restaurant has its own identity. There's nothing like those delicious smells—the baked clams at Umberto's Clam House, the mozzarella carozza at La Mela, and the lobster fra diavolo at Da Nico. I've been going to Little Italy since I was a little boy, but I think I really started to appreciate it when my wife, Jodie, came into my life. She's the pasta princess of New York. She loves pasta and anything with red sauce. So now Jodie and I go to Little Italy almost every week. It still has that feeling and romance of when I was a child. And besides having the best baked clams in the universe, Umberto's has the best waiter, Big Joe.

Umberto's Clam House, 386 Broome Street; (212) 431-7545; www.umbertosclamhouse.com

La Mela Ristorante, 167 Mulberry Street; (212) 431-9493; www.lamelarestaurant.com

Da Nico, 164 Mulberry Street; (212) 343-1212; http://danicoristorante.com

. . . .

Fred Armisen, actor

I love having sushi at Sushi of Gari. I almost don't want anyone to know about it. But it's all right. It's perfect deliciousness. I want to eat every piece of sushi there. I really love the spicy tuna. I also like it because I feel like it's good for me.

Sushi of Gari, 402 East 78th Street; (212) 517-5340; 347 West 46th Street; (212) 957-0046; www.sushiofgari.com

....

Ruth Reichl, best-selling author, editor, and host of the television show, *Gourmet's Adventures with Ruth*

Your question is a great question. It really made me think of what I do. I thought oh God, I should say something like I go to the Morgan Library, which I would do sometimes too.

The real truth is if I have an hour, I love to get on the subway, head downtown, and go food shopping. There are three different places that I visit. Probably the route I like best is down to Chinatown. I wander around and load up on roasted meats and shrimp. I go to Super Taste and get frozen dumplings and then I go to Di Palo's in Little Italy and get the best parmesan cheese in the city and pasta. And then I go over to Russ & Daughters and get their smoked fish and Turkish pistachios.

I could spend hours just walking in and out of those stores and watching people and smelling. The aroma changes as you move from one neighborhood to the next. So you're in Chinatown and it smells like fermented soybean paste, garlic, and dried fish. And you see frogs escaping off into the street. Then you get into Little Italy and it's fresh ricotta, other great cheeses, and olive oil. And you go over to Russ & Daughters. My grandmother went there at the turn of the century. When I go, I think about her telling me about how her mother would visit and she'd be wearing long, long gloves. And she would take off her gloves and stick her hands down into the pickle barrel. And then I go to Yonah Schimmel and they've got a 150-year-old yogurt culture. If you make your own yogurt, it makes such a great starter. I love that it tastes of history.

In the '70s I lived down there and would wander around when it was a really scary neighborhood. The butchers were always so great. I learned about food wandering those streets. It's still totally thrilling to me and keeps changing as new immigrant groups come in. I've watched Chinatown go from being Cantonese to having Fujianese come in. And now there are all these people doing hand-pulled noodles and Shan foods. It's just fascinating and it's always something new. I could spend days. I mean that's my problem. I'd have an hour and I jump on the subway and the next thing I know, the day is gone. And I don't stop until I can't carry one more thing. Also, all these people are so generous. You talk to them and taste things and you get ideas for recipes.

New York is the most exciting place to live and the greatest walking city. I'm a walker and keep fit by walking. I don't belong to a gym. You can just get on the subway, get off somewhere, wander around, and there's always something to do. I love the fact that I can walk across the park and spend a half an hour at the Met.

I also like being a New Yorker because I feel that my history is here. Around every corner—my parents, my grandparents. I feel sort of connected to the earth in the city. I walk past my old school or my father's office and suddenly they're there with me. I feel like I could turn a corner and my father is there.

The city is also just so rich in ethnic delights. You can get fresh turmeric and hundreds and hundreds of different spices here. I'll take the subway out to Jackson Heights and go wander around the Indian supermarkets and bring back curry leaves and snake gourd and all the makings for dosa. The Patel Brothers is a huge market there.

Sometimes I just follow people and watch where they're shopping. In Chinatown I'll just find these little old ladies and follow them in and out of stores. And I'll find some butcher I don't know about. Food people are very generous. If you ask someone what do you do with this, they're happy to give you recipes. Maybe not the first person. Maybe it's the second person. You know New Yorkers have this reputation for being rude and brusque. But I find if you stop in the middle of the street, within ten seconds someone will come up to you and say, "Can I help you?"

Super Taste Restaurant, 26 Eldridge Street; (212) 625-1198

Di Palo's Fine Foods, 200 Grand Street; (212) 226-1033; www.dipaloselects.com

Russ & Daughters, 179 East Houston Street; (212) 475-4880; www.russanddaughters.com

Yonah Schimmel Knish Bakery, 137 East Houston Street; (212) 477-2858; www.knishery.com

....

Cat Greenleaf, Emmy-winning television host of her series, *Talk Stoop with Cat Greenleaf*

I have been going to Tom's Restaurant in Prospect Heights since 2003. My husband and I looked at an apartment right next door, and the very existence of Tom's sold us on the apartment. Everything is right in the world the minute you get there. Often the line is around the block and you don't get to go in immediately. But no matter what the weather, they bring you coffee or cookies or french fries or an orange.

Gus Vlahavas, the former owner, who has since sold it, is there all the time and treats everyone like family. In the city where my husband and I don't have any grandparents, it is amazing to have this grandfather who is always happy to see us and does the embarrassing stuff that a grandfather does. He'll say to everyone in the line, "You know she's on TV." He felt proud when he watched me on television. But it's not just me. He treats everyone like a star.

When we adopted my son, you know how you keep the baby inside for a couple of weeks? The first stop when we got out was to Tom's. Gus is from Eastern Europe and there's a tradition that they throw coins into the baby carriage for good luck. So upon seeing my son, he threw a handful of quarters at us.

I love the egg white omelet with turkey bacon and cremated onions and dry rye toast and french fries with their special chipotle sauce on the side. I think about it all week long. And the decor? Imagine your grandmother's kitchen exploded with tchotchkes and memorabilia everywhere. And the staff, who have been with him for years, are all nice, they're all practically trained in improv—they're all funny, they remember you. Tom's doesn't take reservations. It's not open for dinner, there are no mimosas or Bloody Marys. It's really one of my favorite places to be.

Tom's Restaurant, 782 Washington Avenue, Brooklyn; (718) 636-9738

....

Elisabeth Moss, Golden Globe– and Emmy-nominated actress

I've always loved New York since I was a little girl. There's the architecture, the art, the energy, the amount of options, the walking, the restaurants, the subways.

It's like no city in the world. I've been to a lot of cities, but this is my favorite. And I love the Bowery Hotel and Gemma, the restaurant next to it. In fact, Gemma is my favorite restaurant in New York. They have all kinds of delicious crostinis. The buffalo ricotta one is amazing. I go there a lot.

Gemma, 335 Bowery; (212) 505-9100; www.theboweryhotel.com

....

Rachel Dratch, actress

I love living in New York. It has everything, it's open all night, and there are neighborhoods that don't make you feel like you're in a big city. If you feel overwhelmed, all you have to do is look at a map and get out of midtown.

One of my favorite restaurants is Supper on 2nd Street. It's Italian, has a super fun vibe, and the food is amazing. The spaghetti al limone with fresh lemon and parmigiano cheese is awesome; so is the tagliatelle Bolognese, which I usually order. You can't go wrong with the place. It's really inexpensive for that quality of food. And the Tasting Room Wine Bar is super fun. The bartender there is a neighborhood fixture.

Supper, 156 East 2nd Street; (212) 477-7600; www.supperrestaurant.com

The Tasting Room Wine Bar & Cafe, 72 East 1st Street; (212) 358-7831; www.tastingroomnewyork.tripod.com

....

Kelly Cutrone, founder of the public relations firm People's Revolution, star of *Kell on Earth,* and author

For twenty years, the maitre'd at Angelo's of Mulberry Street treated me really badly. I'd go there with David Lee Roth and the maitre'd would grumble and say, "HOW MANY!" and I'd say "three" and he'd say "WAIT AT THE BAR! IT'S GOING TO BE AN HOUR!" But then one day he just became really nice to me. I thought, he must have seen my TV show, but he just became really nice. No matter what, I love going there. The food is amazing. The waiters sing happy birthday to me in Italian. There are a lot of old-school New Yorker types and a lot of tourists. And you can see the wonder of New York through the eyes of a tourist and the heart of New

York through the old-school Italians. It's very like Carmine Ragusa kind of *Happy Days* old school. Unfortunately, I love the spaghetti in garlic and olive oil, which is very fattening. But I love it. I eat there a lot, like twice a week. With my job, I have to visit very super cool places. So my idea of a fun night in New York is nowhere cool or trendy. My idea of a good restaurant is if it's not cool or trendy, it's safe to eat.

Angelo's of Mulberry Street, 146 Mulberry Street; (212) 966-1277; www.angelomulberry.com

....

Molly Shannon, Emmy-nominated actress

Manhattan is about neighborhoods. They are our backyards. When I'm in a really good mood, I walk to my favorite neighborhood, the West Village. It's like a small, quaint town and almost reminds me of River City in *The Music Man*. One of my much-loved spots for lunch is La Bonbonniere, a little greasy spoon. I always have the chicken salad sandwich on white bread while I read the *New York Times* and the *New York Post*. Afterwards, I walk to Magnolia Bakery, which makes me so happy. I love visiting just to smell the butter.

La Bonbonniere, 28 8th Avenue; (212) 741-9266; www.labon.com

Magnolia Bakery, 401 Bleecker Street; (212) 462-2572; www.magnoliabakery.com

....

Michael Stern, author

My favorite place in New York is Katz's Deli on Houston Street. It's an experience you will find *only* in New York City. And to have them slice the corned beef or pastrami in front of you, get a little nosh while they're making the sandwich, take the sandwich back to a table and sit in that din is sensational. Never mind the fact that *When Harry Met Sally* was filmed there and she had an orgasm thinking about it; it's a great place to eat.

....

Sherri Shepherd, actress, comedian, and Emmy-winning co-host of *The View*

New York is a city that truly never sleeps. It 's exciting to be here. Los Angeles shuts down at 2 a.m. The only thing open is Kinkos. I love the vibe of New York. It's just so diverse. [My son] Jeffrey will have a play date with a Chinese boy. He's got a little boy from Armenia that he plays with.

And I enjoy riding the subway. Because as an actress, I like to look at people and figure out their story. Everyone has a story. And I love watching people and imagining it. So I'll ride the subway to Katz's Deli. I'll go right before they close, right after I perform in a comedy club.

On Fridays, I arrive around 11 p.m. or midnight; during the week, I get there about 9 p.m. And not only can I watch people at Katz's, their pastrami is to die for. I never get anything else but the pastrami on rye bread with lots of mustard. If you want to go close to heaven, Katz's pastrami sandwiches will get you there. It just melts in your mouth. It's funny. I don't even like pastrami, but I discovered it when I asked for corned beef. But one of the little old ladies who worked there made me order the pastrami. I'm so glad she did. It's just so tender.

Katz's Delicatessen, 205 East Houston Street; (212) 254-2246; http://katzsdelicatessen.com

....

Katrina Bowden, actress

I love ceviche so much, I'll try it every place that offers it on the menu. But Yuca Bar in the East Village has the best salmon ceviche that I've ever tasted. The restaurant has a mix of Mexican–South American flavors and also offers a cool, funky bar scene. In fact, I was just in Mexico and had ceviche and it wasn't as good as Yuca Bar.

Yuca Bar, 111 Avenue A; (212) 982-9833; www.yucabarnyc.com

....

John Legend, Grammy Award–winning musician, and **Christine Teigen,**
supermodel

John Legend: New York is the best city in the world. There's so much to do. I
moved here in 2000 and most of my music is written here. It's a great place to
collaborate and I'm always inspired by the city. It's endless.

Christy Teigen: And if you ever have a day where you are alone, you can feel
comfortable eating by yourself reading. We also live in Los Angeles, but it feels
harder to be alone there.

John Legend: The city is company enough.

Christy Teigen: And the people watching is amazing.

John Legend: A lot of our favorite things in New York revolve around food.

Christy Teigen: If it's a Sunday, we'll order in Thai and watch football for the entire
day. But on most other days, we'll go to the Washington Square dog park and
have brunch.

John Legend: We love brunch at Frank Restaurant.

Christy Teigen: It's small, tiny, and the people are fun.

John Legend: The baked eggs ragu is amazing—to die for. It has the best tastes you
can have in one dish. Parmesan cheese, eggs—

Christy Teigen: Meatballs.

John Legend: Tomato sauce. It's simple but too good to be true.

Frank Restaurant & Vera Bar, 88 2nd Avenue; (212) 420-0106; www.frankrestaurant.com

....

Mario Cantone, comedian, writer, and actor

My favorite thing to do in New York? Dine. Dine. Dine. I'm a big foodie whore.
New York has everything. I go to Per Se, Robuchon, Del Posto, Esca. I love those
restaurants. They're brilliant! They just know how to do it. Per Se is brilliantly
designed, the food is impeccable, the service is outrageously brilliant, and I've had
many meals that changed my life there. Del Posto has these poached oysters in

pearls with caviar and tapioca. I could eat 20 of them. That's just the beginning and it goes from there. Daniel Boulud of DANIEL is one of my heroes. I'm kind of a chef nut. I want to know and meet them. So I've gotten to know many of them. In fact, when Lidia Bastianich approaches me, I kind of stand up like she's my mother, bow my head, and adore her. I can't say that one place or chef is better than the other. It depends on the night. All of them are the greatest.

Per Se, Time Warner Center, 10 Columbus Circle, 4th floor; (212) 823-9335; www.perseny.com

L'Atelier de Joel Robuchon, Four Seasons Hotel, 57 East 57th Street; (212) 829-3844; www.fourseasons.com

Del Posto, 85 10th Avenue; (212) 497-8090; www.delposto.com

Esca, 402 West 43rd Street; (212) 564-7272; www.esca-nyc.com

DANIEL, 60 East 65th Street; (212) 288-0033; www.danielnyc.com

....

Jason Sudeikis, actor and comedian

When my friends come to town and I want to give them a true New York dining experience, I take them to Lupa restaurant downtown on Thompson Street. Everyone is seated really close together and the food kicks ass. I like to order the fettuccine noodles with pork shoulder ragu and olives. It's really, really good. And they have lots of good antipasti. Besides, at the end of the night, you're too drunk to care about the bill.

Lupa, 170 Thompson Street; (212) 982-5089; www.luparestaurant.com

....

Mayor Michael Bloomberg, 108th mayor of New York City

I like to run in the park. And I like to eat at my favorite Greek diner, Viand. I always go there. Everything's quick. Everything's good. The people are nice. [Favorite dish?] Fried chicken. Not even close.

Viand, 1011 Madison Avenue; (212) 249-8250

....

Amar'e Stoudemire, power forward, New York Knicks

When I was first looking to sign here, I factored in everything that comes with New York. The city is very diverse, it lets you be yourself, and it's fun. And once I signed and got the deal done, I was extremely excited. I love that there's so much going on. Going to a cafe and grabbing brunch is always fun. I love Pastis. It's a great French brunch spot. Normally I get steak and eggs there. It's early morning for me.

Pastis, 9 9th Avenue; (212) 929-4844; www.pastisny.com

....

Harry Shum Jr., actor and dancer

I'm a foodie so I love trying anything that's good. I don't care what type of food it is; as long as it's good, I'm down for it. Eating in New York is an adventure. I love the variety here. We shot *Glee* at Mario Batali's massive Italian emporium called Eataly. And I love that you can go from that to a little corner spot like Totto Ramen. It's a hole-in-the-wall place and one of the best ramen spots in New York City. You can quote me. You have to try it. It's really incredible. Their soup base is awesome. Their noodles are a little crunchy, but there's softness to it.

And you know what I love about Lea Michele? She loves New York. If you need any kind of tip about New York, you can ask Lea and she will be able to tell you the best place to go for anything.

Eataly, 200 5th Avenue; (646) 398-5100; http://eatalyny.com

Totto Ramen, 366 West 52nd Street; (212) 582-0052; www.tottoramen.com

....

Will Ferrell, Emmy- and Golden Globe-nominated actor

My favorite thing to do in New York City? Well, New York is my favorite city to run in, because I can go in any direction and find a new neighborhood or new street that I haven't been on before. So there's that and the fact that my wife and I love getting coffee at Ninth Street Espresso in Chelsea market. It's just the best coffee ever.

Ninth Street Espresso, Chelsea Market, 75 9th Avenue; (212) 228-2930; www.ninthstreetespresso.com

....

Arianna Huffington, author, columnist, editor in chief, and founder, *The Huffington Post*

I love being downtown—walking around and discovering new restaurants. In fact, I love the whole area around the Italian restaurant Morandi. The food and the energy is so vibrant and wonderful. You feel like you're in a real family restaurant. Their Sunday brunch is perfect, especially since the egg dishes are so fantastic.

....

Bethenny Frankel, best-selling author, television star, and chef

What do I love about New York? Every single day offers something different and new to discover. There's always something to do. You don't need a car. And you can explore a new pocket of the city. My husband, Jason, and I love walking for an hour and then going to a restaurant with Bryn for lunch. We like to experiment with different restaurants, different kinds of foods and neighborhoods. We'll often go to Morandi. It's not far from our apartment. It's cozy. It's Italian. They are very sweet to us with Bryn. Although we like any place that has butternut squash soup because that's one of her favorite foods.

Morandi, 211 Waverly Place; (212) 627-7575; www.morandiny.com

....

A.J. Calloway, television correspondent, *Extra*

A lot of people do the Meatpacking District now. But I'm old school and stick to the SoHo route. I love hanging out in SoHo and getting corn at Cafe Habana. It's a great place for Cuban food and almost one of the best-kept secrets in New York.

Well, it's not a big secret, but they have really great corn with parmesan cheese and spices. It's pretty awesome.

And you know, there's no place in the world like New York City. You can find nooks of different parts of the world. You'll be in Little Italy, cross the street, and all of a sudden end up in China. And you'll have authentic meals from both regions. I've traveled the world and there's nothing else like this town.

Cafe Habana, 17 Prince Street; (212) 625-2001; www.cafehabana.com

....

Paul Dano, actor, and Zoe Kazan, actor

Paul Dano: I like to take my woman on a walk around the neighborhoods in Carroll Gardens, Brooklyn Heights, Cobble Hill, and hopefully end up at one of our favorite places to grab a little bite to eat. New York and good food!

Zoe Kazan: Brucie is our new favorite restaurant in New York City. It's run by a woman named Zara. She's around our age, is really cool, and an amazing chef. She makes fantastic Italian dishes.

Brucie, 234 Court Street, Brooklyn; (347) 987-4961; www.brucienyc.com

....

Brooke Lyons, actress

Growing up in Connecticut, I often took the Metro North line into Manhattan. Even now, when that train barrels toward Grand Central, I get goose bumps from the approaching city's outstretched energy. The feeling of stepping off the train is as intoxicating now as it was years ago: that unmistakable aroma of hot dogs, pretzels, and peanuts, that familiar sound of echoing conversations and shuffling footsteps, and that glorious view of backwards constellations on the main concourse ceiling. I rarely go to New York with a plan. I love to step out onto Vanderbilt Avenue and be swept away by the city's unparalleled sense of possibility. In the winter, I find myself wandering toward the Rockefeller Center Christmas tree and the festive Saks window displays. In the summer, I'm all about the Strand Book Store, the

Angelika Film Center, and any of various benches where one can sit, sip an iced coffee, and experience some of the best people-watching in the world.

Last December, we bundled up and ventured out into the freezing afternoon. The city draped in freshly fallen snow is breathtaking. We meandered over to the Grey Dog on Carmine Street for some delicious coffee and the best slice of pecan pie I've ever had, and sprinted from there to Barrow Street Theatre, where we watched a matinee showing of David Cromer's *Our Town.* Treasures around every corner. A perfect New York day.

Grey Dog, 33 Carmine Street; (212) 462-0041; also located at 242 West 16th Street; (212) 229-2345, and 90 University Place; (212) 414-4739; http://thegreydog.com

Barrow Street Theatre, 27 Barrow Street; (212) 868-4444; www.barrowstreettheatre.com

....

Nina Garcia, *Marie Claire* fashion director and *Project Runway* judge

New York is the center of fashion. When I first got here, I was very inspired by the energy of the city. New York was a dream to me. And I thought, this is where my dreams will come true. This is where I really want to be.

There are so many restaurants in New York, it's hard to pick one or two. Right now I really like the Lion. It's not too big. But it's not too small. It's small enough and perfect. There isn't one particular dish there that I always order. But the food is phenomenal. The service is terrific. A lot of my friends in the fashion business go there. And the other restaurant I really like is ABC Kitchen. It has a really interesting menu with local organic food.

The Lion, 62 West 9th Street; (212) 353-8400; www.thelionnyc.com

ABC Kitchen, 35 East 18th Street; (212) 475-5829; www.abckitchennyc.com

....

Robert Lopez, Tony Award–winning composer and lyricist

I like going to old coffee shops on MacDougal Street. I grew up in the city. And when I was in high school, I used to go to Caffe Dante every Friday. I still like going there. It reminds me of the history of Greenwich Village: the intellectuals who used to live here and the artists—all the beat poets. It's the heritage. And I always get a pignoli tart and espresso. I was a boring kid. I didn't have a fake ID. So I just went there.

Caffe Dante, 79-81 MacDougal Street; (212) 982-5275; www.caffe-dante.com.

....

Henrik Lundqvist, New York Rangers goalie

I'm no chef. I'm terrible in the kitchen. I eat a lot, but cannot cook. So I love going to different restaurants and hanging out with friends. I like brunch at Eatery because they have great omelets and desserts. And I enjoy the real neighborhood feeling at 9. In fact, I recently opened my own restaurant with a few friends called Tiny's in Tribeca. Part of why I'm involved in the restaurant is so I can eat. Tiny's is small and, I think, a cool place. The building is more than 100 years old. It's actually called Tiny's and the Bar Upstairs.

Matt Abramcyk is the brain behind the restaurant and he's done a great job designing the whole place. I trust Matt. He has other restaurants in the city, like Smith & Mills and he was running Beatrice Inn for a while. He has cool taste. When you go, you have to try the turkey chili. It's great! I just love it.

One thing I love about New York is the mix of everything—culture, restaurants, and entertainment. And you can live a pretty normal life, be whoever you want to be and people don't really care. I'm from Sweden, a small country. So I was just excited to come here and play the game. But then you realize you're lucky to play in this city. It's a tough city but when you do well it's good.

Eatery, 798 9th Avenue; (212) 765-7080; www.eaterynyc.com

9, 800 9th Avenue; (212) 956-3333; 9restaurantnyc.com

Tiny's and the Bar Upstairs, 135 West Broadway; (212) 374-1135; www.tinysandthebarupstairs.com

....

Eddie Kaye Thomas, actor

I like to buy the *Daily News* and have breakfast alone at a Greek diner, any Greek diner. Actually, I was just at Joe Jr. this morning and ordered the corned beef hash, eggs over easy. I love the smell of the coffee. All I need is the paper and I feel like I'm in a cool detective novel. I feel like I'm living a cool life when I do that. I don't know why.

Joe Jr. Restaurant, 167 3rd Ave; (212) 473-5150

....

Mike Birbiglia, comedian, writer, and actor

My wife and I got married at City Hall. And afterwards, we took the subway to Big Nick's on the Upper West Side and ate pizza and hamburgers. It was just the two of us and we took photos on our camera phone. That was the most offensive-to-parents wedding that you could imagine. Actually, we wanted to go the opposite of your typical wedding, which would be over the top and flamboyant. We just wanted something simple and no frills, so we went bare bones.

We eat at Big Nick's a lot. We live nearby and we like the laid-back nature of the place. Besides, they take pizza very seriously. And so do I. For example, on the menu, there's a number you can call—a hotline for late night pizza emergencies. So if you really need pizza in a medical way, they will help. I'm a purist, so I just like their plain pizza. Also, the staff is very nice. They're a good group of people.

Big Nick's Pizza Joint, 70 West 71st; (212) 799-4444; www.bignickspizzeria.com

....

Petra Nemcova, supermodel, author, television host

I live in New York and sometimes it's hard to relax here. So my favorite thing to do is actually relax in New York City. One of the best ways for me to do that is to walk along the West Side Highway in the summer during sunset. The river makes you feel connected to nature. Seeing the sunset there is one of the most magical moments during the day. When you go north, on the right side, you have Manhattan. And on left side is all this nature, so it's brilliant.

At night, my friends, family, and I relax by going out for a great dinner. We'll go to Lure in SoHo. Everything on the menu is fantastic. They have lots of great fresh seafood and salads. It's always buzzy and edgy. We love seeing all the people there who are very much on top of everything and the owner is brilliant.

Lure Fishbar, 142 Mercer Street; (212) 431-7676; www.lurefishbar.com

....

Russell Janzen, dancer, New York City Ballet

Frankies Spuntino in Carroll Gardens is an amazing southern Italian restaurant and bakery. While it's not family style, you feel that abundance of food, with lots of pasta. I love the cavatelli with sausage and sage butter. The vibe is really comfortable. The food is amazing. And, they have a cookbook that just came out that's incredible. One of my friends started going there for brunch a few years ago, and he took me once. And then I moved to the area and now I go regularly. I may go once every week or two. But when I'm working I can't go that much. But sometimes I'll go after a show and just get food to go.

Frankies Spuntino, 457 Court Street; (718) 403-0033; www.frankiesspuntino.com

....

Jon Stewart, actor, Emmy-winning writer, television host

For me, New York is all about going to restaurants. You know, low down restaurants like Veselka. Why Veselka? It's the pierogies. Anything wrapped in pierogi flour, that's what I go for.

Veselka, 144 2nd Avenue; (212) 228-9682; www.veselka.com

....

Megan Sikora, actress and dancer

I am a vegan. I have been one for twelve years. So, I enjoy seeking out vegan or vegan-friendly restaurants in New York City. Cafe Blossom is one of my favorites. I can take anybody with me and they can eat there as well. They don't think it's crazy food. And I enjoy a really nice, organic glass of red wine with my meal. Blossom on 82nd and Columbus has delicious sandwiches, like a tomato BLT but with tofu that's so good.

Blossom, 187 Ninth Avenue; (212) 627-1144; www.blossomnyc.com/blossom.php

Cafe Blossom, 466 Columbus Avenue; (212) 875-2600; www.blossomnyc.com/cafeblossom.php

....

Nick Adams, actor and dancer

I love going to different restaurants in the city: especially venturing to new places. Actually, every week I go out with a group of guys from the cast [of *Priscilla Queen of the Desert*] to a new restaurant that we've never been to for a different kind of food. We choose a place out of a hat at random. Beauty & Essex in particular has a fabulous atmosphere and the food is incredible. It really stands out. Also, I've been to HK on 39th and 9th with my family. The rigatoni with hot Italian sausages, plum tomatoes, and shallots is to die for and really special. It's near the theater district and easy to go to after shows. It has a nice vibe, it's really sleek and I know that I can count on always having good food.

Beauty & Essex, 146 Essex Street; (212) 614-0146; www.beautyandessex.com

HK Restaurant, 523 Ninth Avenue; (800) 781-0466; www.hkhellskitchen.com

....

Sutton Foster, Tony Award–winning actress

I love New York City. There's no other city like it. I feel like I could possibly move somewhere else, but after a couple of weeks, I would get bored and miss the energy here. I love that every time you walk out on to the streets, the energy sweeps you away and it's hard to actually stay still in the city. I just bought a house outside in the country because I needed to stay still for a day.

My favorite place in New York is a restaurant called Good Enough to Eat. It has the best breakfast ever. They have an omelet called the Gramercy Park Omelet with cheddar cheese and apples. And they have the best biscuits with strawberry butter. That's my favorite place in New York. If there's ever a destination, I go there. It's my total comfort food.

When I first got here, I was intimidated at first and scared. But I've never felt safer in the city now that I've lived here for almost 15 years. It feels like the safest city to the world to me. It took me a while to fall in love with it, but I truly have, especially over the last five years.

Good Enough to Eat, 483 Amsterdam Avenue; (212) 496-0163; www.goodenoughtoeat.com

....

Karen Olivo, Tony Award–winning actress

I like going to Blue Sky Bakery in Brooklyn. They make the best muffins I've ever had. They come with fruit in the center. The mixed berry muffin is my fave. You can only go from anywhere around 8 in the morning to 3 in the afternoon. And then they shut down.

Blue Sky Bakery, 53 5th Avenue, Brooklyn; (718) 783-4123

....

Rick Newman, original founder of Catch A Rising Star and producer

When I was about ten years old my older brother brought me down to Little Italy and took me to Vincent's. I never forgot it. It had already been there forever. It's 105 years old now. They serve the best fried shrimp and calamari I have ever tasted. I've taken celebrities there. I've sent people there. Everybody goes crazy.

They have a wall of photos and it seems every celebrity that lives in New York is there—from Regis to the Sopranos to Billy Joel to Robert DeNiro. Vincent's is just so traditional New York. They are famous for their medium and hot sauce. They have a mild sauce that is also a wonderful marinara sauce. But I don't recommend the hot sauce, even though they've made it milder over the years. Do not order anything stronger than the medium sauce. The hot sauce is only for professionals. Actually, about ten or twelve years ago they started selling their sauces in stores. But having it fresh there is ridiculous—ridiculously, wonderfully delicious.

Vincent's, 119 Mott St; (212) 226-8133; www.anotherreason.com/vincents

Hannah Yelland, Tony Award–nominated actress

It's 8:00 a.m. on a Wednesday morning. And when most other actors are still hungover on adrenaline or a late night drink with friends who were "in" to see the show the previous night, I am woken from my very deep and much needed sleep by the pitter patter of tiny feet on the wooden parquet floor of my apartment. I say my apartment—I mean the dream apartment that has been found for me by the production company I am working for while here in New York City to perform *Brief Encounter* at Studio 54.

I can see the Hudson to my left and the Hearst Building in front of me, and the patchwork quilt of tiny brownstones and restaurants up and down 9th Avenue. It's quite a view, particularly at sunset, when the Hearst Building catches the setting sun, and it casts an orange glow over the rest of the buildings below.

"Five more minutes Henry—just five more minutes . . ." Poor Henry. Any normal canine friend would demand to go out for his first walk way before 8 a.m. But my intent when having Henry with me in New York was to train him to be the perfect theater dog. After all it is simply uncivilized in my line of work to be up with the birds on a two-show day.

December. Freezing. The last leaves of the autumn have fallen, and it is now *cold*. One thing I miss about England is that it is never the sort of cold where you can't take your hands out of your pockets for fear of frostbite. But those New York winds whip past me on 50th Street as Henry races ahead of me, in a furious mix of trying to stay warm, and the excitement that we are at long last going out for his morning walk.

And once I am outside, even though it's 8:30 a.m. and the prospect of two shows still feels like a very large mountain to climb, I am instantly more relaxed. New York is just waking up. People are rushing around with coffee cups and papers to be at work by 9, and I am suddenly the luckiest person around. My work which never feels like work anyway, doesn't start until noon with my wig call.

My first port of call is La Bergamote, a wonderful French patisserie that my husband, Michael, and I found on one of our first weekends in New York in September while we were discovering the area. I stick my head around the door (as no dogs are allowed inside) and ask for a double soy latte to go. They now know me and my order. Henry is tugging at the leash, desperate to get on, but I can't do anything without my coffee. And it is such good coffee.

On Saturdays, when Michael comes up to be with me for the weekend from DC (where we normally live and where he works), it is our Place to Go before a two-show day on the weekend. They have the best pain au chocolat I have ever had—including the ones I've tasted in France—and their omelets are all so delicious and unusual; blackberry and brie I think was my particular favorite.

And so, coffee in hand, and with a newfound caffeine-filled spring in my step, Henry and I arrive at Clinton Dog Park, on the corner of 11th and 52nd. Henry is in heaven. Sophie the dachshund greets him and he runs off, leaving me to sit and watch and chat to the other theatrical dog owners who are lucky enough to be among the few who are able to enjoy this aspect of New York—the dog world on a two-show day in Manhattan.

La Bergamote, 515 West 52nd Street; (212) 586-2429; http://labergamotenyc.com

De Witt Clinton Park, West 52nd to West 54th Streets, 11th to 12th Avenues

....

Joy Behar, Emmy-winning co-host of *The View,* host of the *Joy Behar Show,* comedian, and best-selling author

I was born in Brooklyn. I had a couple of depressing forays into other states. I spent a year one weekend in Providence, Rhode Island. I lived on Long Island and, you know, I was reading Sylvia Plath. That's how depressed I was, and so I always come back to the Big Apple, because I only feel happy and alive here.

When I want to eat, I stay in my neighborhood, the Upper West Side. So, I eat dinner a lot at a place called Gennaro. It's run by a real Italian and it's very authentic food. You couldn't get any better food in Italy. The pasta Bolognese is great. They have kale salad that's a killer and very healthy. They have a linguine with grouper that's delicious and tuna. They make everything fresh. It's very delicious Sicilian cuisine—seafood and pasta. Also, I like the vibe. It's not a fancy joint. They have artwork on the walls. They have lovely waiters. Everybody's nice.

They do not take reservations, so it's always crowded, but it's worth it, because the food is so good.

Gennaro, 665 Amsterdam Avenue; (212) 665-5348

....

Bonnie Hammer, chairman, NBC Universal Cable Entertainment and Cable Studios, NBCUniversal

One of my favorite things to do in New York is lunch in Tribeca, home to some of the best dining in the city. From Bouley to Bubby's, you can find any cuisine you're in the mood for, in a cool, laid-back atmosphere. But as I dig in to something like the delicious "Grandmother's ravioli" at Locanda Verde, I can't help thinking I'd trade in a minute for some pollo con arroz at the Cuban joint across the street from what used to be my father's factory at 453 Greenwich Street. It was one of the few places to eat back in the days before the uniformly industrial neighborhood became trendy Tribeca. But it was part of the routine after school or on Saturday, when I'd help out at my dad's office, honing the typing skills that still serve me well today.

I make a point of passing 453 Greenwich every time I'm in the area. It's still standing, though now it's home to condos and design firms rather than factories like my dad's. I'd give anything in the world to see his reaction to the fact that his strictly utilitarian workshop—not to mention the neighborhood—became fashionably chic.

Locanda Verde, 377 Greenwich Street; (212) 925-3797; www.locandaverdenyc.com

....

Jeanne Adlon, author of *Cat Calls: Wonderful Stories and Practical Advice from a Veteran Cat Sitter* and cat expert columnist on www.catchannel.com

I grew up on 96th Street and still live on the Upper West Side of Manhattan—one of the New York City's great neighborhoods, particularly for food. Anything your heart desires is here and then some—but my favorite is Indian cuisine. As a full time cat sitter, I rarely have time to eat out but when I do, I love the lunch buffet at Tandoori. It's a real neighborhood place loaded with charm and good food, and a true find for those who want a nice lunch in New York for a decent price ($8.95). Owner Tara Singh Gill makes it a wonderful experience for newcomers and regulars. As soon as I walk in he greets me and sees if my favorite table by the window is free, and there is never a rush to shoo you out. I like the variety of food on the buffet but am particularly fond of the chicken tikka masala, spinach with tofu, and of course the tandoori chicken!

Tandoori, 210 West 94th Street; (212) 932-7720; www.tandoorimanhattan.com

....

Jonathan Cheban, reality television personality on *The Spin Crowd;* designer of his own jewelry collection, JETSET for Richrocks; and founder and CEO of Command PR

I'm a food guy. You have to trust me on my food. The best thing in Queens is Benfaremo, The Lemon Ice King of Corona and their peanut butter ice. I don't even eat peanut butter, but this peanut butter ice is so unbelievable. It's literally the flavor of peanut butter and comes with peanut butter chips. These ices are the best thing in the world—there's a line around the corner. It's been around for decades and the ices cost around two dollars. I drag people there. The place is shown in the opening of the TV show *King of Queens.*

There are other food treasures. New Park pizzeria in Queens is amazing. The best burger in New York is J.G. Melon. I know my stuff. Why is it good? The meat is ground and mushy. Get it medium with the fries well done and pickles on the side. The best fried chicken and strawberry pancakes are, of course, at the Pink Tea Cup. It's a must. It's very urban in there and has a very cool vibe. You have to be cool to go in.

Benfaremo, The Lemon Ice King of Corona, 5202 108th Street, Queens; (718) 699-5133

New Park Pizza, 15671 Cross Bay Boulevard; (718) 641-3082; www.newparkpizza.com

The Pink Tea Cup, 88 7th Ave South; (212) 255-2124; www.thepinkteacuprestaurant.com

Marci Klein, Emmy-winning producer, *30 Rock* and *Saturday Night Live*

If I had a free afternoon or evening in New York City, I would walk all through Central Park with my kids and we'd end up at J.G. Melon to meet up with our friends, and I would run the jukebox all night!

J.G. Melon, 1291 3rd Avenue; (212) 744-0585

Kelsey Grammer, Emmy- and Golden Globe–winning actor and Tony nominee

Keste is a great pizza restaurant that is so Neapolitan. It's just really simple. We were in Chicago and called Roberto [Caporuscio] who set up Keste to see if we could find a place that is similar. He said "Yes! It's called Spacca Napoli." So we go there in Chicago.

New York is the heartbeat of the world. It is the most extraordinary city. If you have a good idea or even a bad idea, you can make it happen in New York. New York is a piece of rock. It's solid rock that I think is informed with some kind of strange energy that makes crazy people do great things. Like build buildings so tall. It's just insane what it does. But it's a creative foundry. I think anyone who wants to actually figure out what they feel or how they think, has to throw their ideas up against New York.

And doing theater here is the greatest trip in the world for an actor. It's instant. It's energized. It's always a challenge. It is the most extraordinary place to play. [In 1982] when I did *Othello* with James Earl Jones and played Cassio thirty-something years ago, it was the greatest experience of my life. And you know, every time I come back and do theater, I say the same thing.

Keste Pizza & Vino, 271 Bleecker Street; (212) 243-1500; www.kestepizzeria.com

....

Joe ("Joey Pants") Pantoliano, Emmy-winning actor, director, and author

They just built a hotel on Grand Street where an old diner used to be. And literally this hotel is about twenty stories high and no more than seventeen feet wide. David Burke has a new restaurant on the bottom floor. When you go outside and you look down Sixth Avenue, you can see the car wash and Canal Street. I just love the view from that vantage point. And they always have good food. David's got a filet mignon on the bone that I like very much. But also, the restaurant is my age group. A lot of places in the city have been overthrown by the anti–baby boomers—like those kids who are thirty. The ones that want to eventually stick us all in old age homes. So this is a place for grownups.

David Burke Kitchen, The James Hotel, 23 Grand Street; (212) 201-9119; www.davidburkekitchen.com

....

Jean-Georges Vongerichten, Michelin-starred chef with restaurants around the globe and author of several cookbooks

When I first came to New York City in 1986, I was just passing though. I was working for a consulting chef [Louis Outhier] who sent me here for one year to do his food. But when I landed here, New York captured me. I remember coming in from the airport. We were stuck in traffic and just before the midtown tunnel I could see the whole city in one shot, like a photograph. And I said, "Wow! Wow! I'm here. I'm here." And I never left. I'm a country boy. I grew up on a farm in Alsace with cows and chickens. And now, my country is Central Park.

I've been adopted by New York, which I love. When I opened one restaurant, people kept saying, "What's next, what's next, what's next . . .?" New Yorkers push me. They inspire me. I meet all kinds of people. I'm friends with Hugh Jackman, who is so wonderful. People may seem so untouchable, they're just people.

I live in the Village and I say, it's my little Village. Walking around there makes me so happy and is one of the reasons I love New York so much. I love walking on Perry Street. And I'll go to the Pier and bicycle along the water by the West Side Highway. Or I'll stop in a little neighborhood cafe like the 11th Street Café. It's a very simple, wonderful place where you can grab a sandwich or a smoothie. They do breakfast with egg sandwiches and great espresso. They are friends of mine now. It's close to my house. And just a few blocks from the cafe is the river. So afterwards, I can walk over and watch the water. It's magical.

11th Street Café, 327 West 11th Street; (212) 924-3804

. . . .

Edward Norton, Oscar- and Emmy- nominated, Golden Globe–winning actor, director, screenwriter, and producer

There are so many things about New York that are great. It has a great cultural life, a great physical life. It has everything. I love New York. There are so many restaurants; my Zagat guide is dog-eared with my favorite spots.

I love Blue Hill. I admire what Dan Barber is doing on every level. I think he's trying to figure out how to do food in a holistic sense.

Blue Hill New York, 75 Washington Place; (212) 539-1776; www.bluehillfarm.com

NOCTURNAL NEW YORK

 My favorite thing to do in New York City is to go to the theater. What do I love about the theater? Everything!

—Sarah Jessica Parker, Golden Globe-
and Emmy-winning actress

Author and media darling Truman Capote once said, "New York is a diamond iceberg floating in river water." So imagine the jewel of a party he threw in November 1966 to fete *Washington Post* publisher Katherine Graham (and in part celebrate the insane success of his book *In Cold Blood*). His Black and White Ball was called the "Party of the Century." It was where the super famous (Frank Sinatra) and not as famous (the UN Plaza doorman) mingled, dined, and danced in the Plaza Hotel's Grand Ballroom. Picture a dazzling mosaic from the art, fashion, society, politics, celebrity, and literary worlds.

Capote worked for months on the guest list. He found inspiration in the ravishingly classy Ascot scene from *My Fair Lady* where everyone was dressed in black and white Cecil Beaton costumes. "I want the party to be united the way you make a painting," he had said. Most alluring was that he asked everyone to wear masks. (Although, ever the rebel, Andy Warhol didn't wear one.) "I haven't been to a masked ball since I was a child," said Capote. "That's why I wanted to give one." Some masks were elaborate affairs made by Halston, Adolfo, and Tiffany window designer Gene Moore (who created a golden unicorn head). In fact, one woman remarked, "The only people I can't recognize are those with their masks off."

The Grand Ballroom shimmered. In the spirit of something akin to the court of Louis XV, guests sauntered around the fringe of the ballroom surveying the parade of invitees. One observed, "It's weird, there is only black and white and red in this room, and yet everything's so . . . so colorful." The guest list included a not-too-shabby Rose Kennedy, Cecil Beaton, Richard Avedon, Henry Fonda, Walter Cronkite, Frank Sinatra, and his pixie-haired new bride, Mia Farrow.

The revelers feasted on a midnight supper featuring the Plaza's famous chicken hash. Four hundred fifty bottles of Taittinger champagne were popped. Lauren Bacall and choreographer Jerome Robbins waltzed and cut a rug in pure Fred Astaire and Ginger Rogers–style. Peter Duchin and his orchestra didn't stop playing until after 3:30 a.m.

Capote later said that the memories of the affair "whirled like a flurry of snowflakes" in his head. "It was just what it set out to be," he told reporters. "I just wanted to give a party for my friends."

While not every New York evening may be on the level of a black-and-white ball, many have the potential for something extraordinary. Historian Arthur Schlesinger says, "History begins after midnight." And such is true in a city that buzzes way past bedtime.

. . . .

Woody Allen, Academy Award- and Golden Globe–winning screenwriter, director, actor

New York is a great city. It's a great city and I've been to all of them and worked in many of them. I've shot in London. I've shot in Paris. I've shot in Spain. I've visited all the cities—and New York is New York. Even when you love these other cities—which I do—the people in those other cities all want to come to New York. It's just great. It has a nervous excitement and a creative excitement that's unequaled anywhere.

I live in New York and I have many, many favorite things. I usually go for a walk with my wife. We walk in Central Park, on the Upper East Side where I live. We go out to restaurants all the time. I go to Madison Square Garden. I go to movies. I do the same things that anyone does. It's about enjoying one's neighborhood.

But one thing I really like is to play jazz at the Carlyle. My band plays Monday nights. It's something that I look forward to in New York very much. It's pure pleasure. It's just pure pleasure for me. I go in and play and it's great. It's like getting paid to play baseball. It gives me a great feeling. It's a wonderful, wonderful feeling. It's not my profession. I don't have anxiety about it. It's transporting. Actually, I'm not good enough. The only reason I get a chance to play is because I succeed in another field. I'm not that great but I'm carried by the other guys.

....

David O. Russell, Oscar- and Golden Globe–nominated director

Bemelmans Bar at the Carlyle Hotel is an extraordinary place. The beautiful murals all over are painted by Ludwig Bemelmans, the same artist who did the Madeline books. It was in the opening scene of the Woody Allen movie, *Hannah and Her Sisters*. Bobby Short opened there. It's classic old-school New York, and the hotel was one of the only privately held hotels in the city. It also has an amazing dining room, piano bar, and a great lounge bar. Everyone from John F. Kennedy to Warren Beatty had suites there. I once met Tom Cruise there and he had two suites. And you should have a martini. It's very good.

The Carlyle Hotel, 35 East 76th Street; (212) 744-1600; www.thecarlyle.com

....

Joan Rivers, Emmy-winning actress, comedian, and television personality

I loved going up to the top of 30 Rock and having a drink when the sun set around New York City. It's amazing. It just made me realize that the city is magical, magical, magical. I was a tour guide there every summer all through my college years. I don't really miss anything about it. But it was always so exciting to take people around Rockefeller Center and NBC. So going to that spot brought me back to how lucky I am that I'm no longer saying "EVERYONE FOLLOW MISS MOLINSKY!"

While the Rainbow Room at Top of the Rock is no longer open, visitors can still go to Top of the Rock's sky high Observation Deck, 30 Rockefeller Plaza; (212) 698-2000; www.topoftherock.com

....

Will Shortz, puzzle creator and editor of the *New York Times* Crossword Puzzle

I'm very passionate about table tennis and play five to six nights a week for about two and a half hours a night. I love the game because it's fast paced, it's great exercise, requires quick thinking, and is a sociable game. I looked up myself and I think I'm 181 in New York State according to the USA Table Tennis Association. Most places just happen to have tables and people go and play and they develop friends there. But Spin is a bar/restaurant/ping-pong emporium and the first table tennis club of its kind in the world. They have up to 16 tables depending on how they are spaced out. They have deluxe finger food.

Spin is a cool place to hang out any day of the week. But it's really fantastic on Friday nights. They have a weekly feature called the Dirty Dozen. They invite 12 of the top players in the New York area to play for a $500 or $1,000 prize. If you just go to watch, you can drink and have some food and watch some very high-level table tennis. If you go to watch the Knicks or a baseball game, you're in the stands somewhere—you're not that close to the action. But the great thing about table tennis is it's not that well known a sport and you're feet away from some top players. It is a great respite for me. For most people, crosswords are their respite and that's what takes them out of their regular world and focuses them on something completely different. And they are relaxed and refreshed when they're done. Since puzzles are my business, table tennis relaxes and refreshes me.

Spin New York, 48 East 23rd Street; (212) 982-8802; www.spinyc.com

Jason Sudeikis, actor and writer

What is my favorite thing to do in this town? Hands down, private room karaoke. This is something anyone can do. I recommend Sing Sing Karaoke; there are two locations, Avenue A and St. Marks Place. One Saturday, I got there at 10:30 p.m. and was there until 4:30 a.m. You pay by the hour and I put together these karaoke super jams and invite a bunch of people. And you have the room to yourself.

Sing Sing is nice because you can have your friends singing over and over again. You call on the phone to the staff to keep the pitchers of beer coming and you pass the microphone around and everyone sings and it's all friends. We do a lot of TV theme songs. So everyone sings songs from *Good Times*, *Family Ties,* and *Cheers.*

One of the most fun things about this kind of karaoke is that it's not in front of a big group of people. You don't have a long wait. You'll sing six or seven songs in an hour and can take chances. You can take risks. You can finally sing that Broadway song that you have always wanted to sing. I did "Look Over There" from *La Cage Aux Folles* and really got to belt it. My friend did songs from *Shrek*.

Will Forte, Emmy-nominated actor and writer

Ninety percent of the time Jason (Sudeikis) and I spend together will end in a late-night karaoke session at Boho Karaoke or Sing Sing Karaoke. We like doing standards, like REO Speedwagon's "I Can't Fight This Feeling" or "Heart of the Matter" by Don Henley. Although we do it "Meart of the Hatter" because we used to do a "Jon Bovi" skit at *SNL*—the opposite of Bon Jovi—well, you have to see it. And we'll also enjoy doing deep cuts. Usually Jason does more the lead and I do the harmonies. I'm the harmonizer.

Karoke Boho, 186 West 4th Street; (212) 255-0011; www.karaokeboho.com

Sing Sing Karaoke, 81 Avenue A, #1; (212) 674-0700; 9 St. Marks Place; (212) 387-7800; www.karaokesingsing.com

....

Derek Cianfrance, director and screenwriter

My favorite place in New York is the Film Forum. They program the best movies. I've spent so many days of my life there just studying and learning about movies. Their programming is like one of the greatest film schools. They do crime movie repertories with Michael Mann or Michael Powell or Emerica Pressburger. It's such a great place to learn about movies. The first time I ever went to the Film Forum was in 1997 when they were showing the re-release of Jean-Luc Godard's *Contempt*. I saw it seven days in a row. And maybe it's just because I love that film so much, but everything was so special about the place.

When I ultimately moved to New York and started regularly going to the Film Forum, I stopped choosing what movies I was going to see. I would just go there and see what they had playing. It's a real experience. I can disappear into it, and they have the best popcorn and coffee so it really gets you amped up for a movie. When I moved to New York from film school, New York was so lonely. The Film Forum became my place that kept me company. It's always my dream that my film will play there someday. The Film Forum—that's a theater.

The Film Forum, 209 West Houston Street; (212) 727-8110; www.filmforum.org

....

Janet Carroll, actress

Every Tuesday night, but only on Tuesdays, Bella Luna, a great restaurant on the Upper West Side, features live guitarist Jack Wilkins. He essentially plays jazz guitar but he also does the great American songbook, flamenco, blues—a whole range of music. I met Jack Wilkins through mutual friends, and I've been going there for about six years.

Jack plays from seven to ten and he'll often have a guest artist like the legendary Bucky Pizzarelli, John Pizzarelli's father. And John will sometimes sit in and play. Bucky is the master. He's probably the most recorded guitarist in all of recording history.

There's no minimum or cover charge. They have a bar so you can just have drinks. Or you can sit at a table and have a fabulous dinner for a very affordable price. The entrees are maybe eight to twelve bucks. It's an Italian restaurant so they have wonderful pastas. Their fresh fish, like the sea bass, is glorious. And they feature incredible vegetable combinations, like great sautéed cabbage. The hors d'oeuvres are marvelous. The waitstaff has been there for years and they're really darling. It's an extraordinary New York musical experience and not that well known.

Bella Luna, 584 Columbus Avenue; (212) 877-2267; www.bellalunanyc.com

....

Patrick McMullan, premier nightlife photographer, columnist, and author

I adore walking through the city late at night after work when there's no one around, especially in the village. I mean 5 or 6 a.m., when the light just starts coming up. At night, the city is spectacular. Some people are starting the day and some are finishing it. And the great thing about the city is that there's always something open at night. Keep walking and eventually you'll find a deli to get a cookie or a Milky Way. The western part of West 4th Street around Bedford Street almost looks like a movie set. From the arch at Washington Square Park you can see the Empire State Building. It's so beautiful when the sun comes out in the morning, and there aren't many cars around. When you wake up in the daytime and there are a million people, you can't walk down the street without having to dodge everybody. But late at night, you feel like the city is yours.

....

Lee Zalben, founder and president of the famed sandwich shop, Peanut Butter & Co.

I was born in Philadelphia and always thought I would live there my entire life. But after college I found a job in New York City and quickly fell in love with the Big Apple. I've grown so accustomed to being at the center of the universe that now I can't imagine living anywhere else.

But New York isn't easy. The summers are too hot and the winters are too cold. The price of everything is outrageous. Getting around town is a nightmare. The only things not stressed out by the rat race seem to be the rats! Ask any New Yorker why they choose to live here despite all the hardships we New Yorkers endure and no doubt most will mention "all of the cultural activities" that we have access to. I wholeheartedly agree, only it seems like I never have time to take advantage of all of the fascinating exhibitions, lectures, concerts, and shows that are all around me.

But every few weeks I do find myself with an unexpected free night or a rather empty weekend. I used to pick up a copy of *New York Magazine* or *Time Out* and pore through the listings, trying to find something worthwhile to do. But after many years of scrambling, I've settled on a de facto bit of culture whenever I have some free time on my hands. I head right over to the TKTS Booth in Times Square for some half-price theater tickets.

I love the TKTS Booth. But the thrill of live theater is only half the fun. I love standing in line with all of the tourists, listening to them debate over which play to see, where to eat afterward (please not McDonalds or TGI Fridays), the sights that they've seen, and all the other things that tourists chat about with each other.

I try to play the jaded New Yorker and remain aloof and quiet, minding my BlackBerry while waiting for my turn in line. I usually crack after a few minutes and then feel obliged to chime in with some helpful advice. "No, ma'am, *Cats* closed several years ago. Yes, sir, the performers in *Naked Boys Singing* really are naked. *Avenue Q*? No, it's not on the Lower East Side, it's playing right down the street."

For me, the exuberance of tourists, many of whom are seeing our city for the first time, is the perfect start to a theater-filled afternoon or evening. The half-price deal is the icing on the cake!

TDF/TKTS Discount Booth (Theater Development Fund), Duffy Square (47th Street and Broadway); (212) 912-9770; www.tdf.org

. . . .

Matthew Settle, actor

To me, New York is about the collaboration of cultures and the experience of different ways of thinking in such a small area. And it's a great place for people to expand themselves. I love having a good dinner and then going to hear some good blues or some jazz. Terra Blues has really authentic blues. And jazz is almost like a religious experience. I developed a passion for it later on in life. It touches a foundational element inside you that helps you process things. It's a combination of guitar chords and the person's voice that just makes it so special. And there's a jazz place that I love called The Bar Next Door at La Lanterna. A lot of session players from NYU and world-famous people play there. It's very intimate. There's a fireplace. I go about twice or three times a month.

Terra Blues, 149 Bleecker Street; (212) 777-7776; www.terrablues.com

The Bar Next Door at La Lanterna di Vittorio, 129 MacDougal Street; (212) 529-5945; www.lalanternacaffe.com

....

Bill Ayers, WPLJ talk radio host and executive director and co-founder of Why Hunger

I'm a jazz freak. The best place in the world to hear jazz is in New York City. I recently went to the Village Vanguard a couple of weeks ago on a Saturday night and heard Joe Lovano play some great jazz. He is probably one of the three or four greatest living tenor saxophone players. But there are a lot of great new clubs that are very tiny and they have a lot of younger performers.

On Fridays, the *New York Times* has a whole listing of jazz performances for the week. Typically, there are about twenty or thirty items. And there's no place better in the world to hear jazz. Jazz is very international here. You go into a New York jazz club most of the people are from Asia, Japan, and Europe and not Americans.

Many musicians moved here in the '30s and '40s. Fifty-second Street was called the Street, where there were lots clubs for musicians to play. That's all gone now, and jazz clubs are spread around the city. There's a lot of them in the Village.

For example, Cornelia Street Cafe is a very intimate space, and I've heard some really good jazz there. You're something like twenty feet from the musicians. They're up-and-coming or people who are not in the jazz mainstream—and they even have jazz legends sometimes. I heard Lee Konitz there. He's in his eighties and one of the leading jazz alto sax players who plays with everyone. There is this great jazz musician on this little stage and you're paying twenty bucks to hear him. Or the next week you can hear someone you've never heard of before who is good. Jazz is alive in New York City.

Another great place to hear jazz is St. Peter's Church. They have a whole jazz ministry. On Sunday evenings, the jazz vespers services are free and open to everyone. I knew the original pastor, the late Rev. John Garcia Gensel. About thirty years ago, I was on a radio show with him for NBC one night and he said, "Why don't you come with me and experience this all-night jazz session," and I said, "Well, I have to get home," and he said, "No, no, no." So I stayed out all night and heard all these great jazz performers at the church—one right after the other. It's extraordinary. Every year, they have a tribute to Lester Young, one of the great tenor sax players. And it's only about fifteen dollars to hear these great performers. They have these fifteen- or twenty-dollar concerts. It's truly wonderful.

There's also a lot of great outdoor jazz. I've also heard some wonderful performances at the Charlie Parker Jazz Festival on the Lower East Side in Tompkins Square Park. (The festival also has performances at Marcus Garvey Park in Harlem.) Top jazz performers come to the two neighborhoods where Parker lived and worked and the concerts are free.

The Village Vanguard, 178 7th Avenue South; (212) 255-4037; www.villagevanguard.com

The Cornelia Street Cafe, 29 Cornelia Street; (212) 989-9319; www.corneliastreetcafe.com

St. Peter's Church, 619 Lexington Avenue; (212) 935-2200; www.saintpeters.org/jazz

....

Amy Sacco, lifestyle and nightlife entrepreneur

One of my favorite experiences is riding my old bicycle at sunset over the Brooklyn Bridge. My friends and I head to the original Patsy's Pizza, now called Grimaldi's, in Brooklyn for an extra-large pepperoni pie and beer. Then we get ice cream and walk it all off on the Promenade afterwards. And sometimes we go to the River Cafe, sit on the deck outside, and have drinks and watch Manhattan. The top of the Brooklyn Bridge is reserved for walkers and bikers. When I look at

Manhattan from that vantage point, I think, I live there, that's my town! I'm filled with happiness and love.

Grimaldi's, 19 Old Fulton Street, Brooklyn; (718) 858-4300; www.grimaldis.com

....

Les Marshak, national voice-over artist, network announcer, and the voice of the *Today* show

In the past ten or fifteen years, I've been really getting into jazz. One of my favorite things is to hear cool jazz, preferably Brazilian bossa nova. I've never been to Brazil but I love beaches. So when I hear this music, it reminds me of different times in my life. It takes me back to the '60s and the days of bossa nova, Stan Getz, and Antonio Carlos Jobim. I just feel like I'm on a beach watching the sunset. No matter what time of the year, where I am, it just brings me to that place.

About three years ago, I discovered Dizzy's Club. It's part of Jazz at Lincoln Center at the Time Warner Center and the smaller of the venues there. It's a little old-fashioned intimate jazz club named after Dizzy Gillespie.

They have two shows, but the early show is magical. During spring, summer, or fall, you can get there at 6:30 for dinner. There are these enormous and completely massive floor-to-ceiling windows behind the stage. And looking at the stage from the table where you're sitting, you're facing those windows. When the show begins at 7 or 7:30, it's still light but getting towards dusk. The music starts and ever so gradually it gets darker out, dusk begins, the lights start coming on outside and all of a sudden, New York is transformed with this background of the soundtrack of New York. That's the way it looks. It just blends so beautifully and before you know it it's nighttime. It's this incredible transition from day to night with this music. And it's both an aural and visual experience.

The food at Dizzy's is great. It's everything from jambalaya to pulled pork sandwiches to great burgers. It's not serious food but it's very good Southern food. And I'll sip an apple martini, so all the senses are satisfied.

Jazz at Lincoln Center harkens back to an era before my time when clubs, supper clubs, and nightclubs were very big. While other jazz clubs are great, you can walk out of there and easily spend $300—especially if you have food and pay the minimum. But the food here is fairly reasonable so it's a lot more friendly to your wallet.

Dizzy's Club Coca Cola—Jazz at Lincoln Center, The Time Warner Center, 10 Columbus Circle; (212) 258-9595; www .jalc.org

....

David Wright, third baseman, New York Mets

I love going to Madison Square Garden during the winter. I am a big Knicks fan and I love to see them play. The garden has a certain aura about it. When you go, you never know what celebrity you might run into. It is a great place to be.

I became a Knicks fan because my friend David Lee used to play for them, although he's now with Golden State. I invited him to Mets games and he invited me to Knicks games. I became hooked on the Knicks. And I just like being in a place that's usually filled to capacity where I can watch other people play. And honestly, I like to go there just so I can watch someone else play and I can relax.

Madison Square Garden, 4 Pennsylvania Plaza; (212) 465-6741; www.thegarden.com

....

James Braly, writer, performer, monologist

During the Christmas season, I like to go to the Guggenheim Museum to hear Vox, a wonderful ensemble of singers and musicians led by a brilliant conductor named George Steel. (Not that I would know a brilliant conductor from a slightly less than brilliant conductor, but the ensemble sounds spectacular, and the proof is in the Christmas pudding.) Vox sings many of the old favorites, only in four-part harmony, sometimes inviting the audience to sing along (in itself a Christmas miracle—New Yorkers lowering their voices to blend in together) as well as madrigals and ancient carols that you (or at least I) may never have heard but that sound strangely and beautifully familiar. The combined effect is to be transported to a primeval, quintessential Christmastime—inside the snowball on a block of the nicer row houses after the fashion of Dickens's London or Clement Clark ("A Visit from St. Nicholas") Moore's New York—only warm and dry and sitting on your folded parka.

That this ancient music is performed in the Guggenheim adds an interesting element of artistic tension. When I first started going, my boys were young, three and six, so they'd walk up and down the concentric circles, and return to ask me why someone's finger painting was hanging on the wall. I don't understand modern art much better than a first grader, so it felt nice to have my childish sensibilities affirmed, like getting an early Christmas present.

After the concert, museum workers pass out trays of cookies and juice boxes, another nod to endless childhood, wisely having held back the sugar till the end, launching the revelers back through the revolving doors.

So that when you walk out on 5th Avenue, in addition to sweets, you really are filled with the love of your fellow man—or woman—and the sense that anything is possible, if you work hard enough. It's the dream that brings you to New York to begin with: to be a part of a group that knows what it's doing. This is that group, all the way around. These people are masters. And you can see on their faces that they know that you know how good they are. They can see how much pleasure they bring you. Just as importantly, you can see how appreciated they feel. It's a perfect, transcendent, single organism: glorious music performed at the highest level, in beautiful surroundings filled with friendly, appreciative people, and treats. All for free! Merry Christmas!

Vox at the Solomon R. Guggenheim Museum, 1071 5th Avenue; (212) 423-3500; www.guggenheim.org

....

Elizabeth Berkley, actress, author, and founder of the organization, Ask Elizabeth

I love seeing theater. I've done so many plays here. And when I do them, I can't see other shows. So when I'm not in one, I see all the theater that I can. My first Broadway show that I ever saw was the musical, *On Your Toes.* My uncle took me to see it when I was a little girl. I was a dancer at the time, so for me, I was in heaven.

....

Zach Braff, Grammy-winning, Golden Globe– and Emmy-nominated actor and writer

I love the culture in New York. My family is here. We consume all the arts. We love it. I'm a theater geek. My father was bringing me to Broadway and Off-Broadway shows when I was seven-years-old and couldn't understand any of the plays. It got ingrained in my childhood. So my favorite thing is to see theater. It really moves me. It's really powerful. I like art that makes you walk away obsessing about what you just saw. Nothing does that more to me than a great piece of theater.

....

Kate Shindle, actress, singer, dancer, and former Miss America

When I have a free Monday night, I love going to *Jim Caruso's Cast Party* at the legendary Birdland. *Cast Party* is basically an extreme open mike—like a turbo open mike night. People like to come to New York and see shows. But most of them don't play on Monday nights. So *Cast Party* is the ideal alternative.

You never know if Liza Minnelli will get up and sing and she has, and probably will again. You can hear everybody from NYU students to people starring on Broadway. Jon Bon Jovi, Tony Bennett, and Hugh Jackman sang there. And Jim Caruso is pretty much the best host of anything and a delightful, kind person. That always makes the experience better because you can be good at something and not be very nice. But it's better if you are.

I've sung there many times. Sometimes I'll say "Oh, can I get on early?" And suddenly it's 1:30 in the morning and Jim's saying, "Come on up Kate Shindle!" You never know exactly who is going to show up, or what they are going to do or how late you're going to be there, but it's a blast. For anyone who comes in from out of town who is looking for a real kind of inside Broadway experience, this is the place to be.

Jim Caruso's Cast Party, **Monday nights at Birdland,** 315 West 44th Street; (212) 581-3080; www.castpartynyc.com

Jim Caruso, singer/performer and host of *Jim Caruso's Cast Party* at Birdland

I moved to New York twenty years ago, and one of the main reasons was for the spectacular theater. I treasure the experience of seeing a show with a friend, then walking to Joe Allen, a theater restaurant and hangout, which has been around forever. You can see the whole theater community, star gaze, see friends, catch the latest gossip, have a burger, and discuss what you've just seen. I love seeing chorus kids in their first Broadway show, bringing their parents from out of town: the girls with their wig hair and lashes, and the boys looking so proud. I never get tired of the experience. It brings me such joy.

A few years ago, I was finally in a Broadway show, called *Liza's at the Palace*, starring, of course, Liza Minnelli. Every night, we'd have the very cool experience of leaving that historic stage door, and walking the few blocks to Joe Allen, feeling like we owned the world. We'd sit at Liza's favorite table—the round one in the back—rehashing the show and who had been in the audience. Sometimes we'd drag folks with us—friends who had seen the show—and we would spend hours talking about New York theater and basking in the afterglow!

Joe Allen has so many special memories for me. I've sung Happy Birthday to Adolph Green in that room. One night I was at a table with Liza, Whoopi Goldberg, Frank Langella, Mary Louise Parker, Billy Crudup, and Matt Dillon—when we were joined by Dr. Ruth Westheimer. I was the only person I'd never heard of! Joe Allen is post-theater theater. A real movie goes on in there every night and has for many years. I love that. Let it always be there.

Joe Allen, 326 West 46th Street; (212) 581-6464; joeallenrestaurant.com

Muriel "Mickie" Siebert, Chairman and CEO of Siebert Financial and the first woman to own a seat on the New York Stock Exchange

My father had a rough illness. He had cancer with five years of nurses off and on, around the clock. We moved from a house to a one-bedroom apartment and I was in the living room. And after a long battle, he died at fifty-two.

At the time, I was living in Cleveland, Ohio, going to college, cutting class, and playing bridge. It was just too much tension to see him dying that way, so I dropped out. My sister had gotten a divorce, moved to New York, and had a good job. And I had a couch to sleep on.

So I was in my early 20s and a college dropout when I came to New York in 1954. I lied to get my first job as a trainee in research at Bache & Co. Sixty-five bucks a week. I said I had a college degree but changed that application when I put the bid card in for the seat on the Exchange. I realized that was a historic application.

That job created my career. I changed jobs for a research job, but the men had been making between 50 and 100 percent more than I was. So, the New York Society of Security Analysts had a placement bureau. They sent my resume out with my initials on it. I got an interview and a job at Shields. I increased my salary to over $10,000 a year, which was a lot back then.

The first day I was employed at the company, I got a call from Madison Funds. They said, "We made money on a report you wrote. We owe you an order." That started me. Only in America. In New York, I found the talent where I flourished. New York packaged it and helped give me those opportunities and I flew. It's what the city stands for.

Sometimes living in New York has a crazy pace. I welcome the time when I can go someplace nice, that I enjoy. I love music. And I love jazz. In school I was the solo clarinetist in the band and orchestra, but that's a long time ago.

Jazz Standard is a special place for me to hear music. I don't have to make reservations or buy tickets in advance. You don't have to stand on your head and eat peanuts to get in. They have very good people who play there. It's not a place where you'll spend an amount of money and then say, "Gee, did I want to do that?" So if I find I'm doing nothing at five o'clock I can call a friend and say, "Hey, how about dinner at Jazz Standard?"

Blue Smoke is their restaurant. Their spareribs are wonderful. And there are a couple different kinds. Kansas City Spareribs are sweet. You can have a half or full rack. So I can eat, and listen to great music. And it's a casual place where I can go in pants and a sweater or a jacket.

Jazz Standard and Blue Smoke, 116 East 27th Street; (212) 576-2232; www.jazzstandard.net

Michael Urie, actor

Employees Only in the West Village is a really cool little speakeasy bar that's new, but feels old. They make the most delicious cocktails. Of course, who doesn't like a gin and tonic or a Jack and Coke? But this place takes these drinks to a whole other level, to an art form. And it's fun to have a professionally made fancy cocktail.

I like to try new things there, but they have a great twist on a Manhattan. All the juices are completely fresh. The ingredients are all just top notch.

Employees Only is sort of secret. You have to kind of know where you're going. You don't just happen upon a place like Employees Only. And I like that. When you enter, you feel like you've stepped back through time when people dressed for dinner.

Colin Donnell, actor

You know what I love to do? Find a restaurant with an outdoor cafe on a nice day, and be able to have a cocktail in the afternoon. It feels so quintessentially New York to be able to enjoy a nice, well-made martini on a sidewalk somewhere.

One of my favorite cocktail joints is Employees Only in the West Village. And, while it doesn't have an outdoor cafe, it has some of the best made cocktails in the city. My favorite is their gin martini straight up with a twist. They have some amazing bartenders and a very quintessential, old-school New York vibe. I love the idea of harking back to the '50s, '30s, '20s—when cocktails were in, and people dressed up in suits. And we're lucky at *Anything Goes*. We've got a couple of great places like that around our theater like the Algonquin Hotel and the Lamb's Club.

Employees Only, 510 Hudson Street; (212) 242-3021; www.employeesonlynyc.com

Algonquin Hotel, 59 West 44th Street; (212) 840-6800; www.algonquinhotel.com

The Lamb's Club, 132 West 44th Street; (212) 997-5262; www.thelambsclub.com

....

Ken Davenport, Broadway producer

One of the most famous dinner spots from folks in the Broadway biz is Joe Allen on 46th Street. You'll always find it bustling with folks on their way to the theater, coming from the theater, or talking about the theater.

But that's not where I go.

Above Joe Allen's, behind an unmarked door and two heavy velvet curtains that make you feel like you're entering some Middle Eastern treasure-filled lair, is one of the few secrets that Broadway has been able to keep.

It's called Bar Centrale. And it's known for . . . well, not being known.

It's a quiet respite for some of Broadway's most elite players. (I could name names, but then I'd be hauled off to Broadway jail so fast it would make your tap shoes spin.) And whenever I find myself in midtown with some time to kill, I head there for a snack (the shrimp quesadilla is my favorite, because the shrimp is always incredibly fresh and the cheese is always . . . well . . . cheese), and a beverage (you name it, they'll pour it) . . . and because I never know who will be sitting in the booth next to me.

....

Kathleen Marshall, Tony Award–winning director and choreographer

And the best little secret of Broadway is Bar Centrale. It's a great little hangout for theater people. Either before a show or after a show, it's the perfect spot. It's not marked, so you have to know where it is. It's like a little speakeasy. And you know what? I love it because it feels like a club. It feels private. It's a cool little place that's sort of half restaurant and half lounge, so it's very comfortable. And I love their guacamole. It's really good.

Bar Centrale, 324 West 46th Street; (212) 581-3130; www.barcentralenyc.com

Danny "Kootch" Kortchmar, acclaimed guitarist and songwriter

I very much love the bar at the Ritz-Carlton. The bartender there is named Norman. He is the greatest bartender in the whole world. Norman is the archetypal New York City bartender, the likes of which you don't see anymore. He's a grown-up and I'm sure he would hate to be described this way but he's kind of a Damon Runyon kind of guy. That doesn't really say it all. He's just friendly, warm, and wonderful.

It's just an absolute delight to go in there and have a martini. And by the way, Norman makes the best martinis I've ever had anywhere. That's another thing, that he really knows how to make drinks—any kind of drink. It's rare to see someone that goes back to the great old days of New York bartenders.

Once I asked Norman, "What makes a good martini?" And he said, "I make them with love." I said, "How come other people's martinis aren't as good as this?" Norman says, "They don't care." But there's just something about it—the texture and the taste of it. The entire experience is not like any I've had with any other cocktail. It's just the smoothest, best martini. I've watched him make it. He doesn't seem to do anything that much different than other people do, and yet the drinks are absolute perfection.

In the olden days of bartending you talked to your bartender. Your bartender talked to you and you took care of each other and traded stories and ideas. You'd also cry on his shoulder. There was a lot of interplay, which I find absent. It's not like I go to tons of bars, but the thing I love about this bar is it's an adult bar. It's not trying to be hip. It's not for kids. It's not loud. There is a piano player playing classic standards. That's a rare thing in the city. It's not like I need a full diet of it, but it harkens back to when I was a kid and would go into these hotel lobbies with my parents before or after theater. You get the flavor of the real deal of what New York was all about back in the day.

Norman harkens back to those days. It's not that he's a raconteur. He concentrates on his clientele. He knows them all. He knows a lot of people. A lot of people know him and are thrilled to know him. He's one of those guys everyone wants to know. I don't know how it got to be that way. It's an underground kind of thing.

I find that the best bars are hotel bars, anyway. Like I said, they're not quiet and not loud, not trying to be hip, not youth oriented. Not that I have anything against young people. But when I want to go have a drink or meet someone for a drink, the last thing I want is loud disco or techno music. I like being in a place that's kind of adult. It's a novelty, actually. And Norman fits right in. He's right out of central casting for the great old-school New York bartender.

The Ritz-Carlton New York, Central Park, 50 Central Park South; (212) 308-9100; www.ritzcarlton.com

....

Ron Delsener, legendary concert promoter and producer

After a concert, I like visiting many, many places.

I usually start uptown in Harlem for a drink at the Seville Lounge. Then I'll head to St. Nick's Pub. There's a lady there who brings in some hotplates and cooks on aluminum foil. She makes macaroni and cheese and chicken and you give her a few bucks. And everyone is satisfied.

Sometimes there's great music—someone belting Billie Holiday. Stevie Wonder has played here. You have to be lucky to catch it. They don't really tell you what's playing. It just happens when it happens. Sometimes it's a "drive by" for me. I pop in, sometimes there is a young lady on the microphone who needs money to pay her rent, you never know.

Afterward I may hit the Showman's Lounge, which is a very famous place too. Although it is not in the same location it was years ago, they do have a set schedule of what is there every night. So on Tuesday, it's Joey Morant, a trumpet player who plays straight Dixieland jazz. He's a very affable gentleman, who goes to Europe in the summertime and plays in the clubs over there. And he's been around a long time and he is fun.

Thursday is usually tap dance night. In the "old days," the Nicholas Brothers, Chuck Brown, and Dr. Jimmy Slyde were around. And the Sand Man would throw sand on the floor and tap and slide on the sandy floor. Sadly, those old days are over. But they do have good live music every night, so it's pretty consistent. So I'll say, "Let's go uptown, it's tap dance night at Showman's, it will be a lot of fun."

I also like to stop by the bar at DANIEL for a quiet chat with the bartender and Chef Daniel Boulud before they close. Daniel is charming and a friend. And there's a mixologist there who makes these fancy drinks without tiny paper umbrellas. They take what looks like a hypodermic needle and inject strawberry into a drink and mix it and crush with something else. That will make you crazy!

At least once a week, I visit the restaurant Antonucci and get to see my new friend, Ben Gazzara, there. You know, Ben Gazzara the great actor and his wife, Elke. You can buy a bottle of wine for 40 dollars at Antonucci's and it's good. Everything is fresh (of course), nothing canned or frozen. Francesco Antonucci was the chef/co-owner of REMI on the West Side. Now he is on the East Side with an excellent cooking team!

Twice a week, I'll head to Sette Mezzo restaurant and sit with proprietors Oriente, Nino, or Gennaro and discuss Italian music, politics, and the universe over a glass of red wine and one of Oriente's grand homemade desserts. These three guys came over from Italy with nothing. They started working at Elaine's and Elio's and decided to open a restaurant together because they all came from the same area in Italy. They all are partners now in Sette Mezzo and VICO, their other excellent restaurant on Madison Avenue.

Oriente comes from a family of bakers. His mother and father had a bakeshop where he learned to bake. He comes in every morning to make the desserts. They usually are blueberry, strawberry, or banana tarts. Or he'll put peaches in their own syrup or poach them in wine. Or he'll make apple strudel. He always sits down late at night at 11 p.m. when nobody's in the place, and we'll have a glass of wine and he'll bring out the desserts—instant acid-reflux.

Sette Mezzo only takes house accounts and cash. No credit cards. I've been going there since they had a little hole in the wall on 2nd Avenue 25 years ago. I used to get take out food from there. Folks like Mike Nichols and Diane Sawyer would come in and take food out. Or Charlie Gwathmey, the great late architect used to go there with Bette-Ann, his wife. It was a small neighborhood joint, then. Sette Mezzo is really upscale.

If I am at the Gramercy Theater or Irving Plaza for a concert, I might go to the roof-top bar restaurant of the Gramercy Hotel. I don't go there as much as I used to because it's not as private as it should be. But it's a fabulous place to go anytime to get away from the buzz of the Rose Bar downstairs, which is crazy, but fun. All the rock bands want to go the Rose Bar.

If I don't have a concert, I always try to stop by any opening my friend Larry Gagosian has at one of his art galleries. I like Larry. I'm always going to his shows. He represents the most interesting artists. The top contemporary artists in the world.

Larry gives the best dinner parties. I don't mean parties, with hats, horns, and dancing like the Studio 54 days. But he has great dinner parties at fabulous restaurants with an eclectic group of people from all over the world. That's what makes it fascinating. The crowd might include Marc Jacobs, Gianni Pigozzi, Daphne Guinness, Mick Jagger, Cicely Brown, Richard Prince, Jeff Koons, or Damien Hirst and on drums, Ronald O. Perelman with Jon Bon Jovi on vocals! Larry educated me about pop art, he is one of my best friends.

Seville Lounge, 2121 Seventh Avenue; (212) 864-8624

St. Nick's Jazz Pub, 773 Nicholas Avenue, Harlem; info@stnicksjazzpub.net

Showman's Lounge, 375 West 125th Street; (212) 864-8941

DANIEL, 60 East 65th Street; (212) 288-0033; www.danielnyc.com

Antonucci Restaurant, 170 East 81st Street; (212) 570-5100; www.antonuccicafe.com

Sette Mezzo, 969 Lexington Avenue; (212) 472-0400

Gramercy Park Hotel Roof and Garden Bar, 2 Lexington Avenue; (212) 920-3300; www.gramercyparkhotel.com

Gagosian Gallery, 980 Madison Avenue; (212) 744-2313; www.gagosian.com

. . . .

Paul Shaffer, musical director, *The Late Show with David Letterman* and Emmy-nominated and Grammy-winning composer and musician

In New York, everywhere you look there's something interesting to see and it's usually in human form. I love Lincoln Center. It's my favorite place. I love the architecture. I'm no maven, but I love to look up and say, "Wow, that's pretty." I love how they're redoing it. I was worried because it was always my favorite. I thought, they're going to wreck it when they redo it, but they're doing a great job. Little by little, it's getting better and better.

I really like walking around Lincoln Center outdoors, especially when they have Midsummer Night Swing in the summertime. I love being outside. I don't know how to dance. So many guys in bands don't dance. We are always playing at the dances. But I like to listen to the music and stroll around and look at the people. It's fun.

Midsummer Night Swing, Lincoln Center for the Performing Arts; 70 Lincoln Plaza; www.midsummernightswing .org

SAUNTERS, STROLLS, SAILS, RIDES & RAMBLES

✱ What do I love to do in New York? Walking the streets. You can go through so many neighborhoods. And what should somebody do coming here from out of town? Walk the busy streets in all the five boroughs. You'll see a more diverse group than anyplace else.

—Mayor Michael Bloomberg, 108th Mayor of New York City

Since 2008, during three Saturdays in August, a 6.9-mile stretch from the Brooklyn Bridge to Park Avenue and 72nd Street becomes off limits to cars. The idea for the "Summer Streets" program is to unleash the streets (even the most highly trafficked ones) for play, create a nirvana for pedestrians and cyclists, and inspire New Yorkers to use sustainable means of transit.

But long before Summer Streets, before development of the majestic Hudson River Park along the water and the High Line, a group of seriously devoted walkers called the Shorewalkers trekked along New York City's diverse waterfronts and shorelines. They've been traipsing around town for nearly three decades. On their first hike in 1982, the nonprofit group, which is run by volunteers, banded together to meander along piers, through Penn-Central railroad yards, and into Riverside Park. They lunched in Harlem, explored the rugged wilderness above the George Washington Bridge, and ended up at an Irish bar in Inwood, which served 15-cent glasses of beer.

"Walking around the edge of a big city along an unknown path can change you, expand your horizons, knock you around for a while," writes Shorewalker's president Cy Adler. So in addition to their hikes throughout the year, each May they trek 32 miles around the rim of Manhattan on a part-endurance, fully scenic jaunt called "The Great Saunter." The leisurely walk (which most certainly is not a race) circumnavigates the island. In the process they encounter the Statue of Liberty, four boroughs, nineteen bridges, twenty parks, and 360-degree views. In fact, Adler and folk singer Pete Seeger created a song about the jaunt, aptly named "Shorewalkers' Saunter."

The Shorewalkers are always happy for people to join their jaunts (membership costs as little as $20 annually; www.shorewalkers.org). Otherwise, get your walking (or riding) inspiration from these people.

Candace Bushnell, best-selling author

In *Breakfast at Tiffany's*, Holly Golightly walks down 5th Avenue and looks into the window at Tiffany. My equivalent would be walking down Madison Avenue. I would start at around 75th Street and walk south and look into the jewelry store windows. The jewels belong in a museum. I'd wonder who on earth can afford them? But it's like when Carrie in *Sex and the City* walked down Madison Avenue. She thought, you own this town.

Blake Lively, actress

What is the best thing about being in New York? Walking down the streets and not knowing if you're going to find something great—someone playing the saxophone or a street performance. I also love the cobblestone streets.

. . . .

Edie Falco, Tony-nominated, Emmy- and Golden Globe–winning actress

Why do I stay in New York City? The city is home. It's where I live. And I love to ride my bicycle along the West Side Highway. They've done such a phenomenal job with the bike path along there. It's New York and you can forget for a while and experience trees and water and smell the flowers. It's really well thought out.

. . . .

Matthew Broderick, Emmy- and Tony Award–winning, Golden Globe–nominated actor

I grew up here and I like being able to walk places and I like the variety of the city. And I like what a mess it is. Unlike Paris, which is beautiful, New York is sort of a messy, ugly, and beautiful place.

There's a very nice bike path that goes all the way up the West Side Highway way up to the George Washington Bridge. And on a nice day, I like taking out my bike and doing that—riding the path along the river. It gets you away from the city a little bit. New York has never had anything like it before. It feels like you're a million miles away. For me it's very nice, and I get to see parts of the city I don't often get to see. Sometimes I go off the path up at 160-something Street and it's pretty interesting. There's a little red lighthouse under the George Washington Bridge. I have a very nice road bike, a nice bent over bike. I don't listen to an iPod, I just like to be quiet. And when it's warm out, everybody has tailgate parties and listens to a lot of music along the path uptown before you get to the bridge. There's always music up there. I feel like I'm in another country.

Hudson River Park, (212) 627-2020; www.hudsonriverpark.org

Riverside Park, (212) 870-3070; www.riversideparkfund.org

. . . .

Gay Talese, acclaimed author and legendary journalist

I have been living in New York for more than 50 years, since 1958. I'm a very, very, very old resident of the city. And I have a very old house that I've lived in for 51-plus years of my marriage. I have lived here so long that I know the history of this block and the surrounding blocks. I know the people in the stores by name.

I work all day in solitude. Two stories below my house, I have a subterranean office. I call it a bunker. It's a 60-foot-long room completely contained with furniture, kitchen, shower, bed, everything down there. There's no phone, no connection to the outside world, and no connection to the building on top of it, which I own.

When you work alone, you don't have an interconnection with people during the workday. I'm all by myself with whatever is in my head. There are times when I really want to escape, and when I escape I just have to go up the steps of my subterranean world. I usually have chores to do. And everything I have to do is on Lexington Avenue, within 2 blocks of where I live. And while doing chores, I have conversations with the people at the establishments that I visit. It's an escape for me that I always love.

So I get to see the whole world within just 3 blocks of my neighborhood. I walk around without going far, and I get to practically circumnavigate the earth in terms of getting to know people who have come a long, long way to be my neighbor. New York is a city of very international neighborhoods. And it's that way throughout the city. In fact, New York feels like the most international city in the United States. I sense that more than ever because people on cell phones are talking in the street and you can eavesdrop very easily. And if you wander through New York as I do, you can easily hear the voices of faraway continents—easily. Even if you don't understand what they're saying, you know that they're saying something.

Just 3 blocks from my house are store owners and employees from Asia, Korea, Haiti, Scotland, and India. My neighborhood is both an international neighborhood and a peculiarly personal place. I make a left outside as I leave the steps of my subterranean office. My doctors are steps away. My gym is here, so is the place I buy the newspapers, get my haircut, the food market, the restaurants—it's all here.

On the northwest corner is my favorite restaurant, Brio. There's an attractive bartender named Zara who makes a wonderful martini for me. The only time I really unwind is at night around eight o'clock, and I really do look forward to having a gin martini. For me, it signals the completion of a day, good or bad, makes no difference. It's completion. The day is over. And I'm celebrating that I've gotten through the day and that's done by a beautiful chilled martini with a little lemon floating.

Zara gives you the full measure of the drink. She fills it right to the top. Sometimes you have martinis they cheat you about a quarter of an inch. But I trained Zara to fill it up and she uses a big glass, but it's not cheap. They also have the best veal in New York, like the veal piccata. Nearby is my favorite Brazilian restaurant, Circus. They have wonderful Brazilian food and every time I go, and hear the staff speaking Portugese, I feel like I'm in Brazil.

Across the street from Brio is my tailor shop, L&S Custom Tailors, on the second floor. The owner is Sal Cristiano. I sometimes have him make things for me like a new jacket or vest, or maybe he'll alter my suit. Much of my style is cultivated in that place. The Bread Factory is where I buy pumpernickel bagels and sometimes pastry. The people who work there are from Ecuador and Brazil. I'm a writer and I use pens. And I buy all my pens and filler for pens at Joon, a stationery store. Mr. Joon lived in this neighborhood when I first moved in. There are guys like Mr. Joon here and many others who I've grown up with.

Further on after I make a left to go north on Lexington Avenue, there's a newspaper stand that sells newspapers from all over the world, A & A Foreign Magazine Shop. They have thousands of magazines—ones you've never heard of, and every newspaper in every language there is. The guy that runs that place is from India. And if there's anything that you think they don't have, although I can't conceive of anything they don't have in terms of the foreign periodicals, across the street is competition from a place called Infinity News that also sells foreign newspapers and magazines. So you're really covered in this neighborhood.

I don't go to really fancy places for lunch. Instead, I eat at a place called Eat Here Now. And I sit on the far left side of the counter by the kitchen so there's no one on my left. And if you're reading the newspaper, nobody's banging against your left shoulder. I'll have a salad with anchovies. And they have wonderful soup. Or I'll go early and have two poached eggs with ham on the side and a cappuccino. And the women who work there are Russian. The guys who own the place are Greek. They're talking in Russian all the time.

You can have a personal relationship with people, even if you are separated by a counter as you would in a store. You can get to know people, and they help you keep in touch. And what they tell you about themselves might not be representative of the daily newspaper or the television news. But these people give me a more balanced picture of the state of the nation and the state of the world. When I go to my gym, Equinox, Vladimir who runs the locker room is from Port-au-Prince, Haiti. When they had the earthquake there, I got my news from him. I'll say to Vladimir, "How is your mother doing down there?" I'm getting reports not having to go to Port-au-Prince but just going to the locker room of Equinox on 63rd and Lexington.

People talk about the economy and how nobody is staying in business and Main Street is suffering. Well, this is Main Street. Lexington Avenue is Main Street. It's a service street. It's a business street. There's nothing elegant about Lexington Avenue. But these places survive. They're persevering.

Brio NYC, 137 East 61st Street; (212) 980-2300; www.brionyc.com

Eat Here Now, 839 Lexington Avenue; (212) 751-0724

L & S Custom Tailors, 138 East 61st Street; (212) 752-1638; www.lstailors.com

Bread Factory Cafe, 785 Lexington Avenue; (212) 355-5729; www.breadfactorycafe.com

Circus, 132 East 61st Street; (212) 223-2965; www.circusrestaurante.com

Joon, 795 Lexington Avenue; (212) 935-1007; www.joonpens.com

A & A Foreign Magazine Shop, 838 Lexington Avenue

Infinity News, 837 Lexington; (212) 223-3240

....

Rosie Perez, Academy Award–nominated actress, activist, and artistic board chair, Urban Arts Partnership

I started going to H&H Bagels for various reasons. 1. They are big, fat, delicious, cheap, and have great smears; 2. It was close to the "Tunnel" (a house/hip-hop/reggae club in the '80s that unfortunately turned into a ghetto fabulous club in the '90s); 3. The true urban legend of the story behind the owners was so f'ing cool.

Helmer Toro, born in Puerto Rico, and his brother-in-law, Hector Hernandez, hence H&H bagels, started the company. Some say that they didn't reveal their nationality because back in the '70s, when they started the business, they felt that some people, through their ridiculous prejudice, would be stupid enough not to buy them because they were both Puerto Rican. Who knows if this is true. I just loved that they were Puerto Rican and made kick-ass bagels . . . only in New York!

It was a ritual. We would party all night, go to H&H, and then head home. One summer, in the wee hours of the night, after we got our H&H bagels, my friend and I grabbed a cab and headed back to Brooklyn. There was this great summer breeze flowing so, on a whim, just before the cab hit the entrance to the bridge, we decided to jump out and walk over it. There were maybe two people on the bridge, no kidding, and the city and boroughs were still kind of quiet. As the sun was just about to rise, we stopped at the middle of the bridge, sat on the bench, which faced the Statue of Liberty, and watched the day come alive while we ate our delicious H&H bagels. It was a wonderful, special moment.

I don't pull all-nighters anymore, well, just not to the break of dawn, but once in a while, I'll get up really early, buy a bagel and a coffee, sometimes from H&H, sometimes just from a bodega, walk over the bridge, cop a squat, and enjoy my own *Breakfast at Tiffany's* moment—Brooklyn style.

H&H Bagels, 639 West 46th Street; (212) 765-7200; www.hhbagels.com

. . . .

Edward Burns, actor, writer, director

Before I had kids, I liked to go to Pier 25 in Tribeca near where I live. It was always the place I walked to as I was thinking about a screenplay I was writing. Or I would visit to read a script.

When you're working on a screenplay and trying to flesh the thing out or you've come to a part in the story that you can't figure out, I always find it's good to walk. In New York it's tough to find some peace and quiet. I remember that this was a pier that nobody used. Any time of the day you would go down there and it was empty. That became my spot. It's been closed for a couple of years during the construction but just reopened. So I've got my spot back.

And since they've redone it, I do everything there from playing tennis at the courts to playing basketball at the basketball courts. They just completed an incredible field. And my daughter and I were there the other night until 8 p.m. while she worked on her gymnastic moves. There's a great kids' playground. They're about to open a miniature golf. When the weather gets warm, I probably spend a minimum of six hours a day there. And anyone can go. It's a public park on the river. In fact, I have a new film called *Triangles Below Canal*, which was originally inspired by the neighborhood.

The walkways are beautifully landscaped and you can walk along the water. It's a great escape from the city. My favorite part is all the way at the end of Pier 25, it's an ideal place to just sit and think. You look south and you've got a great view of the Statue of Liberty. And it's the perfect spot to be at sunset in Manhattan. It really is my ideal place in New York for a little bit of quiet time.

New York continually inspires me. And for bridge and tunnel kids like me, there is always that moment when you're on the Long Island Expressway and heading down towards the midtown tunnel, and the skyline comes into perfect view. That's the moment where you know the day is about to change or the night is about to get very different. I have that memory from when I was a young kid coming into the city for the St. Patrick's Day parade with my father. And I have it when I was in high school driving in to see a Knicks game. And I still get it when my family and I return from a weekend away. Once you cross the river, it's a whole new ballgame.

Pier 25, Hudson River Park, between Franklin and North More Streets at the Hudson River; www.hudsonriverpark.org

. . . .

Eric Bogosian, actor, novelist, Tony Award–nominated playwright, and performance artist

I first saw 42nd Street when I was ten years old. My father and I were in town for the World's Fair. He said if you stand here long enough, everybody in the world will pass by, and I believed him. I still feel that way.

....

Ally Sheedy, actress

I'm a native New Yorker. And one thing that I love about the city is that no matter what you want to do, you're able to find it here. If there's anything you want to study, anything at all, you can do it here. You can learn to play nearly any instrument, study any kind of singing, take any kind of dancing or acting or exercise, or discover any kind of bookstore. If you want to take yoga, there are so many places—everything is here. The other day, I was at the New York Public Library and I was thinking, we even have one of the best libraries in the world right here.

If I have a free hour, I figure out a great walk from wherever I am—especially if I'm in Midtown and walking home to the Upper West Side. There is a yoga class at Yoga Sutra that I take near the New York Public Library. So I'll start at the New York Public Library around 42nd and 5th Avenue and I walk west over to Times Square. I love walking by the area where the mayor closed off Times Square to cars so I can walk right down in the middle of the street. I grew up here and it's still wild that I could walk right down that street and it's all pedestrians and no cars. It's like a movie. I like how people have their chairs out and during lunch hour, office workers are hanging out. And I love that during summers, people sit in the middle of Times Square with suntan lotion. It's so bizarre—getting a tan in the middle of the street.

And I'll go up Broadway and right past the theater district so I can look at all the Broadway theaters on the side streets. I'll see the Naked Cowboy taking pictures of people. Who is the Naked Cowboy? He's a man who walks around Times Square wearing just his underwear and a cowboy hat. The guy carries a guitar and takes pictures with people. He's like the other mayor of New York—welcoming tourists. It's funny. There are all these characters like that. They're all over the place. I love it. It gets really crowded and people are giving away tickets to shows. It's wild—just like a circus.

When I get all the way to Columbus Circle, I like to skirt around by the Time Warner Center. And then I walk straight up Broadway. I guess I pick that street because you get to walk past Lincoln Center, which is always gorgeous. And I can check out what's playing or going on. And there's always cool people hanging out by the fountain there. See, it's all about people watching. Depending on the time of the day, there are all kinds of people out.

My neighborhood is from 59th Street up to 96th Street—and every block gives me a memory. I know the stores. I know the people who run many of them. I always bump into people who I know. On the way I might stop at Fairway, a huge grocery store that has great produce and all kinds of things for stuff for salads. Actually Fairway has almost everything in the world. Further uptown, Zabar's is great for olives, and they have amazing coffee and really good fresh baked bread.

Then there are some little markets in my neighborhood that I really like. Hopefully they won't go out of business. One of the best ones is Mani's Market on 94th and Columbus. It's a little grocery store that has great produce from local farms.

In New York you really see the world. There are so many different people from different cultures just walking the street and taking the subway. I grew up in New York and my whole family is here and I wanted to raise my daughter here and her dad's whole family is here too. My daughter, who is 15, is very independent getting around the city, and her friends hang out in Chinatown. I like giving her the kind of childhood I had.

Fairway Market, 2127 Broadway; (212) 595-1888; www.fairwaymarket.com

Zabar's, 2245 Broadway; (212) 787-2000; www.zabars.com

Mani Market Place, 687 Columbus Avenue; (212) 662-4392; www.manimarketplace.com

....

Sebastian Unger, author, journalist, and documentary filmmaker

I really like just walking around. I live in New York because of the New Yorkers. It's just the most incredible piece of theater ever. You walk down the street and there's every race in the world, every religion, every nationality, rich people side by side with street vendors with whatever. It's humanity all in one block. It's incredible.

I live in a weird neighborhood by the Lincoln Tunnel entrance. I think it resists gentrification. But I remember when I first got here in 1996. I just moved from Massachusetts. I was living in the East Village and there was a blizzard every weekend. I would walk around with a book in my pocket and I'd find a nice bar and sit down and have a drink and read my book and that is how I got to know the city.

....

Rosie Lani Fiedelman, Drama Desk award–winning performer for *In the Heights* and a member of the dance company Jennifer Muller/The Works

When I auditioned for *In the Heights,* I was completely out of my element. I had been dancing for years with the modern company, Jennifer Muller/The Works. I had never danced in heels before. I'd never really done hip-hop. It was crazy. But I loved it. I absolutely loved the choreography and the music. And I walked away thinking if this is the only experience I have with this, that's enough for me. It was a fun experience.

And then I got a callback but was leaving to go on tour with the company to Thailand and had to miss it and was really upset. A day or two after I came back from the tour, I was on the 1 train and it was packed. I looked up and saw Andy Blankenbuehler, the choreographer of *In the Heights,* across the way. This was the second time in my life that I'm seeing this man and I thought this is crazy, this is serendipitous, this is a vibe. I thought, I have to say something even if I just stumble over my words. This doesn't happen. So I got up and said, "Excuse me, excuse me," pushing people out of the way and he looked up and I said, "Hi" and he said, "Hi. I've been thinking about you. Can you come to a callback . . . ? There will be another callback."

So I got to the callback and it was down to four of us. And there was a moment where we were doing all this choreography, and it was beautiful, fast, and crazy. We did double pirouettes and stopped and stood there and the focus was up. And I remember Andy said, "You know, everything looks great. The battement, the turns, the counts—all that stuff. But when you land I want to see what it felt like to see Times Square at night for the first time in your life." I thought, that's what I do. I feel that. That is why I dance.

Times Square, Broadway and 7th Avenues, West 42nd to West 47th Streets; www.timessquarenyc.org

....

Raquel Bruno, producer, Drive Entertainment Group

I really adore going to the Christopher Street Pier—even in wintertime. But mostly I love it during spring and the summer. In the morning when a lot of people really aren't around, I'll grab an ice coffee and a doughnut and sit on a bench and read magazines and catch up for the week. And then at sunset it's fun to see everybody enjoying, winding down. And sometimes there's music outside on the edge of the Pier. You can see the Statue of Liberty. You can see party boats going out. There's a real festive feeling, especially in the spring and summer.

Or after a long week, my friends and I will get a blanket, grab some takeout food, and sit in the middle of the grassy knoll. We'll have a picnic and watch the sunset. It's basically our concrete beach. And there's a dog park near there. And I love watching the dogs from all different walks of life in every size and variety. The dogs are so completely uninhibited, just having a great time.

Just a little bit north of Christopher is the High Line, which used to be an old elevated railroad track that was above the highways. Now it's a pedestrian walkway with grasses, shrubs, flowers, and really interesting lighting. It's like something from the film *Metropolis*. Picture an outdoor artistic art museum, high in the sky. It's really an exhibit that everyone can really enjoy and watch and walk through buildings. There's something very New York and cool about it.

....

Carson Griffith, columnist for *New York Daily News*

When I first moved to New York City, I didn't have an apartment, I didn't have a job. I had nothing. I stayed at a friend's apartment. But all I wanted was to get my own place and to be downtown. So, during the day, I would plug in my iPod, head downtown, and look around for apartment-for-rent signs. I remember walking up and down, all over the West Village, and thinking like how amazing it was.

I stumbled on Perry Street, the 1-block stretch between Bleecker and West 10th Streets. The cobblestoned tree-lined block is lined with gorgeous brownstone townhouses. It feels like you've stepped back in time. It's almost like a movie set—like you're on the Warner Bros. lot in LA. You expect someone to walk by and say,

"No smoking on the set." I remembered thinking, these homes look just like the townhouses in Back Bay in Boston where my parents live. And it was the one block that I would always visit over and over again.

So Perry Street is reminiscent of when I first moved to the city. It also reminds me of where my parents live. Visiting that street makes me a little homesick, but it's also a little comforting. The two things together make that block very special.

I didn't end up living on Perry Street and I don't have any personal connections to it. It's actually where Sarah Jessica Parker's character, Carrie, in *Sex in the City* had her brownstone and that stoop. One of the buildings is actually roped and says NO TRESPASSING. I was thinking, how ironic it is. The one block where I want to live and there's a NO TRESPASSING sign on one of the buildings. What does that say about my housing choices in New York?

I remember a real estate agent asked me, "Where are you thinking about living?" I said, "What about Perry Street?" And she said, "Honey, everyone wants to live on Perry Street." And I just started laughing. But I don't live too far away on Horatio Street, so I can walk there anytime. I mean the homes on my street are gorgeous, but there's just something about that one block on Perry Street. Sometimes it's the little things like a smell or a tree that can make you homesick or can help you kick homesickness, and Perry Street helps me a little bit. It's calming.

....

Elettra Wiedemann, fashion model and founder of One Frickin Day

I grew up in Greenwich Village and after years of living outside the United States, I have finally resettled here in the Meatpacking District. When I was a kid growing up on Perry Street in the '80s, my father used to take me to the little park on Hudson and tell me that I should never go beyond Hudson towards the river, which at the time was pretty dangerous and, I suppose, somewhat derelict. Now obviously, the Meatpacking District feels like the center of it all, and Greenwich Village has become very chic and always seems to be buzzing with New Yorkers and tourists.

My favorite thing to do whenever I have free time is simply to walk around the Village and Meatpacking District and look at all the stores and cafes, and remember what they used to be and my memories associated with them. There is not much here now that existed when I was child, but I can still remember people, bakeries, florists, and small businesses that knew my name when I was little and would give me little candies or say hello to me as I walked down the street.

The apartment building on the corner of Perry and 7th Street was built the year my father was transferred to the West Coast for work, and we called it the Wicked Witch of the West's house because it has a steeple that looks much like her hat. I also remember climbing the tree outside a wonderful diner on Bedford Street (now I believe it is a Greek place), while my dad talked inside with the chef and his wife, who ran the place.

When I walk down these streets, it's more than just a stroll. It's a time to reconnect to my childhood and my family. I moved away from New York years ago, thinking that I would be much happier abroad. Everything in New York City always seemed to be moving so fast and always changing, and I felt it was a place that was too loaded for me. I think I went to Europe in part to search for a city that felt fresh and new, but also a city that was more stable and constant and somewhat softer.

But now I know that New York is not just my home, it is also a part of me. And its constant movement and change is exactly what makes it so beautiful. It never stops, it's always changing, always staying young and fresh and creating new memories for the millions of people who walk these same streets.

....

Kathleen Turner, Golden Globe–winning, Academy Award– and Tony-nominated actress

I live in New York and love to walk. Every block offers something different. Mostly, I stay on the West Side. I feel more at home there.

I just love living here. I love the people. There are so many possibilities. All you have to do is walk a couple of blocks and you'll discover something. A lot of times I like to walk down the Hudson River Park. It's gotten really, really lovely. They've done such a great job with it. And in better weather I bike.

....

Sam Champion, weather anchor, *Good Morning America*

During spring, summer, and fall, when I have a free afternoon, I head to the west side bike path along Hudson River Park and the Manhattan Waterfront Greenway. I almost don't want to talk too much about it. But it's one of the saving graces of New York City's city life. You have this incredible path along the Hudson River, this beautiful stretch of water that is now planted, green, and connected. So you can bike and run all the way up to West Side from Battery Park all the way past the George Washington Bridge.

From my years doing Channel 7 weather, I never got up in the morning and never knew what morning was. I got up around ten because I worked the evening shift. So it was a midday activity for me to be outside. But now that I'm on the morning shift, I can go in the evening, during mornings when the show is done, or in the afternoon. So whenever I find spare time, I'll grab my bike and hit that path.

I live on the Upper West Side in the 60s. So I always hit the path right in front of the Trump buildings. My first ride south, down to Battery Park, doesn't count. That's just a scenic ride and I'll get things along the way. I'll stop by Toga Bike Shop, the oldest bike shop in New York, and make sure the bike is in good shape and the tires are all right. Or I'll stop and get sunscreen. And that ride to Battery Park is a leisurely, warm-up ride. Then I'll go from Battery Park all the way up to the George Washington Bridge as an exercise ride. Once I do that stretch to get my exercise, the rest of my time on the path is pure enjoyment and free time.

I'll come back down south and hit places on the way down. I'll make different stops depending on my mood.

All the way up north, right under the George Washington Bridge is a little lighthouse. It's picturesque. The water gently laps right onto the shoreline there. It's bordered by rocks and you can't get to the water, but it's almost like a little bay. And you can take pictures there that look like you're nowhere near New York City.

I stop at Fairway, the big grocery store right along the water on 130th Street, and get a sandwich or whatever and have a picnic by the water. I love the parks and fields that are up there above the water treatment plant. From the George Washington Bridge to 125th Street, it's kind of a hidden spot. On the weekends it's crazy with families, picnics, parties, ballgames. Everything goes on up there on the weekends. But during the week, you practically have that place by yourself.

One of the great spots on the path is around 68th Street, a place called Pier i Café. It started out as a little open grill. They used two oil drums cut in half with real charcoal to grill burgers. They had a couple little cafe tables so people who knew about it would go because you can't have a grill in New York City. How do I know? The fire department made me take mine off my terrace.

So if you crave grilled burgers you're kind of out of luck. But this place, which started out of these oil drums, has now turned into a full-service open-grill cafe. There are about fifty or sixty cafe tables and umbrellas and chairs. You can get alcohol, french fries, salads, burgers. You sit outside beside the Hudson and watch everybody go past. It's gorgeous. It's not so crowded, and they have really nice quality chairs and tables with flowers on them. And during the day, it's actually kind of peaceful.

Then I pass a lot of cool things. I pass the Intrepid Museum, which is really interesting. I pass the heliports and see all the helicopters that come up and down and enter New York. And just north of Chelsea Piers is a section of giant rocks in the grass. In some cases, these rocks are the size of small cars. And in my opinion, that is the best place to watch the sunset in New York. Period.

All of a sudden, the sun gets over the buildings across the river in New Jersey. The sun kind of drops through them and it's a typical kind of sunset until it gets to about building height. There's a giant railroad sign that says Erie Lackawanna. And then when the sun drops, you get the most spectacular colors that bounce up on any clouds that are there. It's orange. It's yellow. It's pink. It's red. It's the most dramatic sunset anywhere.

Biking further south I get to the piers past Canal Street—right toward the Village. Those piers were once such an eyesore of New York, but now they are all renovated. They are parks where people can lay out on the grass. It's where real New Yorkers, downtown New Yorkers, hang out and get their sun. It's almost like New York's beach, where everyone goes. So that's a good place to chill and get ice cream, water, and Gatorade. And there are bathrooms. The one thing everyone always asks about New York is "Where are the bathrooms?" But this spot has bathrooms, they're clean, free, and you don't even have to buy a Starbucks coffee.

Further south is Nelson A. Rockefeller Park. It's a big open space behind all the apartment buildings at Battery Park. I always see people playing Frisbee or just taking a break. And I can watch the ferries going across and the boats going up the Hudson there.

That boat basin at North Cove Marina is another favorite part. I see all the giant mega yachts of the world parked right there at the boat basin that's near Battery Park. And I can get within feet of them and really see just how huge they are. And if you're lucky enough you'll get to talk to the folks who crew it. Because they're usually hanging out on the yachts or washing them. And so you just start up a conversation with them about where they've been and where they're going.

Between the marina and Museum of Jewish Heritage there's a great green space that's all the way down in Battery Park. I love to hang out there. You kind of have to walk around to it and not many people know where it is. There's a thicket of trees and bridges. It feels like you're in a waterside forest and it's absolutely beautiful.

As soon as spring comes, I'm on the bike path all the time through the fall. And I miss it during winter, but the wind along the river is just too cold for me. But I believe what keeps me in New York, besides the fact that this is where my job is, is that in the summer, I don't feel the need to leave.

I know that I can get away and have an outdoor experience without having to truly go away. If I want the experience that people in America have of going to the backyard and grilling a burger, I have my burger spot. If I want to sit and get some sun, I'm down at the piers watching the ferries and the boats go by. If I want to have a picnic, I stop at Fairway and head to the park up there. There are so many things I can do to get away. New York really opens up for me because of a path that allows me to stay here, live it, and enjoy.

Hudson River Park, (212) 627-2020; www.hudsonriverpark.org

Toga Bike Shop, 110 West End Avenue; (212) 799-9625; http://togabikes.com

Fairway (Harlem), 2328 12th Avenue (at 130th Street); (212) 234-3883; www.fairwaymarket.com

Pier i Café, Riverside Park, Riverside Boulevard and 68th Street; (212) 362-4450; www.piericafe.com

....

Jay Jay French, Twisted Sister guitarist and founder of the Pinkburst Project

There's a new promenade on the Hudson River South of 72nd Street to around 60th Street that is absolutely stunning. It's almost like they built it for a club of twenty people because no one's on it. There are sculptures, futuristic seats, and steps that lead right down to the water so you can sit right by the river's edge. At 70th Street and Riverside Drive there's a pier that juts out halfway across the Hudson River. There are grasses. I walked it last summer with my girlfriend and it was so empty. I said, "It's open for you and me."

....

Tom Kitt, Tony Award–winning Broadway composer and musician

I love walking around New York City, especially with my kids when it's nice out. We live in an age where are we are constantly working. Walking really allows you to turn off, enjoy being in New York, and see the architecture. I find it very inspiring. We live in the lower Fifth Avenue area. And it's really nice to go from around 12th Street up to Madison Square Park. We'll stop to get coffee and a paper and hopefully my daughter falls asleep and I can actually read.

....

Bunny Williams, interior designer and author

The High Line is extraordinary. The fact that you're walking sort of above the city and looking at the river and lower Manhattan is really one of the most thrilling things in New York.

The High Line was originally an elevated railroad bed. So it's an elevated garden. You climb steps and walk along a wide meandering path from Gansevoort Street to 20th Street. And eventually the plan is for it to end up at the Javits Center. I live uptown, so it's fun to go down there in the late afternoon, particularly when the days get longer. You can walk and see the sunset, and then have dinner downtown. It's just a magical evening.

I'm a gardener, so from a plant point of view, the High Line is very interesting. The plans of plants are as interesting as any I've ever seen. They've used prairie grasses, a number of different perennials, and some annuals. You see things that could grow in the Midwest, but they've been transported to this urban garden.

We live in a very hard landscape of sidewalks, cement, tall buildings. But when you have this oasis of gardens, it's just such a gift in a city. And all along are benches and places to sit and really enjoy it. As New Yorkers, we tend to be inside a lot. We work inside. We live in apartments, and I think that anytime that the city creates these spaces, it allows us to be outside and that is so exciting.

The High Line, Gansevoort Street to West 20th Street, between 10th and 11th Avenues; (212) 500-6035; www .thehighline.org

....

Richard Kind, actor

If I have an hour there's only one thing I do. I start at Columbus Circle, walk across Central Park South to 5th Avenue, pass Rockefeller Center, turn right, and walk down Broadway. It makes you feel alive. It's amazing that one city can accomplish all of this. You see all the things the city has: the beauty of architecture, the beauty of nature, and the beauty of people. That's what I love about New York.

....

Jason Oliver Nixon, creative director of John Loecke Inc. interior design and global lifestyle editor, *Delta Sky* magazine

I love going places that capture the glamour and sophistication of New York, and I try and do things that harken back to Nick and Nora Charles in the *Thin Man* movies. Nowadays, when everybody is dressing down, it's really fun to dress up. And once a month on a Saturday afternoon, I'll put on a suit and walk across Central Park and hit the Frick Museum at 70th and 5th Avenue. It is really magical. They have such a fantastic collection. And to be in this incredible setting, in this wonderful house, you get to take in a very different slice of life. And then I walk down the street and around the corner and have a glass of champagne at DANIEL. It's a jewel box of a setting with great Brazilian music. What a perfect high glamour afternoon that doesn't end up costing that much.

The Frick Collection, One East 70th Street; (212) 288-0700; www.frick.org

DANIEL, 60 East 65th Street; (212) 288-0033; www.danielnyc.com

....

Orfeh, Tony-nominated actress and singer

My favorite ritual is to go to the Lower East Side and haunt all those amazing boutiques that just get better and better. They're always there. They haven't been destroyed by the recession. I start at 3rd Street between around A and 1st Avenue and make my way to 12th Street. I'll maybe hit some places towards 2nd Avenue. Once you pass 2nd, it's over.

Seventh Street in particular is a real treasure trove. At Fab 208, the owner and his wife design all these amazing clothes. I've been going there my whole life. Just so you know, the owners are fab, everything in their store is fab, and almost everything is made by them. They design and they get a couple of pieces from here and there. It's hip and it's really cool. And right across the street from there is a vintage consignment store, AuH20. You can find a vintage Gucci bag if you really search—or you'll find vintage denim or leather motorcycle jackets. It's on the north side of the street on 7th. You can't miss it because it's the only vintage consignment store on the entire block.

After shopping and shopping and shopping, I dip into Veselka because I've walked enough to earn my meal. It's Ukrainian comfort food with big portions. I always have the vegetarian plate. You get pierogis, stuffed cabbage, soup, salad, bread. You get everything for about $12.95. They also have amazing desserts like nuclear-size Rice Krispies treats. It's a fantastic meal but you have to walk a few hundred miles before you can eat it without any guilt. I love the food and atmosphere. When I was a kid, the dining room was really small. And then they expanded and now it's a huge space. And it's open 24 hours. So it's the one place we could go to after we were in the recording studio. I have really good memories of the restaurant.

I have my meal and then walk all the way downtown and back home. I mean it's like a trek. It's my favorite, favorite thing to do in the world. This ritual gives me a sense of peace. I feel like the city is mine. There are not a lot of people down there in the middle of the day during work hours—especially in the warm weather. People aren't going down there. They go to tourist attractions. It's still a nice little untapped treasure. So I put on my most comfortable sneakers and go.

Veselka, 144 2nd Avenue; (212) 228-9682; www.veselka.com

Fab 208, 72 East 7th Street; (212) 673-7581; www.fab208.com

AuH2O, 84 East 7th Street; (212) 466-0844; www.auh2oshop.com

....

Bebe Neuwirth, Tony- and Emmy-winning actress, singer, and dancer

I love to walk in neighborhoods that I don't know very well. My husband is a very serious photographer and he has a really great camera, and the two of us will just walk and walk and take pictures together. And we'll look at something and he'll take a picture of it and then I'll look at the same thing and then I'll take a picture of it. He likes to say, "One camera and four eyes." It's nice for the two of us to discover a new place and share what we see, how we see, and know each other that way. You can always tell, that's a Chris shot, that's a Bebe shot. And it doesn't matter where you walk. In New York City, there's a photograph to be taken. There are cobblestoned streets that I like. Down in Battery Park there is a beautiful statue in the water for the merchant marine. There's a man in the water and he's being helped up by another man, and it's beautiful and haunting and provocative. There's all kinds of things to discover if you just walk and look.

American Merchant Mariners Memorial, just to the south of Pier A, Battery Park; (212) 360-8143

....

John Ortiz, actor and artistic director/co-founder, LAByrinth Theater Company

New York makes me stronger, makes me feel more alive and gives me a purpose in life. And I love walking in Spanish Harlem. I grew up in Bed Stuy, and Spanish Harlem was a big part of my life. I love that I can just duck into any kind of cuchifrito place and pick up a delicious fried pastel. And I'll get a nice cup of coffee and people are so friendly and warm. It's like going back to Puerto Rico.

....

Atoosa Rubenstein, founder of *CosmoGirl* and former editor in chief of *Seventeen,* president, Big Momma Productions

Every time we are on the West Side Highway, my 2-year-old daughter Angelika reminds me of our favorite activity when she points toward the Hudson River and squeals, "Bike riding!" If I had a free morning or afternoon (and sadly this isn't a year-round activity), I would hop on my bike and ride up to the 79th Street Boat Basin and go kayaking. I can't tell you how many times I drove by the bike path in a taxi or walked by the FREE KAYAKING signs when I lived on Riverside Drive. But back then, I was working full time (or I should say "all time") and these opportunities didn't even register with me. It's as though they were for someone else.

It took me a good few years to thaw out from that hectic pace of life. But now that I have, there's nothing I like more than the freedom I feel biking and the peace of sitting in that kayak as my husband rows and my daughter giggles as she dips her toes in the water. Okay—so sometimes she gets yelled at by the "free kayak" volunteers. But when that doesn't happen, what a beautiful moment of serenity we enjoy together. And of course my daughter, without fail, falls asleep in her bike seat on the way home and then we are the laughingstock of the bike path with a dangling helmeted toddler head in our backseat. Makes for great laughs, great pictures, and great memories.

Biking and kayaking on the west side of Manhattan without fail, for me, creates those amazing moments when I am so present and aware of my blessings that even writing about it now in the middle of the cold winter brings a tear to my eye.

From mid-May to mid-October, the volunteer not-for-profit organization, New York City Downtown Boathouse, offers free kayaking from several piers along the Hudson River. For more information visit www.downtownboathouse.org.

....

Ana Gasteyer, actress and singer

My husband loves to go biking on Governor's Island with our kids. It's very peaceful and affordable and there aren't cars. There's a great sense of context that is very private and spiritual. You kind of feel like you left your life a little bit and it's a quick ferry ride from Manhattan.

The Trust for Governor's Island, (212) 440-2200; www.govisland.com/html/visit/biking.shtml

....

Fred Armisen, actor

I'm from Long Island and my mom used to bring me to New York when I was growing up. I would see shows. When I got older, I'd come to see the Clash and go to record stores. I always loved it. It's the coolest city in the world. Don't you think? Just walking down Central Park West—around 72nd Street by the Dakota, is exhilarating. It's something that you can't describe. And I love the sounds of New York. Everything is so loud and I like it that way. I like constant noise. I hate quiet. When I go out and it's dead quiet, I hate it. I like noise.

....

Abigail Disney, documentary filmmaker and co-founder and president, the Daphne Foundation

My favorite thing to do is to go for a run on Broadway at rush hour. I know it sounds nuts, but I drop my son off at 78th Street at about 8 in the morning for school and sometimes run home for exercise down to 26th and Broadway, which is a little under 3 miles. It usually takes about a half an hour, and that's right during rush hour.

It is just the coolest thing to see the range of humanity on its way to work and to dodge in and out on my way downtown. It's very fun! And I see basically everything! Sometimes I bring a notepad and write things down, because some things are so strange and unexpected that I know I'll never remember them. However, I only carry a notepad if I have a pocket in my sweatpants (though I confess to sometimes carrying money in my bra).

Once, I was fast walking, and feeling very fit and together, until I was passed by an orthodox Jewish man with curls and a hat and everything—that traditional outfit. I thought I was walking so fast and he just left me in the dust! And once there was a homeless guy waking up and three different people offered him food because they felt so bad for him and he refused all of it, saying he was fine and didn't need their help.

From 78th down to 59th it's pretty much just families heading over to drop their kids at various schools and moms and nannies shopping for groceries at Fairway and Citarella. From 59th to 42nd there's a bizarre combo of businessmen and women with their very serious game faces on, ready to kick some MBA's butt when they get to the office. They're trying to dodge the slow-walking tourists gawking of course at Times Square.

The tourists are a menace in many ways more than the slow walking, mind you, though that's bad enough for a girl bent on a good workout. They also have a way of suddenly darting left or right, with absolutely no warning. Every self-respecting New Yorker knows that you walk in a straight line unless you absolutely have to veer, and then only at the last second and minimally.

Below 34th is what's left of the garment district. Sadly, most of the actual garment making is over in this area, has moved east to Brooklyn and Queens and *way* east to China and such places. But the buildings are there, with their big generous loft spaces, and little by little they are being commandeered by creative types, so the neighborhood is a weird mix of great restaurants (what is it with artists and the way they always have great restaurants in their neighborhoods?) and depressingly identical and repetitive notions shops that sell wigs and sequins and bows of every description. Then I'm home! Every day is an adventure, no two days the same.

....

Eugene Pack, Emmy-nominated writer, actor, producer, director, and co-creator of *Celebrity Autobiography*

Growing up on Long Island, New York City was just an hour away by train. But that ride from Massapequa in to New York was so dramatic. When I was a kid and we were going to New York, it seemed like the biggest trip in the universe. The transition from suburbia—passing Queens, going into the darkness of the tunnel, getting out into Penn Station, walking up the stairs, and seeing Macy's and all that energy—was utterly astonishing. I thought, here you go up these steps and there you are in the middle of the greatest city in the world. I just thought that was such a gift that it was so accessible.

In New York, everyone's in motion, in progress, right there in front of you—in the moment. There's something so exciting about that. It's overwhelming too. You can absorb all this different energy—everyone walking and hurrying on route to different places that is so important to them. Everyone has a story and it's right in your face. It's so fun to see it. It's like watching a movie, the best movie, right in front of you all the time. There's the person with their yoga mat, the person with their *New York Times*, the person with their dog, the person with their kid, the person with their ideas and their dreams.

When I went to New York University (NYU), it was a great time in my life. One day, I was with a bunch of friends and we made a seemingly wrong turn. We stumbled upon this place, which was just across from our really modern dorms, called Weinstein Residence Hall. I remember saying, "What's behind this open gate?" There was a sign that said THE WASHINGTON MEWS.

This block was like no other block in Manhattan. It was so foreign, it just blew my mind. Walking down the little street, I remember thinking, where am I? The Washington Mews is a single narrow gated cobblestone street with beautiful carriage homes from the late 19th century. It's on a private road right in the middle of Greenwich Village off University Place. It's just one of these hidden blocks in Manhattan that has to be experienced. Even now, whenever I visit that block, it feels like I'm entering the past going to a different country in a different time. It's like I've popped into a storybook or I've entered a little mini travel machine. I'm completely out of time and space.

I wonder who lives there. Are they professors? Do they have modern appliances in there? It just brings up all these questions and I think, could this street be the most private little block in New York City?

....

Donald J. Trump, chairman and president of the Trump Organization

New York is an exciting city, and to walk it makes it doubly so. You can immediately feel and sense the energy of all the people, the buildings, the neighborhoods, and the architecture. Nothing pleases me more than to walk or drive to my various properties—to check out the action at Wollman Rink, to inspect the renovations at Trump International Hotel & Tower, and to have lunch or dinner at the wonderful Jean Georges restaurant, our signature restaurant named after famed chef Jean-Georges Vongerichten. Sometimes I'll go downtown to our beautiful building on Wall Street, 40 Wall Street, and then to SoHo to visit our hotel, Trump SoHo, and to have superb Italian food at our restaurant, Quattro. New York is a place where one can live and work at once, which for someone like me is a perfect combination. It's a wonderful place to be.

Trump Wollman Skating Rink, 830 5th Avenue; (212) 439-6900; www.wollmanskatingrink.com

Jean Georges Restaurant, Trump International Hotel and Tower, One Central Park West; www.jean-georges.com

Quattro Gastronomia Italiana, 246 Spring Street; (212) 842-4500; www.quattronewyork.com

....

Doug Liman, director and producer

I produce a TV show that shoots in Brooklyn and my office is in Tribeca. So biking across the Manhattan Bridge from my Manhattan office is one of my favorite things to do. The city looks so great and so beautiful from there. And when I'm biking to Dumbo in Brooklyn, I can imagine that I'm younger, cool, and living in Dumbo.

....

John Benjamin Hickey, Tony-winning actor

The easiest way to have your spirits lifted is to walk in New York. I love the Village where I live and I especially love West 4th Street. The brownstones are laid out in a beautiful way. I've lived there for twenty-five years, but I can still get lost in the Village. Yet it's manageable and small—unlike the grid that is the rest of the city. It's a great place to lose yourself.

....

Wendy Diamond, author, TV personality, endangered animal and rescue advocate, and editor in chief, *Animal Fair Media*

New York is beautiful, has the richest architecture, and wealthiest people. But there's also a whole other side to appreciate. There are people who are do-gooders helping people every day.

One of my favorite things to do is to ride on the Coalition for the Homeless van to spend time with them delivering meals to the homeless. There are three different routes—the Bronx, downtown, and uptown. On average, they distribute 1,000 meals between the three. And space permitting, anyone can volunteer.

I'll never get out of my head the image of an old man under the Brooklyn Bridge, which is one of their spots. He had half his teeth and was so grateful and smiling for a ham sandwich, milk, and an apple. It was a simple meal and he was so genuinely appreciative.

That truly made me realize just how lucky we are and that there are so many people who are worse off. Of course there will always be people who are much better off, but there are people who are much worse off. This really hit me that day.

For most of us, to have meaning in life means more than any materialistic things that you can acquire. It's nice to find something that drives you more than money or stuff. After that first volunteering experience, I was inspired to publish two cookbooks and raise hundreds of thousands of dollars for the Coalition for the Homeless and Empty the Shelters.

The Coalition for the Homeless van stops at locations like the South Ferry, Penn Station, and Port Authority. They require that you call in advance to sign up. And then you ride on the van to these various locations and help distribute the meals. You see a side of New York you would never see anywhere else. It brings things down to reality. And it makes me think, no matter what, my life is great.

The homeless people know the locations. And it's every day, 365 days a year. Many people volunteer on Thanksgiving. But Thanksgiving is just like any other day for these people. They always need to eat. The second Tuesday in May, they still need help.

That couple of hours volunteering with the Homeless Coalition changed my entire life. I will never forget that man under the Brooklyn Bridge. I don't know his name. I don't know what happened to him, but he's always in my mind. He touched me at a young age when I was living a pretty opulent life. And it showed me that I've got to appreciate what I have. He gave me a bigger gift than I could ever ask for.

Coalition for the Homeless, to volunteer please call (212) 776-2062 or email volunteer@cfthomeless.org; www .coalitionforthehomeless.org

....

Mark Ruffalo, Oscar-nominated actor and director

My favorite thing to do in New York City is walk around—anywhere. Any part of New York—just start walking. But the West Village is my favorite. It still has its original New York charm. It doesn't feel too overrun by all the new stuff and my friends live there.

....

Drew Nieporent, restaurateur and founder of Myriad Restaurant Group (Tribeca Grill and Nobu)

My favorite thing to do here? Smoke a Churchill size cigar in an area where Mike Bloomberg wouldn't have me arrested. Normally, it's on the loading dock of that very famous restaurant, Tribeca Grill. Or actually it can be anywhere in Tribeca. It's been my home for 26 years. This activity is calming. I can focus. And it can be any kind of cigar but it has to be a big Churchill size. I'm like the frog in that cartoon [Chauncey "Flatface" Frog]. It's like giving a dog the bone. It's a reward for me. And what keeps me in New York? It's an amazing city. Every day there's something to do. Tomorrow it could be a Knicks game or a Rangers game or the Yankees playing. There's theater. Great restaurants. There are a million things going on.

....

Michael Shannon, Oscar-nominated actor

I love going for walks and seeing where the spirit moves me. I live in Red Hook, Brooklyn, so I like to walk along the river from Red Hook to Dumbo. They have a really nice park there now so I like that walk a lot.

....

Julian Niccolini, co-owner Four Seasons restaurant

Cycling gives me freedom and calm. Besides, after working inside for so many hours, it's nice to be outside. And there are so many places to bike in New York. Some of them are not as well known.

There's a great bike path that runs right along the East River. It's a tremendous spot and the best place to see the sunrise. I like watching the drama of the sun as it hits the United Nations building. It's a spectacular view. There is no question about that. I love the crispness and quiet of a morning ride. And when you're heading north on the path, you can cross over to Randall's Island. It's a very beautiful and peaceful spot and there aren't many people around. From April to October there's a footbridge that brings you to Ward's Island, which is also very tranquil, and I'll bike there too.

The first thing that went into my mind when I came to this beautiful city from Italy in 1974 was that I couldn't believe the sea of people walking along 5th Avenue. I used to walk from 24th Street all the way up to Central Park, and was amazed by the number of people constantly walking. I never saw anything like that in Italy—whether in Milan or in Rome, or anywhere. It was really, truly, amazing. And I remember going to Central Park and finding enormous pretzels for sale. They were only 25 cents each.

By 1977, I was working at the Four Seasons and managing the Grill Room. I really never believed that I was going to be here for such a long period of time. I thought that maybe I was going to stay for maybe six months or a year. The owner at the time was very hard to work for and very tough on people. You never knew if on a whim, he would just say, "You're fired," just like Donald Trump would do. Imagine being an apprentice for the rest of your life?

But I managed to please a lot of people, and that's why the Grill Room became so successful. When I first began working here, everybody was going to the Pool Room for lunch. Nobody was coming to the Grill Room. Even at that time, the Pool Room was the most expensive room for lunch. We had a lot of repeat customers who were set in their own ways and basically telling me what to do. And I really didn't like it that way at all. I mean, I think it's much better for me to tell you what to eat than for you to tell me what you should eat. I began to train the customers the right way so now they are very well-trained. So we managed to change their tune. It was very difficult but they came around.

Randall's Island and Ward's Island, www.nycgovparks.org/parks/randallsislandpark

. . . .

Rachel Axler, playwright and Emmy-winning television writer

New Yorkers are obsessed with real estate. But not in a realistic way. In a fantasy, "Ooh, look at that amazing place, what would my life be like if I lived there" sort of way. As a native New Yorker, I'm sort of a Lifestyle Peeping Tom. I love unique architecture combined with huge windows, which can be peeked into from the sidewalk, sparking an imagined life story.

There are several great neighborhoods for this. Sylvan Terrace in the 160s, with its astonishing cobblestone block of painted, wooden rowhouses. Bond Street in SoHo—another cobblestone block, with lofty art-filled apartments seen through windows with curved, stone ledges. Washington Mews, a gated alley (okay, maybe I just have a thing for cobbled stones) by NYU, where an almost fairytale amount of brambles seems to seal some of the entrances shut, but glimpses of books and statues in the windows reveal signs of life. The decrepit skeletons of mansions at Admirals' Row in the Brooklyn Navy Yard, where you don't just see through the windows, but through the crumbling brick walls, to a lifestyle long past.

But my most recent favorite real estate obsession is Verandah Place in Cobble Hill, Brooklyn, where a short, squat row of old carriage houses sits along a slender alley, next to Cobble Hill Park, a tiny, perfect little idyll that feels straight out of London. In good weather, you can get a coffee at Ted & Honey on the corner, take it into the park, maybe bring some travel Scrabble, if you have a Scrabble partner handy, and sit among the dogs, strollers, dogs in strollers, and lovely greenery, facing an old row where horses used to be kept, where people now lead lives. Watch the real estate. Drink your coffee. Make up your own story.

Ted & Honey, 264 Clinton Street; (718) 852-2212; www.tedandhoney.com

Cobble Hill Park, Clinton Street between Verandah Place and Congress Street; www.nycgovparks.org/parks/B32

....

Norbert Leo Butz, Tony Award–winning actor

I want New York to look like it does in Woody Allen movies. And when I go to the West Village and areas like Brooklyn Heights, the locales have that really romantic, cinematic feel. You feel like you're in a Woody Allen movie. It's that architecture. Those brownstones in the West Village. And you find cobblestone streets and hidden bookstores. Also, there's nothing more beautiful than the West Village in the springtime around mid-May.

If I have an afternoon to kill, I go straight downtown to the West Village, around Bank Street, Jane Street. I get a latte and find a bench in one of those little corner parks and just look at the people going by. I bring a camera and take lots of photos of the buildings, I bring a book. I can waste an entire day. It's so romantic. So romantic.

....

Bill Irwin, Tony Award–winning actor

I don't think I could be in Hollywood for a number of reasons. But it's my best hope to make a living here. I have a son in college. And my hope is still to be up for a gig here on stage in New York, because there's nothing ever like it.

My favorite thing is to walk through the theater district. I love 45th and 46th Streets. You walk around, you see—oh a friend of mine is working, oh good. Oh, those guys are working. And you remember, I did something there. I had a nice paycheck there. It's where a lot of us have lived a lot of our lives. And I remember when my son was this big and I was twenty.

The Richard Rodgers Theatre is very special to me. It used to be the 46th Street Theatre, if anybody goes back that far. The Richard Rodgers is where we first did a show called *Fool Moon*. It was two clowns and a five-piece band, and it was a great time of life. We were young enough to fall out of balconies and do all kinds of things.

45th and 46th Streets, between Broadway and 8th Avenue

....

John Oliver, Emmy-winning *Daily Show* correspondent, actor, writer, and comedian

I love walking over the Brooklyn Bridge. It's my favorite thing to do. The structure itself is incredible. The story behind it is amazing. Emily Warren Roebling sort of finished it in the 1880s after her husband [Washington Roebling, the bridge's chief engineer] died. Everything about it is sensational. It's quintessentially American. There was absolutely no need to build a bridge that big, that wide. There was no need whatsoever, but they did it anyway.

Brooklyn Bridge, City Hall Park, Park Row and Center Street

....

Steven Kroll, famed children's book author*

I grew up in New York City, on the Upper West Side of Manhattan. The apartment building I lived in was on the corner of West End Avenue and 73rd Street, one block from the Hudson River. My parents were very stylish. My father, a diamond merchant, had a mustache and wore suits with vests and a watch chain. My mother wore fashionable dresses and big hats. She was a great storyteller, which is probably where my love of telling stories began.

But I also had my Upper West Side neighborhood, a wonderful ethnic stew of Jewish, Latino, Chinese, and Viennese. Wandering those streets, experiencing the restaurants and the pastry shops, delicatessens and the movie theater, the corner drug store and the corner book shop, I began to recognize a wider world, a world outside my own that would make me want to tell stories, travel, and be a writer.

* Sadly, Steven Kroll passed away before publication of this book.

Many of my books have come out of that neighborhood. The kids in my building all played downstairs together, under the watchful eye of Gordon, the doorman. The sharing we did can be found in the *Biggest Pumpkin Ever* and its sequels, the bullying, followed by sharing, in *Jungle Bullies*.

And there was Riverside Park, just a block away, where I played stickball near the railroad yards and cowboys and Indians on the green lawns, and where I watched an endless parade of dogs that morphed into an endless parade of dog stories, from *Is Milton Missing?*, to *A Tale of Two Dogs* and *Pooch on the Loose*, my ode to New York at Christmastime. I may be one of the few authors to have written so many books about dogs without ever having owned one.

Riverside Park, 72nd to 158th Streets along the Hudson River; www.nycgovparks.org/sub_your_park/vt_riverside_park/vt_riverside_park.html

....

Sarah Rose, author and journalist

A few years ago I had a bad break-up—a terrible, devastating, miserable, awful, horrible, ruin your life break-up—the kind you believe you will never recover from. After spending four or five nights a week with my beloved, I suddenly had way too much time on my hands. I was alone and suddenly evenings at home took All. Night. Long.

One autumn afternoon, crossing the park on the M66 bus, I was knitting and the bus driver asked me if I would knit him a hat. I had met the chattiest man in New York, Jimmy Higgins. Could I knit him a hat? He was bald as a cue ball and winter was coming, he was going to be cold. There was an English couple on the bus who asked directions to the Met Museum, they were here visiting their son in NYC, a banker. "I hear there's a lot of money in that," Jimmy said. "Can he get free samples?"

When we came to my stop, I decided not to get off. The bard of the bus was more fun than another night on my sofa wondering if anyone would ever love me. So I circled back from the Upper East Side back toward Lincoln Center again and New York was less lonely. For the next few months, I would seek out Jimmy's bus schedule and just ride in circles.

There was a rotating cast of characters whose stories he knew: the elderly couple who came to New York as professional flamenco dancers in the 50s; the woman who went to the opera at Lincoln Center five nights a week, who kept the stack of recent ticket stubs in her purse to prove it; Lauren and Orrin, the newlywed doctors. As Lincoln Center would let out for the night, he would ask the women in fur coats if they had sons my age—and I even got a few dates out of it.

Riding across the park with a chatty driver is still my favorite thing to do in New York. Alas, Jimmy is on the M79 now, so it's more of a schlep for me to see him. I owe him a hat. Thanks to Jimmy, the cross town remains one of my great joys.

....

David Carr, business columnist and culture writer for the *New York Times*

I think New York is fundamentally a meritocracy. I came here ten years ago with very little in the way of personal connections. By dint of both industriousness and very good luck, along with the kindness of others, I've done very well professionally and personally. I subscribe to the EB White Maxim. I'm paraphrasing here—it's a primary willingness to find a place to stand and a willingness to get lucky. I feel like I've gotten very lucky here.

New York is an island that extracts a toll from all humans who live there. If you want a place to stand you've got to be willing to fight for it, but there are rewards and promises over and over again for people who are willing to fight and find a spot to stand in.

New York does not give up its charms easily. It does not. There might be days where it unfurls and reveals itself in all its glory. And other days, the borough just might kick you from one end of it to the other. All you're trying to do is cross to Midtown and it's physically impossible. So, like most people; I have a very complicated relationship with the city.

I live in Montclair, New Jersey. Every night I'm on the helix, which offers the opposite view. The other side of Manhattan is no less impressive. Every night when I'm leaving, I look over at the city and I either blow it a kiss or I flip it the bird. Or most often, I flip it the bird, but with a kiss. A kind of a bird/kiss. What it is, is you screwed me, but I love you anyway.

Just before sunset, I would go to 59th Street and 2nd Avenue, and I would bring a friend. The friend might be my lovely wife Jill. If it's someone else, it could be whatever romantic interest they have. I would use my metro card to get onto the Roosevelt Island Tram. And I would go out to Roosevelt Island and walk around for ten or fifteen minutes and look at Midtown.

I'm from the Midwest so I'm still riveted by the sight of tall buildings, especially across the river. I find that view of Midtown to be compelling. The best part would be just right after sunset when the lights of Midtown are starting to twinkle, I would get back on the tram.

From the tram, you're several hundred feet above Midtown. The cars on the tram are at each end and meet at the midpoint. They just kiss briefly above the East River and then continue on their way, one to Roosevelt Island, and one to Manhattan. I've always found that to be a very compelling moment. The other reason I like the tram is, I'm a skier. I love to ski and it reminds me of all the great tram rides I've taken to the tops of mountains everywhere.

When you come toward the city, that view of it, you can't argue that New York isn't one of the greatest cities in the world, if not the greatest city in the world. Its muscles and charms are on full display. It's twinkling and bright. All of the sort of quotidian aspects of street life—which is the fight for a taxi or to get on the subway or to get in your cube, you can't really see that part. All you can see is the gloriousness of New York. You're literally floating through the air looking at it. It never ever fails to amaze and make me happy.

The Roosevelt Island Tramway, 59th Street and 2nd Avenue; (212) 832-4543, Ext. 1; www.rioc.com/transportation.htm

....

Susie Essman, actress, comedian, and author

My favorite thing to do in New York is people watch. It's uniquely New York. I mean you can do it anywhere, but you don't get the visual feast that you get here. You don't get the variety anywhere else. If I'm taking a cab, I always make sure to give myself extra time and I get out early, not exactly at my location. So I can walk a few blocks and observe wherever I am.

And I love to listen. Listening is more musical than actually eavesdropping on conversations. If you're eavesdropping on conversations, they're usually boring. But because there are so many languages and so many ethnicities, I like to listen to the rhythm and music of how people talk—even hearing foreign accents.

The great thing about Manhattan is that we're all living, working and functioning in really close proximity. And we all seem to know how to navigate each others' boundaries. I find that so fascinating. New York City is the great experiment of modern living that's really, for the most part, worked.

You can usually tell tourists because they don't have the sense of navigating the space. They'll get into your space but New Yorkers, even if you've lived here just a couple of weeks, get the space navigation. We're all just moving around, doing our thing. We live on this little tiny island together from every possible background, ethnicity, and walk of life.

I like Riverside Park better than Central Park, even though I love Central Park. Riverside Park is less transient than Central Park. Everybody goes to Central Park and it's so beautiful. Tourists go there. Whereas I like the less touristy spots. I like to watch people living in their environment, in their neighborhood.

When I have to go to midtown, I find it incredibly relaxing to take the 104 bus. I just perch myself in the seat by the window. I watch people in the streets who have no idea they are being observed. I like to watch the way people walk. You can do that because you're going slow. Everybody has a different walk—they way they hold their body, gesture with their hands or nod. And I love to walk across 125th Street. It's so alive with so much street life going on. There's all the African merchants selling incense and hair braiding. It seems like a whole vibrant universe.

The thing is, I love the museums, shopping, and theater. And I've done all that in other cities. But New York is the only place that offers the diversity for people watching and listening. Each new group that comes along changes the face of the city and I love that.

My mother grew up on 57th Street, and anytime we're driving around the city, she'll have nostalgic longing and say, this is so different than what I remember. And I'll say to her "Ma what makes this city great is that it's constantly changing. It's always having an influx of new energy and new immigrants." But I imagine that when she was growing up, people her age now were probably saying the same thing about the city. But what really makes it great is that it's not all the same.

. . . .

Elizabeth Swados, Tony Award–nominated director, composer, author and musician

When I was 15 and becoming a folk singer, I wanted to be Joan Baez. I thought New York was so snobby. I was going to travel across the country like Woody Guthrie and tour and play in underground coffee shops. I thought that the theater was the most ridiculous art form there was. All these people talking. What does that that have to do with life?

But then my teacher at Bennington College introduced me to La Mama [the renowned experimental theater company in New York City] and I learned about other forms of theater and music. There were puppets. It was nothing like I thought theater was. It was in the Lower East Side. And I fell in love with New York and gave up the idea of becoming a folk singer.

Now I work in the Off Broadway theater scene. I love the singers and students that I work with. New York is a home for me and it's not just because the business I do is here. I know the streets so well.

When I have free time, whenever I can get away from the piano, my notebooks and rehearsal, I take my Labradoodle Clementine and walk her from Mercer Street to the river along the West Side Highway. We walk south to Battery Park and see the bike riders, rollerbladers, all the parks and freighters. I love tugboats. They're goofy and not pretty, but sturdy. I'm always looking for them.

I like going in the early morning when it's less crowded and the city feels more like it's mine. I treasure every step and breath of air. And I dream and I watch my dog who I love who has panda bear feet. And we meet other dogs and say hello. Sometimes, by chance, words come into my head or I have tunes in my head and I can go home and write.

....

Andy Cohen, Emmy-winning host and producer of *Watch What Happens: Live* and executive vice president of original programming and development at Bravo

I live in the West Village. I'm all about roaming around the West Village. On a Saturday or Sunday, when I have nothing really going on, I love hitting the streets and walking around. I just go where the wind blows me. I love the energy, the vibe, the excitement, the people. And I love that nobody here gets any sleep and that's OK.

....

Jane Rosenthal, producer and co-founder of the Tribeca Film Festival

I work in Tribeca, and it's where I begin most days. In the morning, it has beautiful light, cascading off the buildings downtown. With rivers on both sides you're reminded that New York City is really Manhattan Island when you're here, surrounded—by water, by people, by the city.

I would jump on the Hudson River Ferry, taking the chance to see Manhattan from a different vantage point, reflected from the water. Then, I'd walk to the High Line, starting on Gansevoort Street all the way up to West 30th. It's quintessential New York, you can hear dozens of languages mixing, creating the kind of cacophony of sound the city is known for.

From different vantage points you can see the entire skyline, the Chrysler Building, the Empire State Building, the Statue of Liberty, and even New Jersey! Old and new in a symbiotic relationship, complementing and celebrating each other.

From there I'd head to the Sonnabend Gallery, admire the Clifford Ross film and photography exhibition, and enjoy the art only New York can curate.

As the sun sets I'd find my way home to the Upper West Side, with its baby strollers and every type of dog imaginable. I would stop for a glass of wine at Lincoln, watching the pre-theater crowd rush to catch curtain at Lincoln Center.

I'd take a hansom carriage from the Lincoln to my home on Central Park West and look at the splendor of the park and relish in the fact that as much as things change, so much in this city has remained the same since 1870.

Hudson River Ferries, (800) 533-3779; www.nywaterway.com

The Sonnabend Gallery, 536 West 22nd Street; (212) 627-1018; www.sonnabendgallery.com

Lincoln, 142 West 65th Street; (212) 359-6500; www.lincolnristorante.com

STORES, STREET FAIRS, BOUTIQUES & BARGAINS

 I love the variety of shopping in New York. You can spend a lot of money. You can spend no money. You can find really amazing things in unexpected places. There are 1,001 shops just in my Brooklyn neighborhood alone.

—Zoe Kazan, actress and playwright

It is said that ingenuity is ingrained in Chinatown's cultural fabric. It's a very resilient place. Even during its beginnings, in the late 1800s, people living in small quarters developed unique carpentry skills to build innovative and imaginative furniture to accommodate the tiny spaces and make them habitable. The Chinese living there found ways to adapt. And in turn they served an important niche. They created family-owned hand laundry shops that had low start-up and low overhead costs. And they served the whole upper echelon of New York bachelors who needed laundry done. They developed unique custom tailoring and carpentry skills.

And that spirit of creativity and entrepreneurship in Chinatown has endured to this day. The mantra has been, tell us what you want and we'll make or repair it for you. "My family has lived in Chinatown since 1890, and there's always been that kind of service offered here," says Jan Lee, who owns Sinotique, an antiques and furniture design shop on Mott Street that sells Chinese antiques from ancient pottery to antique rugs to ancestral shrines. "It's about finding a niche in the market."

De Vera

So should you need a wedding dress tailor made, an unrepairable watch repaired, a personally designed herb concoction to treat your ailments, or commission furnishings made from Chinese teak and fruit woods—Chinatown can offer that and more. Imagine all these services within a matter of blocks.

In addition to Chinatown, the city is chock-full of shopping ingenuity. Look at these treasures.

....

Nora Ephron, Academy Award–nominated director, screenwriter, journalist, and novelist

One of the things I love doing in New York is going to the flower district. It's on 28th Street between 6th and 7th Avenue, a street of shops that are mostly frequented by florists. For years I thought they were wholesale only, and never went near the block. But then I started visiting, very early in the morning—I'm talking 6 a.m. The stores are full of whatever is in season. This week it's hydrangeas, thousands of them—and of course every other kind of flower. There are roses in colors you didn't know existed—blue roses, red-and-white-striped roses, and at least seventeen different kinds of roses that are some version of orange—and they're all stacked in the most exquisitely beautiful piles. I go to buy, because you can get three dozen great roses for less than $30, but I would also go just to look. And if I were a tourist, I'd go just to take pictures. If you want to buy, they prefer cash. Almost all the stores are closed by noon.

....

Alain Ducasse, Michelin-starred chef, author, and global restaurateur

I always love to visit my favorite culinary bookstore, Kitchen Arts & Letters. They have a wealth of cookbooks from all over the world, including very old cookbooks. The first time I went there they told me that they had all my books. And I was so happy, I didn't believe it! I've visited many specialty culinary bookstores, even ones in France, and they don't carry all my books. But Kitchen Arts has every one of them. I also love visiting the Vinegar Factory, one of the best food markets in New York. It has one of the finest selections of food, and they have great dried bread.

Kitchen Arts & Letters, 1435 Lexington Avenue; (212) 876-5550; www.kitchenartsandletters.com

Eli's Vinegar Factory, 431 East 91st Street; (212) 987-0885; www.elizabar.com/Elis-Vinegar-Factory-C24.aspx

....

Joel Derfner, author and composer

The Strand is absolutely hands-down, the best place to hang out in New York. I mean, come on. It's a used bookstore with eighteen miles of books. What more could you want? I've found books there I couldn't find online; I've found books there I didn't even know existed. I found one of my own books there once and wrote a little note in it to whoever bought it: "To whoever buys this book from the Strand: I hope you like it very much. Love, Joel Derfner." And later on, the guy who bought it sent me an email saying he liked the note. I guess I feel like the Strand is a place where time stops. And in New York sometimes you desperately need that.

....

Fran Lebowitz, author

I love second hand bookstores. You can go in and browse around and buy stuff or not. Although, I'm pretty bad at not. If I'm uptown, I would go to Argosy, and if I'm downtown, I would go to the Strand. These stores didn't used to be so unusual here, there used to be billions of second hand bookstores around.

Actually, one of my big questions is how does Argosy afford that place? They must own the building. Because commercial real estate in that neighborhood is expensive. If you own a building on East 59th Street, you usually have to sell something a little more popular than books. Plus they have that delightful little outside space with shelves and an open table.

Once I had about 15 minutes before I had to go to the dentist, and I was browsing around outside and I saw a play that until the night before, I had never heard of. I had been at dinner with friends, and this guy was talking about a play called *If Men Played Cards As Women Do,* and there it was, by George S. Kaufman from 1923. So, I bought it because it was a dollar and I sent it to my friend. That was an unusual find. Though, obviously, anything I buy I consider a find. Otherwise, I wouldn't buy it.

The Argosy also has a basement where they have stuff even below quite reasonable. The Argosy and the Strand both have rare book rooms. They both have places there that are pretty expensive. Those spots, I go to deliberately. I go to the Strand Rare Book room, but it's upstairs, next door to the main Strand. I mean, I have to have more than 15 minutes. But if I have extra time, the browsing around is more in the dollar department in both stores.

I really don't know how long the stores have been there. The Strand has been here so long, I think the Dutch built around it. If the Argosy was there when I was younger I would have thought, oh, I can't afford anything there. But I still would have gone in. I mean a bookstore, to me, is a place to buy books if you can, and if not, just to be with them. Just to look at them. They're better than friends. They don't talk back.

Argosy Book Store, 116 East 59th Street; (212) 753-4455; www.argosybooks.com

Strand Book Store, 828 Broadway; (212) 473-1452; www.strandbooks.com

. . . .

Ted Allen, star of the Food Network's *Chopped*

Nearly every weekend, I head to Williamsburg, Brooklyn, and pay a visit to my friends at the Meat Hook. It's a wonderful kitchen supply place and butcher shop. They have a terrific new location with airy, beautiful classrooms for their classes. They teach you how to break down a pig. They make their own vinegar—all different kinds. I also make my own vinegar and I geek out with them on that. They boil their own sausages. They sell stocks and spaghetti sauces. And they have a wonderful selection of cooking gear ranging from new to vintage stuff.

What's really significant to me is that it's an exciting example of what's going on in the Brooklyn culinary renaissance among young foodies. Most of the butchers over there are in their twenties. They're tattooed from head to toe. They're cool and passionate and knowledgeable and they're so into what they're doing.

For decades we've been talking about the butcher and how we're buying our meat shrink-wrapped and raised on nasty seed lots out in Colorado. These guys are buying local sustainable products, cutting it themselves—cutting it into old-school cuts that you can't buy in other places—and it's so much fun. We go almost every weekend and we hang out and talk food and get ideas of what we're going to cook that weekend. They sell rabbit, goat, and anything you can imagine.

It's something that I'm so excited about in New York now. It's almost turned into a community center for the Brooklyn artisanal food folks. These people are making everything from ricotta to liquors to pickles—I could go on and on.

The place is on a bleak industrial street and very close to the metropolitan line on the subway. They have some refrigerator cases where they sell local organic produce when they get it. I bought these crazy bright red carrots a couple of weeks ago. And I was super impressed to discover they sold fresh yuzu lemons; I had never seen one in person. I've only had the juice in restaurants. It's a Japanese citrus fruit that is kind of like a cross between a lemon, an orange, and a lime. And chefs really love it. I don't know where they got their hands on it.

The Meat Hook is headquarters for the young passionate artisanal food geek. I know the guy who makes sausages for me. His name is Brent Young. I don't have to wonder how many thousands of cows were ground up with *E. coli* and swept up off the slaughterhouse floor in my food. I know who is doing it. I walk up to the butcher's counter and Brent says, "Dude, you gotta see this cut of pig I just got." Brent is really into it.

The Meat Hook, 100 Frost Street; (718) 349-5033; www.the-meathook.com

....

Robin Williams, Oscar-, Emmy-, and Golden Globe–winning actor

I like riding my bike everywhere and I'll go to this great comic book store called Forbidden Planet. It's a wonderful giant comic book store and the people who are in it are fantastic. But I just love walking and being in New York. I love that I can blend in here and no one notices me—especially when I have a beard. One time someone looked at me and said, "Who's the crazy homeless guy?"

Forbidden Planet, 840 Broadway; (212) 473-1576; www.fpnyc.com

Vivienne Tam, designer

When I grew up in Hong Kong, everybody looked to the West for inspiration. While Western culture is good, being Chinese, I wanted to use the Chinese culture as inspiration for my work. Now things are different and better. But that time, I couldn't do that there. I wasn't able to make it happen. I wanted the freedom to do something that I love. So I came to New York and I felt such excitement and freedom in New York.

It seems that people here are so open to accept anything good and special. If you have talent, you can make it here. So when I first came to New York, I thought, I can be who I am. It's so great. I can do my thing. My first collection was on the cover of *Women's Wear Daily*. I was so thrilled. I didn't think that would happen.

Ever since I arrived here, I've been going to the flea market on 25th Street. It's called the Antiques Garage. I love secondhand and antique clothes, jewelry, fabrics, and furniture. I found so many treasures there—shoes, bags, embroideries, and beautiful laces. The pieces give me such inspiration. The Victorian lace there inspired my spring collection. I wanted that look. You can see clothing from the Victorian era or from '50s, '60s, or '70s. In fact, the dragon table in my store is from the flea market. You can discover something really cool.

Christian Siriano, fashion designer, youngest *Project Runway* winner, and author

I produce all my collections in New York. I think people are fashion forward here. And you can kind of do anything in New York, which is fun.

My boyfriend and I like antiquing and looking for furniture. I love furniture. So I buy a lot of knick-knacks and antique chairs. That is my little weekend thing to do. There's a great salvage place that is really cool. It's huge and literally, you can get old beams from a church. They have pieces from old buildings and door handles, knobs, mirrors. All the crap that you don't need but is interesting and really has character, which I love. We bought a really cool gold antique gilded little chair. And I've bought some little odds and ends there. It's inspiring just to go look and see it.

William Ivey Long, Tony Award–winning costume designer

My favorite thing to do in New York City is to visit the weekend flea market on 25th Street and 6th Avenue. Every Saturday, I have a whole valuable ritual. I begin upstairs in the garage section on the right, east side at the 18th-century prints and old books. Then I march all the way around, continue counterclockwise, and head downstairs. I describe my perambulation as one that I learned at the Guggenheim. You go to the top, then go around and down. It is really part of my life now.

These flea markets are an important part of each of my productions. They're endangered because they are within high-rise buildings. But it really is something that I count on for my design process. I try to go about 8:30 on Saturday mornings, rain or shine. When I designed *Cabaret* several years ago, I found so much vintage clothing at the flea market. I adapted the underwear that I found there because it was too delicate to really wear. I used it as inspiration for Natasha Richardson's character. The suspenders on Alan Cumming were all from that garage. I found a three-piece suit for Dennis O'Hare, who played Ernst. It was a 1920s-or early-30s-style three-piece suit and fit him perfectly—the length of the cuffs, everything. That was miraculous. Subsequently, when I did *The Music Man* (circa 1912), I found jewelry, brooches, hat pins, and gloves there too.

I also find lots of joke presents to give to people—like funny little flower vases in a head or a hand shape. Or I've picked up body-building sketches for friends who hate going to the gym. Really wrong stuff. My biggest find ever—ever, ever, *ever*, circle in red: a loose-leaf binder filled with fabric samples from the 18th century. The prices can be high, but I'm just happy to find something I want. They understand me. I'm the perfect shopper. I'm not a haggler. So they see me coming and say, "OK, sucker!"

My flea market "Holy Grail" is I hope to one day find the famous brooch worn by Little Edie Beale in the film of *Grey Gardens*. I searched for it when I designed the Broadway production a few years ago, and ended up having it copied for the stage. I keep a photograph of her wearing the brooch by my bed. I would recognize that piece of jewelry even if it were broken in pieces. For me, it is not unlike bits of the Statue of Liberty rising up from the sand in the film *Planet of the Apes*.

Stay tuned . . .

Antiques Garage, 112 West 25th Street; (212) 243-5343; www.hellskitchenfleamarket.com

....

Simon Doonan, author, wit, and creative ambassador-at-large, Barneys New York

If I ever found myself with an hour to kill in New York City, I would head to one of the Japanese bookstores in Midtown and browse, browse, browse. My favorite, Kinokuniya Bookstore, is right opposite Bryant Park on 6th Avenue. I have killed many hours there while waiting for fashion shows to start in the tents. What makes these stores so compelling? Firstly and most important, there are the mounds and ramparts of popular magazines. These give an incredible window into the madness and fabulous perversity that is the popular culture of Japan where the latest aberrant style trends and obsessions—fashion, hobbies, cars, sports, maquillage—are relentlessly documented.

For those with less esoteric tastes, there are stacks of exquisite art and photography books. My personal favorites are the translations of Japanese murder mysteries. In this bookstore I found a strange and horrible book called *Out* by Natsuo Kirino. It follows the lives of four troubled ladies who work the night shift in a lunchbox factory. The action explodes after one of these gals decides to strangle her grumpy husband with his belt. Bon appetit!

After an hour of immersion in this hothouse of Japabilia, you step back onto the NYC street and see everything with refreshed objectivity. Japan might be strange and beautiful, but so is the Big Apple.

Kinokuniya Bookstore, 1073 6th Avenue; (212) 869-1700; www.kinokuniya.com

....

Mary Alice Stephenson, celebrity stylist, television host, and fashion commentator

I love to shop at New York Vintage. It's the best vintage shop in the world. Many major stars shop there. Jennifer Lopez, Scarlett Johansson, Sarah Jessica Parker, and Chloe Sevigny wear New York Vintage. Michelle Obama got the dress she wore last Christmas at New York Vintage. It's a jewel of a place. And it's very unknown except for all the fashion insiders. My great finds there were vintage Balenciaga and vintage Givenchy. I dress a lot of girls in their clothes. Amazing! Amazing!

New York Vintage, 117 West 25th Street; (212) 647-1107; www.newyorkvintage.com

....

Mireille Guiliano, best-selling author of *French Women Don't Get Fat* and other books

When I first came to New York from France, it was really hard to get used to the food. I'm spoiled. I grew up with big gardens and fresh food. But about 16 years ago, the Union Square Greenmarket began. It reminds me of my grandmother's farm in France. During summers, I would visit all my cousins and eat peaches cut from trees just 10 minutes before.

I go to the market every Saturday when it opens at 8 a.m. And I head to my baker, Rock Hill Bake House, which sells 15 kinds of bread. The guy right next to him is the chicken farmer, Knoll Farms. He has the freshest eggs and the best chickens. Cherry Lane Farms has great raspberries, strawberries, and blueberries. PE & DD Seafood sells excellent fish like skate, tuna, cod, mussels, and scallops—caught the day before. I also love stopping by James Durr Flowers to get exquisite and cheap cornflowers, iris, and peonies. If I didn't work, I would go to the market three times a week. It's such a treat.

Union Square Greenmarket, north and west sides of Union Square; www.grownyc.org

....

Peter Pennoyer, architect, historian, and principal of Peter Pennoyer Architects

Having grown up in New York, I love things that remind me of the city in its dustier days. It's so shiny and condo filled—not in a negative way—but sometimes it's good to dip into the past. So I like to visit a store called the Old Print Shop, an art reference and art bookstore. There's a frame section on the ground floor. Upstairs is a wonderful gallery with prints and other art. It has been there forever.

What interests me there are mostly prints, etchings, and mezzotints. Many of them are by artists who documented New York in its earlier days and were some of the greatest artists who I associate with New York. At the gallery, you can see incredibly beautiful views of New York—including etchings by Edward Hopper and Gerald Geerlings. These artists were enchanted with New York as it was developing, They saw the skyscrapers. The skyscrapers look like castles, so it's very romantic.

When my grandma died decades ago, she left me an etching of a harbor by an artist named Joseph Pennell. I found that he was represented at this gallery. They were selling Pennell and also had these amazing prints and wonderful photographs by Bernice Abbott. The Old Print Shop actually represented these artists when they were alive and they still have their work. They also carry contemporary prints. It seems that all the stories that I care about in New York and the history of New York are sort of all represented in those wonderful etchings and maps. It's a different way of looking at New York than through literature. It is literally like being in your own little private museum up there in the second-floor gallery. So to me, that is the real New York at its best. Every time I go, I learn something and it's a charming place.

Also, so many galleries are set for intimidation. But you can go to the Old Print Shop and get some wonderful prints for literally $200. What can you buy in this world that's unique and beautiful for $200? Or you can get an exceptional Audubon plate for $50,000. It's not intimidating, which I think is a good thing.

I think I do more framing than buying at the Old Print Shop. But I find the place very compelling because it's so peaceful. In fact, because it's off the beaten track, you don't get people hustling and bustling through. It's a very cozy place. When you go, you're in this special world and there's the continuity of it. You can find a print that shows the Woolworth building when it was new and had a romantic, old New York aspect to it.

There's one particularly amazing building near the Old Print Shop, which is certainly worth looking at, which is just a block away on 30th and Lexington, called the Women's School of Applied Design. It's a huge temple-like building with a reproduction of the complete frieze of the Parthenon wrapped around the base. It was funded by women to create a place for women to study art at the turn of the

20th century when women weren't admitted to art schools. It's a fascinating bit of New York history and the most bizarre-looking building.

My advice to New Yorkers and visitors is look up. Just make sure you're standing on the curb. Don't look up when you're in the street. But look up and you'll be rewarded.

The Old Print Shop, 150 Lexington Avenue; (212) 683-3050; www.oldprintshop.com

....

Daniel Boulud, chef-owner of New York's DANIEL, Café Boulud, db Bistro Moderne, Bar Boulud, DBGB Kitchen and Bar, Boulud Sud, and Epicerie Boulud

I enjoy returning to places that I like and know. Every spring I go to Arthur Avenue in the Bronx and get baby goat and baby lamb at Biancardi Meats. The baby lamb and goats are lined up by the dozens. In many ways that area is the Little Italy, which we don't really have in Manhattan anymore. Biancardi is still a family-run business and a time capsule that hasn't changed much in the past fifty years.

I discovered Biancardi about fifteen years ago when one of my customers told me that his favorite baby lamb was from there. He took me to the store and I saw the salami hanging on the ceiling and I loved the smoky smell. It's very old European.

When I first visited, I thought, oh God, how could I have missed this. But I don't think it's on the radar of many people living in Manhattan. And even less so on the Upper East Side. It's charming, charming, charming. And it's wonderful to get lost in the neighborhood. The stores are wonderful and Fordham University is nearby, so there's a lot of activity.

I really like to support neighborhoods. I find it exciting to go to the Essex Street Market on Essex Street. I feel like a total foreigner when I visit. It's a very old neighborhoody market. I love that it still exists. Our director of operations discovered Saxelby Cheese at the Essex Street Market, which is a tiny cheese purveyor. He asked me to check it out.

I really fell in love with Saxelby and the market itself. They have a lot of tiny purveyors. Is everything at the market fantastic? No. But a few of them were very interesting. We are now going to work with Saxelby in our store, Epicerie Boulud, on the West Side. They will take care of the cheese program. Anne Saxelby, the proprietor, mostly uses farmers from five states in the northeast. The bulk of her study and the cheese they manage mostly comes from Vermont, Connecticut, New York, Pennsylvania, and New Jersey.

If Anne Saxelby carries a cheese, that means that she knows the cheese maker, she's been to the farm, it's very integral and personal for her. And with the 20 or so different farms who work with her, she has a fabulous array of cheeses. I've discovered a lot of different cheeses through her. She's not trying to give you everything, she's trying to give you what she thinks is unique and special and worth trying.

And if I have a free hour, I love to stop by Di Fara Pizza in Brooklyn. I go mostly because I like observing the old man who makes the pizzas. I'm convinced what makes a good pizza is love. He makes each pie one by one. People line up out the door to get in. His sons only do the dough. It's the old-fashioned Brooklyn pizza—thick, bready dough, good tomato sauce. He stands over each pizza to cut fresh basil over it and grate the cheese. He adds more cheese after it's cooked and lets it melt over the hot pizza, rather than cook the cheese too much.

The first time I came to New York, I had been living in Washington DC. I came to visit David Bouley, who is now famous, but at the time was the pastry chef at La Cote Basque. He cooked a wonderful welcome brunch for me in his home on 55th Street—a *pot au feu.* It was my first meal in New York. And I felt so welcome and we walked down Park Avenue, through all of the Upper East and West Side of New York. And I was in love at first sight. And I'm still not jaded.

Biancardi Meats, 2350 Arthur Avenue, Bronx; (718) 733-4058

Saxelby Cheesemongers, Essex Street Market, 120 Essex Street (at Delancey Street); (212) 228-8204; www.saxelby cheese.com, www.essexstreetmarket.com

Di Fara Pizza, 1424 Avenue J, Brooklyn; (718) 258-1367; www.difara.com

....

Carson Kressley, actor, author, television host, fashion designer, and stylist

I love that New York is home and I've lived here for 18 years. When I'm on a plane, I can't wait to get back. There's a feeling of Christmas morning and you can't get in the midtown tunnel fast enough. And New York feels very neighborhoody to me. It's a little world where everything is perfect in a crazy world.

And if I had a free day, I'd love to lock myself inside Bergdorf Goodman. Imagine. You can window shop, browse, get an amazing lunch, have a manicure and pedicure, and get your hair done at John Barrett. That would be a day in heaven. I can't afford to do all those, but I can pick and choose. When you step into Bergdorf Goodman, it's so unusual and so different. It's like you're transported to 1965 and Babe Paley is there. And you can go to the restaurant and sit with the ladies who lunch. It's really entertaining and the food is yummy and it's not crazy expensive. That's a great way to experience Bergdorf. You don't need the $900 designer shoes. You can just buy the $14 egg salad sandwich. And they have the BG salad and it's a bunch of lettuce and some eggs and you get to chow down and stay skinny. It's a socialite dish.

Bergdorf Goodman, 754 5th Avenue; (212) 753-7300; www.bergdorfgoodman.com

. . . .

Iris Rainer Dart, best-selling author, playwright, and television writer

My favorite hour in New York was always picking up my grandson at school and then having him all to myself for a few hours. The first time I arrived there, the nursery school teacher asked, "Are you Bubbie Iris?" I felt famous. He had obviously talked about me. Jonathan was less than three the first time I picked him up. My daughter-in-law is Israeli and both she and my son spoke a lot of Hebrew to him, so his English was a little hard to understand at times.

That morning when I asked where he wanted to go after school, his reply was, "Toss the Rice." It didn't sound familiar. I thought maybe it was a Chinese restaurant that he liked. I wanted to take him wherever he wanted to go, to spoil him so that Bubbie Time would be special, so I kept probing. "Where is it?" I asked. "Near Mommy's office." My daughter-in-law worked at Morgan Stanley in the 40s. "And what do you do at Toss the Rice?" "Go on the ferris wheel."

The dawn broke. It was Toys R Us on Broadway. And that turned out to be a place we would frequent. First the ferris wheel, then the Thomas the Tank Engine train table, the trains of which have people's names, all of which I have learned and can recite, and have subsequently bought for him over the years. He's seven now, and has moved to Israel. He's coming to visit me in New York this spring, and I'm sure one of our stops will be Toss the Rice!

Toys R Us Times Square, 1514 Broadway; (646) 366-8800; www.toysrus.com

....

Patricia Field, Academy Award–nominated, Emmy-winning *Sex and the City* costume designer and a boutique owner with her own clothing label

I was born and bred in New York and I've never gotten out. It's the most diversified life experience city I've ever encountered. There are many great cities. New York isn't the only one. But it's very unique in that way. Also, people inspire me and New York is filled with all kinds of inspiring people from everywhere. You can walk down the street and hear three languages in one short block. That's New York and that's what I like. That's what I was born in and grew up in. That's my style.

I love shopping at the Pathmark downtown off the FDR Drive. It's a big huge supermarket. The neighborhood is a mix of Jewish, Chinese, and Latin, so the store caters to a lot of different ethnic groups and has a ton of variety. And I can park my car in their lot, do all my shopping, load my car, and easily take all my stuff home just like in the suburbs.

Pathmark, 227 Cherry Street; (212) 227-8988; www.pathmark.com

....

Elina Furman Landauer, author and co-founder of AListMom.com, the popular daily email for moms

I have always loved thrift shops. One of the first times I went to Housing Works, I had just moved to New York from Chicago and there was one on the Upper East Side. I had no idea what they did, what their mission was. I remember picking some costume jewelry. I thought, what a New York thing that I could just go into this random store and find something so beautiful and affordable. At the time, people knew about Housing Works, but it wasn't as well known. Now it has become more of an institution. And when I discovered that they were such a great charitable organization, I felt even better about supporting them. Housing

Works works to help end homelessness and AIDS. You're shopping but you're also helping.

At Housing Works, you feel that sense of community because there's one in almost every neighborhood. The merchandise seems to reflect the character of each locale, almost like a little microcosm of the pockets of New York. The one on the Upper East Side has very specific things there because it seems to cater to people living there. When I go to that store, I don't usually find clothing. I usually look at the costume jewelry because I feel the Upper East Side women have that area covered. When I go to the West Village, I discover great boho pieces and designers. The clothing is more bohemian, a little bit carefree and artsy. The one in SoHo has a bookstore/cafe. It's very SoHo that people would want to stop and have coffee, read, and shop a little more.

One of my best finds was a really cute green designer top, a steal for about ten dollars. It was a really airy green tank top with white appliqué that almost looked like doilies. It ties in the back and is backless. I remember grabbing it and not even trying it on. I just knew it would look cute and it did. I finally gave it to my sister because she's in the East Village and I'm not boho anymore now that I'm a mom. I love that I've passed it down to her.

I read a story about a man who found a Cartier watch at a Housing Works and had it refurbished. That inspires me. I always think that maybe I'll find that great piece. There's something very New York about thrift shopping. Like anything can happen. There's that wonderful possibility when you walk in you could find a real treasure. It's almost like the dream of bumping into a producer who wants to turn your book into a movie or getting noticed and becoming famous overnight. There's the sense of, "Oh, maybe I'll find that Cartier watch." Of course you realize that's not going to happen—especially because Housing Works has gotten very good at curating. It's become a great business. But secretly, that hope is always there.

Housing Works, Upper East Side: 202 East 77th Street; (212) 772-8461; West Village: 245 West 10th Street; (212) 352-1618

Housing Works Bookstore Cafe, 126 Crosby Street; (212) 334-3324. For additional locations visit www.housing works.org

....

Kelly Killoren Bensimon, author, model, television reality show star

The corner at Spring and Lafayette Streets is my favorite corner in America. It's filled with really interesting people—hot chefs, babies, teenagers, fashion people, skater boys. It's an eclectic, fun neighborhood. And I just love that corner. For me, it embodies what New York is—understated, cool, educated, and interesting. For example, I love the magazine store there, Lafayette Smoke Shop, which has everything from Italian *Vogue* to *Us Weekly*.

Lafayette Smoke Shop, 63 Spring Street; (212) 226-3475

....

Lola Ehrlich, esteemed milliner and owner, Lola Hats

My local magazine store is great if you want to pick up a bag of M&Ms, a pack of rolling papers, or the odd copy of *Town & Country,* but since it's always packed with people buying lottery tickets, it's not the best place for clandestine reading. That's why I love Spoonbill & Sugartown Booksellers. Frequently in the morning, on the way to my studio, I stop in Williamsburg for a cup of coffee and some serious magazine perusal.

Spoonbill & Sugartown's idiosyncratic magazine selection is endlessly appealing, as is the store itself. The ceiling is pressed tin, the concrete floor was once painted lavender, and there's lots of raw wood displaying small-press books with offbeat covers filled with poetry I don't understand. Not many customers are in the store at that hour, but the few who are there look as intriguing as the books they pick up.

What I like most, though, is the magazine rack just to the right of the entrance. There too you never know what you'll find. Just don't expect *Newsweek* or *Glamour.* This rack is devoted to esoteric periodicals in pulp paper with black-and-white photography on a wide range of subjects—from *Paper Monument: A Journal of Contemporary Art* to *Kaiserin: A Magazine for Boys with Problems. Cinemascope* focuses on film, while *Block* and *Apartamento* cover architecture and interior design. I'm not sure how to describe *May*—maybe a literary review?—and *The Baffler* definitely lives up to its name. Here, lines between zines, magazines, and books are blurred. And I find all of it irresistible. I always leave the store with something unexpected to read on the L train out to Bushwick.

Spoonbill & Sugartown Booksellers, 218 Bedford Avenue, Brooklyn; (718) 387-7322; www.spoonbillbooks.com

....

Rachel Bilson, actress

Shopping in New York is great. I love anything fashion related and supporting great designers, like Derek Lam. And the fact that Isabel Marant came to New York is not good for my wallet, but it's good for my shopping addiction. Her clothing is so great, fits so well, and is so well structured. And her prints are beautiful.

Derek Lam, 12 Crosby Street; (212) 966-1616; www.dereklam.com

Isabel Marant, 469 Broome Street; (212) 219-2284; www.isabelmarant.tm.fr

....

Derek Lam, designer

I decided for my store to be on Crosby Street because I was so in love with De Vera right across the street. It's a real privilege to be sharing Crosby Street with Federico [de Vera], who I've gotten to know and is amazing. He also has an amazing eye. I love the mix of his pieces. He designs some of the jewelry but also uses antique ones. He curates, collects, and creates jewelry in such a gorgeous setting. It's the most beautiful store in New York. It's like going into the Metropolitan Museum of Art and seeing the most exquisite, refined, interesting, intriguing items, and you get to take them home. How great is that?

De Vera, 1 Crosby Street; (212) 625-0838; www.deveraobjects.com

....

Bruce Weber, photographer and filmmaker

I usually don't have any time off in New York, but if I do, my favorite place to take a walk is up in Harlem on 125th Street near the Studio Museum in Harlem. It's a beautiful small museum, and the surrounding streets are filled with music and the joy of all kinds of people gathering together. Then I would go for a late lunch at Sylvia's—collard greens, southern fried chicken, and hot home made biscuits, mashed potatoes, and the best lemon meringue pie in town. Obviously not a good place if you're on a diet. Then I would head up to 160th Street to Jumel Terrace Books, one of my favorite bookstores. It's tucked away in a beautiful brownstone, and the owner Kurt Thometz is knowledgeable about books on African art and culture, African-American poetry, and these small paperback books of fictitious stories by drug dealers. I love taking walks with Kurt around the neighborhood as he points out the buildings where Duke Ellington and Billy Strayhorn used to live. Some of the streets still have their original cobblestones, and you get views of Manhattan that most tourists never see. If I'm still there after dark, my favorite hangout is amateur night at St. Nick's Jazz Pub. You'll hear some of the best jazz in the city, and you can just imagine the Nicholas Brothers dancing there, tapping their hearts out. If you go there, have a Manhattan for me.

The Studio Museum in Harlem, 144 West 25th Street; (212) 864-4500; www.studiomuseum.org

Sylvia's, 327 Lenox Avenue; (212) 996-0660; www.sylviasrestaurant.com

Jumel Terrace Books, 426 West 160th Street; (212) 928-9525; www.jumelterracebooks.com

St. Nick's Jazz Pub, 773 Nicholas Avenue; info@stnicksjazzpub.nett

. . . .

Tracee Chimo, actress

When I first came to the city from Saugus, Massachusetts, I immediately fell in love with the vibe of the East Village. It's the one place in the city where I don't ever feel alone. There's something about the energy of the village that brightens me completely. Makes me feel happy and light. Hopeful.

I think it's all the creativity down there. Artists of all kinds strolling the streets with paint on their hands, tattoos covering their bodies, wild hair, wild clothes, smoking, drinking coffee, playing guitar, singing on their bicycles. It's like you've walked back in time. Like when Jimi Hendrix roamed St Mark's. It even smells different there! Like sweet grapes or something.

The East Village is the only place where I don't feel like a freak or a weirdo. I feel like I am among my people. And sometimes I like to just get a cup of coffee and go sit on a stoop somewhere. And I swear, every time I'm in the East Village I end up making a friend.

East 6th, East 9th, and East 10th are my streets. Those streets sort of have the most eclectic feel. There are so many different kinds of wonderful folks around and lots of great shops and cafes. One of my favorite things to do is hang out at Ninth Street Espresso. The last time I was there, I met a dude named Drew and his French bulldog, Murray. I was just sitting outside the coffee shop when he came over to talk to me.

Drew and I share a love of motorcycles, which is how we got to talking. His right arm was in a big cast due to a recent motorcycle accident, and we started chatting about bikes and how I've been thinking of taking lessons and getting my license. He gave me lots of advice and good recommendations on where to learn how to ride, etc. I hung out with the two of them *all day long*, laughing, talking about favorite movies, reading the paper together, and running after Murray who eventually sat on my lap and licked my arms. Drew and I are now buddies.

On East 9th there's also a great clothing store called Tae. The clothes are all made and designed by Tae, so they are one of a kind, unique, and totally original. When I met the owner, Jane, we gabbed for two hours in her little shop. There's a certain realness and quirkiness to Tae. And I just love that it's the size of someone's closet. It's so small that after you try on the clothes, she takes you on the street to fix you, alters the dresses to your figure, and holds up a mirror.

My other two favorite dress shops where I've become friends with the owners are Huminska, which has amazing dresses (I won the Obie wearing a frock from Huminska) and Dusty Buttons. I bought a real 1950s dress from there that I loved and landed on *Star* magazine's "Worst Dressed of the Week" page! The dress was gorgeous!!!! They don't know what the hell they're talking about. I took the issue of *Star* to Dusty Buttons and Amanda, the owner, and I had a huge laugh. She said "All press is good press, right?!"

Ninth Street Espresso, 700 East 9th Street; (212) 358-9225; www.ninthstreetespresso.com

Tae With Jane, 411 East 9th Street; (212) 228-3799

Huminska New York, 248 Mott Street; (212) 477-3458; www.huminska.com

Dusty Buttons, 441 East 9th Street; (212) 673-4039; www.dustybuttons.com

SUPERSTAR STRUCTURES, SEXY SPACES, BEATIFIC BRIDGES & ARTY POCKETS

 My favorite thing to do in New York? There are a lot of great things to do in New York. It's cool to be in love in New York. It happened to me once and it was really fun. The history of the city, the light, the architecture, the energy, the stuff to do—it all heightens the romance.

—Keanu Reeves, actor

On May 1, 1931, at 11:30 a.m, President Herbert Hoover ceremoniously pressed a button from the White House to signify turning on the lights of a new 102-story art deco edifice called the Empire State Building. At the time it was the world's tallest structure and would remain so for decades.

The Empire State Building took just one year and 45 days to build—at a rate of 4.5 stories of framework per week. To this day, that's still a record for a skyscraper of its 1,250-foot height. When construction commenced in 1930, 3,500 laborers worked around the clock for 7 million hours. They poured 62,000 cubic yards of concrete, laid 10 million bricks, and installed 2.5 million feet of electrical wire. The price of construction was originally estimated at $60,000,000. However, due to the Great Depression, labor costs were decreased and the total price tag (including the land) came in at a mere $40,948,900.

Because of the nation's severe financial crisis, after the structure opened, only half of the 2.1 million square feet of rentable space was taken—few could afford it. In fact, the tower became affectionately labeled "the Empty State Building." It took nearly ten years for it to earn a substantial number of tenants. And during that first year, the owners made substantial profits ($2 million) from the observation deck entry fees.

Immortalized in more than 90 films, the building's most famous close-up came from King Kong's lofty climb. His 8-foot hand held screaming human ingénue Ann Darrow (played by Fay Wray). Other visitors taking in the 360-degree views have included President Bill Clinton, Nikita Kruschev, Tom Cruise, Mariah Carey, Rihanna, Ethan Hawke, Pierce Brosnan, Celine Dion, and Princess Grace. The skyscraper was also a stop for a young Queen Elizabeth II during her first New York visit in 1957.

But many famous visitors hoped to connect with the one man whose presence was instrumental to the tower. Two months after opening in 1931, Jack Brod occupied a 400-square-foot box on the 7th floor to house his company, Empire Diamond and Gold. Although he changed offices and ultimately ended up on the 76th floor, Brod remained at his famed 5th Avenue address for nearly eight decades—gaining the title of last original living tenant.

Brod could recall the early days of the unfinished lobby and workers pushing wheelbarrows. He remembered when elevators switched to automatic ones and 6,379 windows were replaced. In fact, he said he met so many celebrities over the years, he couldn't recollect if Queen Elizabeth was one of them (although he was certain that he did meet Princess Grace and Fay Wray).

In 1996, to commemorate Brod's long tenure, the building was lit in gold. The passionate diamond seller worked six days a week until he passed away in 1998. Brod explained that he would only retire when "they plant me." For a man who loved his view "in the clouds," he wouldn't have it any other way.

The Empire State Building is one of many structures to feed and nourish the city. Perhaps Frank Lloyd Wright said it best when he observed that all these buildings "are shimmering verticality, a gossamer veil, a festive scene-prop hanging there against the black sky to dazzle, entertain, amaze."

....

Kenneth Cole, designer and activist

Last night I was at the Metropolitan Museum of Art. One of the most wonderful things about New York is the extraordinary depth and presence of all these forms of popular culture. For example there's an exhibit at the Met about the short life of Alexander McQueen. It's a long and inspiring [temporary] exhibit about the short life of this extraordinary artist. And it is so uplifting. So there are all these great places here where our culture is communicated in all these wonderful and inspiring ways.

....

Peg Breen, president, The New York Landmarks Conservancy

My favorite place in the universe is the Metropolitan Museum of Art. I feel enriched just walking into the Great Hall. Whether I'm there for a special exhibition or just picking rooms at random, I feel calm, intrigued, and happy. I often go with one exhibition in mind and wind up spending hours there because I see something else that looks wonderful. I actually feel upset if I'm not caught up on the special exhibitions.

Most recently, I went to see the restoration of Filippino Lippi's *Madonna and Child*. It brought me through rooms I hadn't been to in ages. And there were the Vermeers, the Rembrandts, and the wealth of great European paintings. I wound up adding an extra hour to my visit and felt like I had just had a reunion with special friends.

After 9/11, I was agitated and down. The Metropolitan Museum of Art had a special exhibition of Middle Eastern art. And I went maybe two weeks after the attack. I stood looking at beautiful vases, lovely calligraphy, and felt at peace for the first time. It was a reminder that we are all capable of beauty.

The museum is a landmark, of course, and they did a wonderful restoration of the entire 5th Avenue facade. I hope one day the museum will have a brochure on its architectural history available for visitors.

. . . .

Judy Collins, singer, songwriter, author, and founder of Wildflower Records

My New York fix involves a couple of things. It includes, without a doubt, the Metropolitan Museum of Art. I don't have as much time as I used to because I do 120 shows a year. But I like to take an artist's date by myself and just wander around the museum for hours. I'll have lunch there and be with this great art. It's so inspiring.

I moved to New York in 1963 and the Metropolitan Museum of Art became a destination for me almost immediately. I have had a close connection with it ever since. My mother, who recently passed away, was a docent at the Denver museum for 25 years. And I've been a museum devotee all over the world. I don't own art that's very exotic but I am a great fan.

I gravitate towards the Impressionists. I have to get my fix of Van Gogh, Matisse, and Gauguin. There is a Monet that was purchased by New York City Parks Commissioner Tom Hoving in 1967. And I got to know Tom because I was singing at Wollman Rink. He is the person who was responsible for giving permission for artists to have concerts at the Wollman Rink in the late '60s. And he invited me to a great party when he celebrated having bought this Monet boating scene on the waterfront. The colors of this work are so magnificent—particularly the blue, blue water. I always have to go look at that painting when I'm there.

I did a concert at the Temple of Dendur and it looks like I'm going to do a Christmas show there. It's a dream. I had to pinch myself. I go to that vast spot a lot. I heard Bill Clinton speak there; Tom Hoving's funeral was there. It's an unbelievable place. And to think that Jackie Kennedy was involved in getting that temple over here. Otherwise, it would be underwater, damaged, drowned, and gone forever.

I long for the beautiful restaurant, which was near the Greek statues. It was of the best restaurants in the city. Now it's filled with sarcophagi—which is magnificent, but that restaurant was special. In the American wing there is a little place where you can get sandwiches and salads and look right onto Central Park. And there's another spot near the Rodin sculptures which also looks into the park. The food downstairs is excellent and has a huge amount of choice, but I love to be with the art.

After the museum, I like to go to Swifty's on the Upper East Side and have a cheese soufflé. It's the best soufflé in the English-speaking countries. Then I will have a massage and facial and get my hands and feet done at Elizabeth Arden. I've gone there since 1964. I'm one of these people who when I find something that works, I don't want to abandon it.

The Metropolitan Museum of Art, 1000 5th Avenue at 82nd Street; (212) 535-7710; www.metmuseum.org

Swifty's, 1007 Lexington Avenue; (212) 535-6000; www.swiftysny.com

Elizabeth Arden Red Door Spa, 691 5th Avenue; (212) 546-0200; www.reddoorspas.com

....

Douglas Carter Beane, Tony Award–nominated playwright and screenwriter

I love going to the Frick in the morning by myself. During the afternoons, it gets crowded. I'll pretend that I own the house. I go from room to room saying, "When's the company coming? They're going to be late!" I imagine the doorbell just rang. It's such a great museum and a wonderful, beautiful place to walk around. And in the middle there's that gorgeous fountain area. Doesn't every house in New York have a big pool like that in the middle?

....

Soledad O'Brien, anchor and special correspondent for CNN

I have always loved going to the Frick. When I was a little girl, my dad used to love taking me there. I think, wow, this was someone's house. It's amazing. There's a little pond in the middle of the house. It's so beautiful. When guests come to visit New York, I'll say, "Let's pop in for an hour." I always find it relaxing.

I have four kids and love raising them in New York. I love that their backyard museum is the Museum of Natural History and that they want to go and sit under the whale there. I love that my daughter, who is 10, knows what's on the fourth floor at the Metropolitan Museum of Art.

At school, they started taking them to museums on field trips at 8 [years old]. The thinking is, you live in New York, these are your backyard museums, so you should visit as much as you possibly can. I love that for kids. I love that.

....

Sidney Offit, novelist and author

When I first walked through the Frick it was like no experience I had ever had. It's like being invited to someone's home. The scale is so intimate. I fell in love with a Vermeer painting there called *Officer and Laughing Girl.* It's right in the hall as you enter.

This Vermeer has been in the same spot for years and is still there. It seems he's speaking and she's listening. You see the back of his head. The light is almost celestial. I always love conversation. And I projected onto that painting a feeling of conversation. When you are speaking and you're entertained, there's something beneath the surface that's a lot deeper than the relationship, than what you're discussing. It just seemed to me that that couple was connecting. The light that came in was almost a little symbolic, like falling in love. I thought of *Some Enchanted Evening.* It had all that romance to it. I identified with it. It was like a spiritual journey to come in and be lifted by that experience.

Another painting that always gets me is Rembrandt's *The Polish Rider.* I'd had some very limited experience in military school where I briefly tried the cavalry. Riding a horse had a certain romantic quality. But I thought that taking care of a horse was more than I could handle. *The Polish Rider* also seemed very different from anything I expected to see from Rembrandt. I was startled to see it was a Rembrandt. I thought Rembrandt was into the portraits, but this one also had a feeling of high romance. And it always captures me. And as you walk around the room, you take a tour of the world with the Turners. I also fell in love with George Romney's *Lady Hamilton* as "Nature." She's holding a sweet dog and it reminds me of my little dog.

When someone comes to New York, I feel that the Frick should be the one place that shouldn't be missed. Sometimes I'll see tourists walking up Madison Avenue heading towards the Whitney. And I confess, on some occasions if I've had a little bit to drink or feeling a little cocky, I'll say, "Hey, by the way, don't miss the Frick." Several years ago I saw a couple, who I believe were German, coming out of the Whitney. And I heard the man say something to the woman like "Where do we go from here?" And I said, "You'd best go to the Frick." And he said, "The where?"

And his wife had heard of it and I was showing them how to get there. I walked them down to the Frick. He said, "You Americans, you are very gracious." I said, "Well, I just think you shouldn't blow through New York and miss this one."

The Frick Collection, 1 East 70th Street; (212) 288-0700; www.frick.org

....

Anthony Malkin, president, Malkin Holdings and an owner of the Empire State Building

One thing I like to do—and it's a moment of zen for me—is to go to the observatory at the Empire State Building at night after dinner. On weekend nights, we have a saxophone player up there and you see this incredible cross-section of anonymous Manhattan if you will. You never know if the visitor is the chairman of some big company or someone over from Ireland or from the mid-West or China. And you look around and it's amazing. Everyone's there for one reason and one reason only, which is to amazed by New York City.

At night, the Empire State Building is not crowded. You can mill around. Up there, the world is silent. Everything is below you. You see planes taking off from Kennedy and LaGuardia. You see all the illuminated buildings. You see the Chrysler Building. The Met Life Building, One Bryant Park, Times Square. The Citicorp Building. You see the GE building and which part of the neon isn't working. There's always something missing in a piece of the GE sign.

You look out towards the Hudson River and sometimes you'll see ships docking or pulling out or boats going up and down the River. You can look all the way down Fifth Avenue to the Washington Square arch. You know you're in the middle of everything. You're surrounded by the excitement of the city. You just feel it. And the people who are up, they're not working. They're not stressed. They're going to the top of the Empire State Building at night to have a fun, peaceful experience—which is kind of cool.

I may be known to the manager or to the employees of the Empire State Building but nobody in the crowd knows who I am. For me to be there anonymously while people are experiencing this connection feels like a moment of weightlessness. It's a completely magical moment for me in New York. Most people who visit the Empire State Building have decided that they've come to see it long before they ever come to New York. So there's palpable excitement, palpable electricity. Everybody, particularly at night, really feel it's theirs. And to sense that it's significant to them—that my work has made it something which they can really enjoy—has real meaning to me.

I'm always reminded of what Samuel Clemens said: All his life he wanted to be a riverboat pilot and he worked and he worked and he got himself to the point where he could be a riverboat pilot. To a child, the riverboat pilot was this mysterious superhuman who stood up above in the wheel house telling everybody what to do because he knew everything that there was in the Mississippi River. He knew every snag. He knew every shoal. And the boat's commerce and safety depended on it. But when he became a riverboat pilot, all the mystery of the Mississippi was gone. He knew everything. Up on the observatory at night, I forget I'm the riverboat pilot.

I really relish those things in New York which remind me of being a teenager in my early 20s and my wife's and my early years together in New York when we were really always going for the corners. We were looking for the wonder, the excitement of New York City.

These are my moments to step away. That's the real magic of New York—when I step out of the business mode and slide back into the wonder-of-it-all-mode.

Empire State Building, 350 5th Avenue; (212) 735-3100; www.esbnyc.com

....

Rudy Tauscher, area vice president, general manager, Mandarin Oriental, New York

For many years, I've had the privilege of working around Columbus Circle, watching its transformation, contemplating it. I remember the old Coliseum building and Amish market that was here. And I've often stood at the windows of the Mandarin Oriental looking down to the statue of Christopher Columbus in the center. Not many people know that this circle represents the original point from which all distances are measured for New York City.

I'm not from New York, but I've been living in the city fifteen years now. First I worked for Mr. Trump at the Trump International Hotel. When we opened that hotel, Beverly Sills, the late famous and wonderful opera singer, said that the hotel served as the gatekeeper of Columbus Circle. Now that the Mandarin Oriental, the second hotel on the circle, has opened, it still rings true to me.

I like looking at Columbus Circle very early in the morning, between 6 and 7 a.m., when the sun comes up from the east and hits the building. The reflection is beautiful. Often, I'll go jogging through Central Park. And when you go around the reservoir, you can see the buildings from there. Everything looks clean and crisp and ready for a new day.

Sometimes in the morning, I'll have a cup of coffee outside in the center of the circle. People are hurrying to work. But if you just pay attention there's a beautiful light. Sometimes I just like watching people trying to roller skate or break dance. It's a real slice of life. All is calm amidst the busyness of life—the flow of life, the circle of it all.

In the evening when the sun goes down, the view changes almost by the hour.

When it's really foggy out, the view of the circle from above almost looks like a Jackson Pollock painting. It's a great canvas with red dots and the red dots keep moving. They are the string of bright lights from all the cars rushing by.

....

Dennis O'Hare, Tony Award–winning actor

I'm a huge museum freak. I like to go to the Chelsea Gallery Center and see things that I haven't seen before. The center is a whole district—a neighborhood from about 18th to about 27th Street, in between 10th and 11th Avenues with many art galleries. I love all those galleries around there and they're all free, which most people don't realize. I've been going for about 10 or 15 years, and you get to see cutting-edge and memorable stuff. You just walk in just like you would a museum.

For a listing of galleries and more information, visit www.nyc-arts.org/categories/17/galleries.

....

David Ippolito, beloved Central Park musician (aka "That Guitar Man from Central Park")

You may be speaking to the least religious person on this island. But one thing that I love is visiting the Cathedral of St. John the Divine. The place is a surprise for most people. If you walk up Broadway to 112th Street, on that corner is the exterior of the diner in Seinfeld. It's actually called Tom's Restaurant. I stand on the corner and go "duh, duh, duh" like the theme song. But then I walk across 112th Street and there's the largest cathedral in the world. St. Peter's in Rome is bigger, but it's a basilica. The largest cathedral in the world is the Cathedral of St. John the Divine.

I've probably walked in there a hundred times. Every single time it takes my breath away. The first thing that hits me is the enormity of it. I think, human beings, with ten fingers and ten toes made of flesh and blood, just like me, can construct something like this.

You can fit a building inside this building. It's like two football fields. It has a stained-glass rose window in the front facade that is bigger than the house I grew up in. It's mind-boggling in its beauty. It's awe inspiring just to walk into that building. And again this is coming from the least religious man you'll ever meet. The reason that it was built probably doesn't impress me, but the fact that it was built, that human beings are capable of that, does. And it's right in the middle of an island that I like to call Florence during the Renaissance.

I love walking up to the support columns and putting the palms of my hands on them and realizing the enormous pressure that is on these slabs of stone. That this thing is holding up a ceiling that is who knows many stories high. The density of it. The power of it. There's a stoic power to that building. It's not moving and yet it's got such energy and power, such strength about it.

When I have out-of-towners with me, I'll take them over to the diner that my friends and I call the perfect diner on 100th and Broadway. It's called Metro Diner, but we call it the perfect diner. We'll say, "So you want to do a diner run? Yeah, where? 6:30 at the Perfect. Okay." The french fries are thin and well done and the right crispness. They have amazing omelets, great burgers, sandwiches. And the waiters are friendly and fun except they've got the one angry waiter we all love. And there's a manager that knows everything about everything in the universe or he thinks he does. And they refill ice coffee for free. The perfect diner. It's great.

After the perfect diner, we'll walk uptown and stand at the corner of 112th and Broadway and I'll surprise them with the *Seinfeld* Diner. And then we walk 1 block east across 112th Street. And from a little silly pop culture exterior like Tom's Restaurant in *Seinfeld*, you're suddenly at a monument, the largest cathedral on the planet. You're in a completely different world. And in a way that's kind of what Manhattan is in so many ways.

The Cathedral Church of St. John the Divine, 1047 Amsterdam Avenue; (212) 316-7490; www.stjohndivine.org

Metro Diner, 2641 Broadway; (212) 866-0800

....

Mehmet C. Oz, MD (aka Dr. Oz), Daytime Emmy Award–winning host of *The Dr. Oz Show* and author

The Museum of Natural History has so many places you can visit. You can learn about fish and dinosaurs. I've got four kids, and Oliver, the youngest one, who is 12, loves to go there with me. We have a family membership so we can just head over. We love the huge room with the big whale. I love looking at aquatic creatures because they're underwater and usually invisible to us.

And since we're on the Upper West Side, we can eat at Pasha, a great Turkish restaurant that has delicious Mediterranean cuisine. I like it because I'm Turkish and the service is fabulous. Also, my wife is vegetarian so she can find great vegetarian dishes that are naturally present there. I don't love going to restaurants where they have to do something special for her.

Pasha's fresh fish is fabulous. There's something called Imam Bayildi that I love. Sometimes it's called Fainting Imam. The story is that the priests loved the dish—which is eggplant stuffed with onions, peppers, and tomatoes—so much that they fainted.

Pasha New York, 70 West 71st Street; (212) 579-8751; www.pashanewyork.com

....

Brad Anderson, director, writer, and producer

I have two kids and we always go to the Museum of Natural History. That's our gig. You let the kids go and they can run all over the place. There are these great exhibits. We've been going for years but never get tired of it. I love the hall of African mammals—seeing the leopard and cheetah. When I was a kid, my first experience in New York was going there. Those dioramas are like movie screens. It's like looking at a little three-dimensional movie. The spectacular nature of it is inspiring.

American Museum of Natural History, Central Park West at 79th Street; (212) 769-5100; www.amnh.org

....

Fisher Stevens, Academy Award–winning filmmaker, producer, director, co-founder of Naked Angels Theater Company, and actor

New York is like an addiction. It's like a drug. I leave a lot for work, but I'll always come back. You can't leave for good. The people and the energy inspire me to stay. And I like wandering into the International Center of Photography and getting lost. It's one of the most incredible places in New York. I love photography and they always have great shows.

International Center of Photography, 1113 Avenue of Americas; (212) 857-0000; www.icp.org

....

Bryan Bantry, producer and entrepreneur

I am a commercial aviation enthusiast, aka "nut." I have had this longtime obsession of recording the tail registration numbers of every aircraft I fly. And I'm in a lot of them. So when I check the list, I realize I've been in this airplane before from New York to London on the 8th of April a few years ago! Or I took this one to Hong Kong 18 months ago. Or this is the third time we've taken this plane on the same route to Rome.

As a child, I remembered flying often on TWA. Walking through that 1960s Eero Saarinen futuristic-looking terminal at JFK always reminded me of being

Jonah in the whale. And when I was a teenager, $199 student fares were popular, so we would go to London every five seconds. I mean, I love New York and I would never want to be based or live anywhere else, but leaving New York has its own special thrill.

Even if I'm not going to JFK to leave, it's still exciting to watch the aircraft. On a clear day it can be mesmerizingly great fun to sit in the parking fields at JFK and watch planes approach and land! Up until 1998, Kai Tak was Hong Kong's airport, which was especially famous for its dramatic landing approach as the pilots would have to make an extreme left turn to avoid a hillside, tipping the plane on its side, which really seemed like you were about to crash to the uninitiated! A Cathay Pacific pilot told me that one particular runway at JFK actually had an even more extreme approach than Kai Tak. So if you go to the public parking lot at the JFK AirTrain stop, you have the perfect vantage point to watch the planes come in, veer to one side, and then land. Although it may seem less dramatic without the hillside!

Airliners.net is my favorite website. It's for pilots and probably a lot of teenage geeks. But there I am, falling somewhere in between. I'm happily one of them.

John F. Kennedy International Airport (JFK), JFK Expy, Jamaica; (718) 244-4444; www.panynj.gov/airports/jfk.html

. . . .

Richard Kirshenbaum, author and chairman of Kirshenbaum Bond Senecal + Partners, one of the nation's largest creative advertising agencies

I absolutely love auctions. I've sort of become a bit of an addict. They're what I call museums with prices. You can visit the Metropolitan Museum of Art or the Guggenheim and they're wonderful, but you can learn so much more about the art at an auction viewing.

When you see a piece of art at a museum, it might list a little bit of information about the artist and when the painting was painted. But what's interesting about auction houses is that not only do they list the artist and when the piece was painted, they also list provenance. You can see the seven or ten owners of the painting. Provenance plays a big deal in terms of who owns a specific piece of art. The catalogue also lists where the piece might have been exhibited. The price estimate is listed, which is usually a high and low range.

What's also great about attending auction viewings is you don't have buy anything. They're completely free and open to the public. And very often, when things come available at auction, they go into a private collection. You have an opportunity to see some really amazing things that you may never see again, because they may go to a buyer in Europe, or Asia, or someone who just wants to be private with the piece.

Auction houses list their schedules and tend to have shows at the same time. Generally, Christie's and Sotheby's will auction contemporary, modern, or impressionist art within days of each other. They're really trained professionals and do a marvelous job.

You can go to a viewing, see the piece, and have someone take it off the wall and handle it for you. You can look at the back of the painting, which I find even more interesting. The back of the painting usually reveals bits of clues, a little history of the piece—which galleries owned it, if there are inscriptions.

The only thing that you have to pay for are auction catalogues, which sometimes can be fairly expensive glossy catalogues. They can also be viewed online for free. And of course, there's the cost if you bid on something and buy it. But there's a very large range of auctions. People think auctions only sell the most expensive things, but there's a number of auction houses in the city that sell lower priced antique furniture, prints, bric-a-brac, and jewelry. There's a spectrum in the city for everybody.

The real exciting part is to attend an auction and bid on something. One of the most thrilling auctions for me was when I brought my 10-year-old daughter to Christie's to her first auction. She is very interested in art. On a Sunday, I'll bring her to the museum with a sketchpad and she'll go into the Impressionist room and sketch. So to be able to take her to see some really wonderful art and then bid was wonderful. I wanted to buy something that she would have a hand in and we bought together. She held the paddle and it was really fun for her. There is such a feeling of exhilaration at an auction. And we actually bid on and won a Man Ray sculpture from the 1920s.

Experiencing an auction gives you a whole other perspective about the art market. There's something about it that's alive. The average person may not be able afford a great painting, but that said, you can view it when it becomes available at auction.

Sotheby's, 1334 York Avenue; (212) 606-7000; www.sothebys.com

Christie's, 20 Rockefeller Plaza; (212) 636-2000; www.christies.com

. . . .

Spike Lee, Emmy-winning, Academy Award- and Golden Globe-nominated director, writer, and producer

I go to Knicks games, Yankee games, Broadway plays, Alvin Ailey—all of that.

. . . .

Neal Shapiro, president and CEO of WNET

One of my favorite things to do is to visit Yankee Stadium in the Bronx with my family. If I could, I would go to every game two hours early and wander through Monument Park. You can see plaques honoring all the great Yankees, those whose playing days ended before I was born, like Ruth, Gehrig, DiMaggio, and those whose careers I watched with my own eyes: Mantle, Munson, Mattingly, Jackson, and Guidry. For trivia fans, there's also a plaque for a Pope and a new bronze plaque for George Steinbrenner, which is impossible to miss. Then, I'd watch batting practice and watch the Yankees hitting long arcs into the late afternoon sky: going . . . going . . . gone!

. . . .

David Cross, actor, Emmy-winning writer, comedian

Part of my joy for New York is that you can get and do anything you want—whenever you want. There's an energy and a close-knit community feeling here that I always loved and missed when I go to other places. And I'm a foodie too. There's a never-ending supply of food, great bands play, and all my friends are here.

My perfect day in New York? I'll get to do it a couple of times a year if I'm lucky. My friend and I will ride our bikes to 34th Street on the pier on the Hudson River and we'll get on the *Yankee Clipper* and take the ferry up to Yankee Stadium to see the Red Sox beat the Yankees [the *Yankee Clipper* has been replaced by the *Delta Baseball Water Taxi*]. I love it that it combines everything that I adore. It combines biking—it's such a great city to bike in. It combines being on the water, which is wonderful. It combines baseball, which I love, and Red Sox which I really love.

Delta Baseball Water Taxi, (212) 742-1969; www.nywatertaxi.com/commuters/baseball-ferry

. . . .

Keith Olbermann, broadcaster, political commentator, and writer

My love for baseball started with the Yankees when I was 8 years old. I have no idea how to describe it. It's like a religion. It was always kind of an entree to the world of an adult. It was like jumping into it.

. . . .

Angelo Vivolo, owner of the restaurants Vivolo, Bar Vetro, and Cucina Vivolo

I am an avid baseball fan. Since I was a little kid, my team has been the New York Yankees. And if I'm not in the restaurant or running my business, I'll always try to take a peek at a game. I'm actually such a fan that I watch repeats of the games at one o'clock in the morning. It's kind of my relaxation. In fact, before he passed away Joe DiMaggio was a client of mine for thirteen years and we became friends. He used to come to my restaurant regularly. I'd think, here an Italian kid from Brooklyn gets to meet one of the greatest baseball players and athletes in America. So one of my favorite things is to go to Yankee Stadium to watch the Yankees play.

Even though the stadium is new, I feel the history, the tradition of the city and the Bronx. The new building is laid out so well, everyone who visits has great views of the field. And the restaurants now are totally different. They're real restaurants, not fast-food places. They're really done well. But at the end of the day I like eating a hot dog with good old deli mustard. It makes me feel like I'm really at a baseball game.

New York Yankees, Yankee Stadium, 161st Street and River Avenue, Bronx; (718) 293-4300; http://newyork .yankees.mlb.com

....

Paul Gunther, president, Institute of Classical Architecture & Art

Since New York existed, people have always talked about the deliciousness of quiet when it's heightened by the hubbub going on around them. Years ago, I remember a poet talking about being in his apartment here and he could hear the subway rumbling beneath him. And the thrill of the coziness of solitude in his apartment was heightened by the frenzy of human activity that was right outside. There's such a wonderful contrast of peace and frenzy.

In that spirit, over the years, I have looked for the mysterious and wonderful opportunity to be in the city and yet, somehow, in a peaceful space, within that frenzy. I've lived here for 35 years. And one of the most ironical paradoxical places is the Metropolitan Museum of Art where you can go into certain galleries, even on the most crowded Sunday, and literally by going down a passage or through a doorway, you're suddenly in extreme quiet.

I find that most extreme quiet at the Islamic Galleries. You can hear a pin drop. And while I love Islamic art, and it's a very important collection, it's not necessarily the objects themselves. It's just a chance to contemplate them in this calm heightened by the frenzy that's going on down the hall. So I savor that funny contrast. It's something that I've always sought out—where time is left behind and yet it's not just nostalgic. It's just a place of more possibility, of sort of silent communion.

A very different place where I also find this kind of joy is the Japan Society. It's a '60s modernist place and still has this magical, peaceful, calm and relatively tranquil feel. You go over a stairway to an interior Japanese bamboo water garden that has a pond with a slight ripple and a glass ceiling. I can sit there in this sweet place for hours. Then you go up to a suite of galleries on that second floor and at one point there is a passage that looks down onto this little garden. There's something deeply comforting about the experience regardless of what's on view.

Here you can be in one of those one of those passageways going from Point A to Point B and just by slipping across the threshold, you're in this sea of tranquility. And when you walk into the garden you know it's just more or less unchanging. For me, it's the magic of the unchanging. The Japan Society has done these Japanese post-war cartoon, edgy, vaguely shocking shows. But nonetheless it's within this unchanging quiet context that I adore.

The Metropolitan Museum of Art, 1000 5th Avenue; (212) 535-7710; www.metmuseum.org

Japan Society, 333 East 47th Street; (212) 832-1155; www.japansociety.org

. . . .

Malcolm Gets, Tony Award–nominated actor

I love to go to the public library—especially the Lincoln Center Library for the Performing Arts. I spend a lot of time there. That particular library has alternating exhibits that are incredible—everything from the history of ballet costumes to the life of Jerome Robbins. And on the third floor, you can watch Broadway and off-Broadway shows on video.

I also adore Madison Square Park. In my lifetime, I've seen the park gloriously restored. It's just dazzling. They have these changing art exhibits there and it's landscaped beautifully. And it's a part of New York that still has a vibe of what New York was like 100 years ago. And I sit there and stare at the park and the Flatiron Building and imagine that Edith Wharton has passed by.

New York Public Library for the Performing Arts, 40 Lincoln Center Plaza; (917) 275-6975; www.nypl.org/locations/lpa

Madison Square Park, 10 Madison Avenue; (212) 538-1884; www.madisonsquarepark.org

. . . .

John Patrick Shanley, Academy Award–winning screenwriter and director, Pulitzer Prize–winning playwright

Grand Central Station is one of the great public spaces in New York. One of the things about being a New Yorker is that when you enter a large public space, you experience a special exhilaration. There is compression to the city in general. And when you enter Grand Central, you suddenly feel a tremendous relief. The guys who designed that vaulted ceiling and sky must have known that. In the most pleasant way, they must have had that feeling of insignificance.

Sometimes I visit Grand Central to rendezvous with someone. But I'll arrive early and enter through the Vanderbilt Avenue side. There's a bar on the immediate left that is part of the public space and you can sit and look down like a Roman emperor.

I always visit Grand Central wearing scuffed shoes. It's the only place in New York where I'll get a shoeshine. For me, I need to have a reason to do something. So I won't aimlessly go to Grand Central. Most people who go there go to leave, to travel. They go with a purpose. The shoeshine motivates me to cross the whole public space.

If you enter like I do through the west side, you have to walk through the entire space to get to the shoeshine stand. And I like to look up at the ceiling, which is painted like the night sky with so many stars. When I get to the shoeshine stand, the payoff is not only the shine (they do a fantastic job) but the opportunity to look at people as they go by, which is my particular pleasure in life.

The first time I visited Grand Central Station, nobody told me to look up. It wasn't until I came back as an adult and I looked up that I really understood how great the room was. And after the renovation, when the ceiling was uncovered, I had a certain sense of anticipation. It felt like the world was opening up and you could fly up right through it.

I adore Grand Central, but you really need to hold out and have scuffed shoes in your closet before you go.

....

Sir Clive Gillinson, artistic director, Carnegie Hall

The place that I adore is Grand Central Station. I think it is the most incredible, spectacular building. And it speaks of the age of which it was built—where everything was built for beauty, for perfection, to sort of create something that was really monumental. It was built at a time when nobody would think, can we afford to do it this way? I just find it incredibly majestic—something so stylish. It's huge, yet feels quite intimate.

The lobby is spectacular. I love looking at the space—the gorgeous ticket offices with their grills, beautiful glass brass handrails, astronomical ceilings, those breathtaking windows where sometimes the beams of light just come in in such an extraordinary way. And I love the elegant staircases, that amazing four-sided clock, and the Tiffany glass clock facing 42nd Street with those statues all around it. Then you have the low arches down below on the concourse. It's just one thing after another. Grand Central is just one of the great places in the world. And all this stuff has been restored like it was originally.

If I'm anywhere nearby, I sometimes go in just to walk around and enjoy the space. And I like eating at the Oyster Bar. The food is fantastic. But it's such a gorgeous environment to just sit and relish where you are. Funny enough, I don't eat oysters. But I love the selection of different fish: smoked salmon, prawns, and crab. They have a lovely clam chowder. It's all very fresh.

I first saw Grand Central in the '70s when I came here to play for the London Symphony Orchestra. And I don't think it was as restored and as beautiful as it is today. I could have never imagined it. It was unimaginable that a railroad station was built like that or that anyone would build a space like that. If it was one of the world's great libraries or one of the world's great institutions, like a museum, you could imagine that conception. It's a bit like when you step inside Carnegie Hall and walk into the Isaac Stern Auditorium. It takes your breath away and you just feel you're in one of the world's magical places. Well, that's what I feel stepping into Grand Central Station.

Grand Central Terminal, 87 East 42nd Street; (212) 340-2583; www.grandcentralterminal.com

Grand Central Oyster Bar, 89 East 42nd Street; (212) 490-6650; www.oysterbarny.com

....

David Hyde Pierce, Golden Globe–nominated, Emmy- and Tony Award–winning actor

I remember my early days as a young actor here. You could be out of work and pretty hopeless, but you walk down the street in New York and you're constantly stimulated by the wild people that you see, the level of discussion you hear in a restaurant, the intelligence of the people, and also the toughness of living here as well. All of that is really exciting.

[If I had free time] I would go to some great piano recital at Carnegie Hall. It's the history. It's the sound. It's the artists who play there. And I have a friend who gets me really good seats.

Carnegie Hall, 154 West 57th Street; (212) 247-7800; www.carnegiehall.org

....

John Leguizamo, Tony- and Golden Globe–nominated and Emmy-winning actor, writer, and director

New York is such a cross pollination of cultures. It continues to be the intellectual center of the United States. There's the UN, all the heads of magazines, some of the best writers, the top thinkers are here. It's a close portal to Europe, Asia, and South America.

The city inspires me in terms of life. Living in New York, you feel part of the world and you feel connected. And there are the restaurants. You can't beat the variety of food. I can easily find Ethiopian food, Spanish, Filipino, and French all here. I grew up in Queens and there was always a bit of a dream to go to Manhattan. The best dances were coming out of Manhattan. People may say rap was born in the Bronx, but it started to come to life in Manhattan. I started doing performance art in the '80s. This was the center of performance art with Eric Bogosian, Spaulding Gray, and Lily Tomlin.

Besides, there's nothing like a pick-up basketball game in New York City. You can't get more fun than New Yorkers playing ball on the street on a public court. They're rowdy but fun. And they're not as aggressive as people would think. Or I sometimes go to West 4th Street and 6th Avenue and play handball. I play a little, just to let off some steam. I either play against other people or play by myself. Usually I play by myself because I'm not as good as I used to be.

And I love museums and bookstores. The Metropolitan Museum of Art is my favorite. I'm Latin and I like to discover where I came from. So I spent a lot of time in the Aztec and Mayan ruins sections. I also love the Roman Empire. I don't know if it's because I saw *I Claudius* and it's one of my favorite PBS movies and books. That history is all so alive. And it's so interesting to see real people in statues who you read about. You look at their real features—those sinister looks—you can almost see them plotting against each other.

I first remember going to the Metropolitan when I was on a school trip when I was about 12 or 13. We got to the Dark Ages exhibits and I looked at all the armor and all the swords and all those elements. That really sank into me.

....

Tom Seaver, New York Mets Hall of Fame pitcher

One thing this city did was make me want to take my children to London and Paris to see the same kind of stuff. I mean, I selfishly wanted to see it myself—see their art, their architecture, people. New York made that possible for me because there was so much energy and so much going on. If you live in New York, well, listen. I can go to London. I took my kids to London when they were babies. Then the next year we went to Paris. Great stuff.

My favorite thing is to have moments shared with my three girls—one of those includes my wife. And one of my great joys is taking my children to museums. If I had to pick one in New York, it would be taking them to the Museum of Modern Art. I didn't have the ability to do that when I was growing up in Fresno, California. But we were lucky enough to have that at our fingertips. I enjoyed it and I know my children enjoyed it so much that my daughter, Sarah, was an art history major by the time she got to Boston College and ultimately worked for Sotheby's.

I am drawn to modern art. If I had to put a name on it's Richard Diebenkorn. His work is almost spiritual for me. There's just some string that clutches onto your heart. And that's what's got me with the Diebenkorns. I was happy to be able to share that with my girls. But they all had different likes and dislikes too.

I remember when I made about a handful of six or eight players from the Chicago White Sox go to a museum of western art in Texas. I said, "Now listen, we're going to an art museum." And they slopped that off and said, "Baloney, we're not going." I didn't tell them it was a museum of western art. The greatest part was that we got there and they found these beautiful western scenes from great western artists and saddles. They said, "Wow! I never knew this stuff was here."

That was fun. Actually, I took them because I didn't want to pay the cab fare all by myself.

I still love art museums. I rue the day when there was a certain Diebenkorn I wanted to purchase in a gallery on Madison Avenue twenty, twenty-five years ago. I didn't pull the trigger on that one. It was way too much money back in those days. That was the one that got away. I admit. I couldn't have paid for it. But I wish I had.

....

Nancy Novogrod, editor in chief, *Travel + Leisure*

For me, going to the museums and galleries has always represented a kind of freedom. Maybe they are signifiers of a kind of worldliness. The art was often from elsewhere. There were big ideas behind it, and it just reflected a broader world. Also it was beautiful. And I liked the privacy of it—that I could wander through these places on my own. You didn't need someone.

To be alone and wandering through a gallery and a museum was a very expansive and exciting experience. And when I was pretty young, maybe 14, I went to museums on my own sometimes. I still remember some exhibits that I saw like the Gertrude Stein show or Cezanne or Bonnard, which were at MoMA. I remember the great exhibition when Thomas Hoving was director at the Metropolitan Museum called *Harlem on My Mind* in the 1960s. All of these experiences were so exciting and so mind expanding.

The feeling that I now have of exhilaration when I go to a museum, show, or gallery is a holdover from that. What I love to do on weekends is to make time to take a route down 5th Avenue. I'll go to the Guggenheim, the Neue Galerie, and the Metropolitan. All in one day. And there are pretty places at the Met and Guggenheim to have coffee. Cafe 3, the coffee bar in the Guggenheim, is wonderful because it overlooks Central Park and the reservoir. I've been there early in the day and I've been there at sunset, and it's just extraordinarily beautiful and a great place to relax. Most recently, I was there with my son. You can sit around. It's not so comfortable, but it's wonderful to sit on chairs and look at the view.

At the Met, I always go to the photography exhibitions, and I'll often stop to see the Asian art. And they have great changing exhibitions including photography from their own collection that are always interesting. And I particularly like Chinese ceramics, Japanese screens, and the Astor court. The ascetic pleases me.

And I believe that the Neue Galerie is one of the best things that has opened in New York in the last 20 years. It is beautifully designed by Annabelle Selldorf. It has a jewel-like permanent collection of Secessionist art paintings and work by Josef Hoffmann, Koloman Moser, Otto Wagner, Adolf Loos, and others. They have some of the greatest objects and paintings from that period, and also changing exhibitions that are really quite wonderful. Cafe Sabarsky, if you can get in, is a great place to go for lunch. Kurt Gutenbrunner, the well-known Austrian chef in New York, has the restaurant concession. It's like one of the great Viennese cafes.

Another place I love is the MoMA. It's wonderful to have lunch at the counter of the Modern restaurant on a Saturday—especially if you're by yourself. And I eat light things at the counter. They have a wonderful egg that comes in a cup.

The Metropolitan Museum of Art, 1000 5th Avenue at 82nd Street; (212) 535-7710; www.metmuseum.org

Neue Galerie, 1048 5th Avenue; (212) 628-6200; www.neuegalerie.org

Solomon R. Guggenheim Museum, 1071 5th Avenue; (212) 423-3500; www.guggenheim.org

The Museum of Modern Art, 11 West 53rd Street; (212) 708-9400; www.moma.org

....

Dick Cavett, Emmy-winning television host, actor, and author

There's a curious ritual that I've repeated, maybe twenty times over the years. Maybe more.

I relive and revisit my first hours in New York City when I got off that train from Lincoln, Nebraska—decades ago—on my way to freshman year at Yale.

Re-enacting my ritual, first I find the approximate track where I emerged from that train and took my first step—although not yet on a street—in the city of my dreams. I had changed trains in Chicago after a fitful upright sleep. I loved Chicago, but knew that New York was the big time.

Speeding along the rails beside the Hudson, I suddenly began to hear the opening lines of that great old radio show, *Grand Central Station*—brought to us "by Pillsbury Baking Flour." Back then I could recite from memory the stirring opening of the show with reasonably assured accuracy.

Pausing just now, I find that I still can recite it, without, of course, the wonderful, chill-giving whistle and speeding locomotive sound effects from the already declining era of the great trains. For those of a certain age, I submit it here for nostalgia purposes, hoping it raises pleasant goose flesh on those who remember it. It still does on me.

As a bullet train seeks its target, shining rails in every part of our great country are aimed at Grand Central Station, heart of the nation's greatest city. Drawn by the magnetic force of the fantastic metropolis, day and night great trains rush toward the Hudson River, sweep down its eastern bank for 140 miles, flash briefly by the long red row of tenement houses south of 125th Street, dive with a roar into the 2.5-mile tunnel which burrows beneath the glitter and swank of Park Avenue and then . . . Grand Central Station! Crossroads of a million lives! Gigantic stage on which are played a thousand dramas daily.

In my re-creation ritual, I find the (approximate) track from which I emerged from the train in mid-evening on that far-off day and took my first step—although still underground—onto long-dreamed-of Manhattan.

I feel sorry for folks who grew up in or near this great city, deprived of that thrill of first coming to it from the heartland, having New York segue from dream fantasy into reality.

My stepmother—who'd been in New York as a U.S. Marine during WWII—had made a map for me that led, still underground, to the lobby of the Roosevelt Hotel next door.

I checked in, and finally fell asleep with some difficulty—the words "I'm actually in New York" repeating in my head as I drifted off, not yet truly convinced that such a thing could be.

Back to my ritual. From the lobby of the Roosevelt, I find the exact door and the exact spot where, on that bright and thrilling morning so long ago I stepped down onto the sidewalk. I thought, and may have said aloud, "Now I, the former Little Dickie Cavett of 1825 South 23rd Street, Lincoln, Nebraska, really am in New York City! It's not there anymore. It's here."

Re-enacting this, I have to be careful not to be recognized so as not to tear the fabric of the reverie I feel each time; wondering then what New York was going to mean in my future life. Would I go back to Nebraska? Could I ever really leave the east and the Manhattan that I seemed somehow destined for?

Might this great city somehow prove to be a major part of my life? Now, more than a half century later, I recall standing there for a moment before taking my first walk in this majestic place. What wondrous things lay before me to discover here, following my magic carpet ride to Manhattan from the Great Plains?

A lot has happened since then . . .

And I'm here.

....

Jon Robin Baitz, playwright and screenwriter

I'm a very big fan of the Neue Galerie on the Upper East Side. And I love just sitting in Cafe Sabarsky on the first floor. It's sort of a quiet and a great place to read. And for some reason, I'm able to write there. I don't know why. And I'll have apple strudel *mit schlag* (with whipped cream).

I've tried all the other places, but I keep coming back to New York. Last week I saw *Nixon in China*, I saw a workshop of a play, and ran into a bunch of painters I knew on the street. Every night to me in New York—whether it's a quiet night or a bigger night—is magic. I mean I stepped on a dead rat to get here tonight—a dead frozen rat. And I thought, in LA that doesn't happen. But I'm much happier here—stepping on a rat to get where I need to go instead of driving.

Neue Galerie and Cafe Sabarsky, 1048 5th Avenue; (212) 628-6200; www.neuegalerie.org

....

Jay Jay French, Twisted Sister guitarist and founder of the Pinkburst Project

In almost every major city in the world, the neighborhoods between the rich and the poor are drastically divided, and people don't cross the tracks. But in this city, nearly every single person from every walk of life, every financial strata, every religious denomination, and every color goes down to the subway every damn day. You see every kind of person. And you know what happens when you see so many different people every day? You have no fear. Fear is brought on by ignorance and by lack of exposure. And New York City exposes you to everything every day to the point that you become understanding, you're more empathetic, you're more charged up, and you're not afraid. And that is one of the intellectual strong points of this city.

One of the greatest things to do in New York is visit the Riverside Church on 125th Street. It's one of the most amazing sights in the city. Riverside Church is a stunning church right along the Hudson River and just across from Grant's Tomb. I love to take the elevator to the top of the tower and walk on a catwalk outside above the bells. It's actually one of the highest points in New York and overlooks the George Washington Bridge, so the view is utterly magical.

On a beautiful day you look north along the Hudson and see up through the Tappan Zee Bridge. And luckily the Palisades are undeveloped and look so pristine. And you can walk around the other side and see Lower Manhattan and the Hudson River down all the way to the Battery and beyond. It's an unfettered view of New York. There's nothing else around that church that is close to that height, so you really get a breathtaking view of the city. Sometimes it's closed due to construction, so call and ask if it's open. It's probably a very underused tourist attraction in New York.

The Riverside Church of New York, 490 Riverside Drive; (212) 870-6700; www.theriversidechurchny.org

. . . .

Maguy Le Coze, owner, Le Bernardin

I live close to my restaurant which means that I am also very close to MoMA (Museum of Modern Art). And so if I have about thirty minutes, I just pop in. I always find something new to see for about fifteen minutes or so. And I'll take another fifteen-minute look at something else on the same floor or gallery. I don't like the contemporary, contemporary art where you don't understand what you are looking at. But I always love seeing the Picassos.

Also, I discovered opera late in life and I'm still in the process of appreciating it. On a Saturday afternoon during the opera season, I'll arrive at about 12:30 and you can always get a ticket. I love the music, but sometimes I'll just go for the singer, like Marina Poplavskaya. And when the orchestra begins it's so magical.

The Museum of Modern Art, 11 West 53rd Street; (212) 708-9400; www.moma.org

....

Lidia Bastianich, best-selling cookbook author, television star, and restaurateur

I love music and adore the Metropolitan Opera. And one thing that I've been doing for years is going to their open rehearsals. Tickets are either much less expensive than a regular performance or sometimes they're free. Anybody can go and you can even bring your own lunch inside. It's so interesting to see the conductor and the orchestra interacting. Some of the shows are dress rehearsals, and the conductor will stop in the middle and will make corrections then move on. So it's kind of hiccupping sometimes. It's great because you notice what the conductor is looking for. Also if you see it again, you get to learn if there are changes to the scenery or the lighting. You are part of all that. I think of it as a front row backstage experience. It's been happening forever.

When I go to the opera, the music transcends me. I relate to the language and the customs, but basically, for me, it's all about the music. I float on the melodies. It lightens me. It makes me feel good and recharged. It's like the gratification that a great flavor of food provides or a wonderful glass of wine. The elements add depth and complexity to your life—through your senses. Opera is life magnified. I think that the cycle goes: setting up the stage, falling in love, and then dying for what you love. Most of the operas have that.

One opera that really stayed with me is *Aida*. I remember seeing it at the old Met with Leontyne Price and Franco Corelli. It was wonderful. I was very young, maybe 16, and I was seated way, way up because that's all I could afford. And it was just electrifying. I remember Leontyne's voice. She just projected and it blew me out of my seat even from where I was all the way up. I also remember the procession of all the animals walking onstage, those camels.

Recently, I saw the new production of *La Traviata*, which is a contemporary take on the classical one. I had my reservations about the scenery but the music was magnificent. The conductor, Gianandrea Noseda, is a friend. And I just I took my grandchildren to see *Rigoletto*. They're young, just 7 and 11 , but they appreciated it. These kinds of memories stick with you. Arias in *Rigoletto* like "La donna e Mobile" stay with you forever. If you're a child, that music is haunting. These kinds of things are beautiful.

During *Rigoletto* we were in the Grand Tier where you can have dinner. It's a whole celebration. The beauty of that is, first you have you have your appetizer and main course. And then before you see the first act, you order dessert. You come back after the first act and your dessert is waiting. The kids were just thrilled by that.

There's a special feeling at the Met—whether you're in a box or all the way up or in the middle of the orchestra behind the conductor. Different places give you a different feeling. If I'm sitting in the orchestra behind the conductor, I actually follow the conductor's energy—how he almost has bolts of lightning on the performers. You can see when he lets go of his hand, there's a reaction. It's beautiful to see— kind of being in synthesis.

The Metropolitan Opera, Lincoln Center; (212) 362-6000; www.metopera.org

....

Joanne LaMarca Mathisen, supervising producer, *Today*

Every time my five-year-old son and I ride over the George Washington Bridge, I say to him, "What bridge is this? What river is this? Where's Mommy?" He's known those answers since he was three. He knows how much the bridge means to me.

One of my favorite things is to walk, run, or ride over the George Washington. I ache for it. I say to my son, "One day, Mommy is going to take you on a bicycle trip and we're going to go over the bridge and down the path all the way to the ferry and ride the river."

There's a path on the upper level and it's often packed with bike riders and runners. You just feel like you're on vacation when you're on it. I think about the history and beauty of the bridge—how it stands there so strong. There's that expansive structure, the big sky, and the Palisades that jets out from behind it. And you think in the scheme of things, your problems are so small because of how big it is.

People worked on that bridge for years. Sometimes I'll stand in front of it and think, OK, before 1931, this bridge wasn't here. There was this big gap between New Jersey and New York. It must have changed people's lives to be able to finally go back and forth all the time. It has meant so many different things to people. I can't help but look at it and think about how far we've come.

When 9/11 happened, I was at work and we were on the air. And soon after that, Tom Brokaw's assistant received anthrax in the mail and they put us on lockdown. They tested us. They gave us Cipro. I remember going home to my apartment that overlooked the George Washington. And I was thinking, what is this world coming to? And the next morning I woke up and there were helicopters going over the bridge and under the bridge and over and under, and I thought, oh my God, they're going to take away my bridge. I thought, my bridge can't go. That's my bridge. That bridge has so much meaning to so many people. And to me it symbolizes peace.

. . . .

Elise Finch, WCBS-TV meteorologist

My favorite thing to do in New York City is to see Alvin Ailey American Dance Theater perform during the holidays at New York City Center. I especially like to catch them on a night when they are performing *Revelations*, the company's signature work.

When Ailey is at City Center around Christmas, they perform two to four pieces during each show. *Revelations* is usually performed around 75 percent of the time because people like me look forward to seeing it again and again. The pieces they perform are always listed, so ticket buyers can choose what they want to see.

Alvin Ailey American Dance Theater was founded in 1958 by a dancer named Alvin Ailey. He used his training in ballet, modern, jazz, and African dance and infused it with blues, spirituals, gospel, and what he called his "blood memories" of growing up in Texas during segregation. To me, *Revelations* is the most touching example of his work. Divided into three sections, the piece uses traditional African-American spirituals to explore what they call "the places of deepest grief and holiest joy in the soul." Every time I see it I am in awe of its beauty and complexity. I cry during each performance I see, but look forward to shedding those tears each year.

Alvin Ailey, New York City Center, 131 West 55th Street; (212) 581-1212

Ana Gasteyer, actress and singer

I live in Dumbo where there's an explosion of beautiful parks. The Brooklyn Bridge Park has become one of my favorite places in the world. And it's incredible for my kids who play there. There's the giant tobacco warehouse and bridge behind you. It's just heaven. I feel so lucky that I get to be so close to that incredible piece of greenery. You just sit there and see the Staten Island Ferry and watch the boats go by. It makes you realize that we live on an island city.

Also what I love about New York is that something as simple as walking across the Brooklyn Bridge can be a heart-stopping experience. As a New Yorker there are a few moments that you can repeat over and over again that echo the original experience of coming here if you weren't born here. There's the heart rush and the intensity of a million people all in one place.

I also get a rush when I'm at the spot where Broadway and 7th Avenue converge in Times Square. When you are facing Times Square looking north, you feel like you are in the middle of the universe. And it's really exciting. It doesn't matter what time you are there. No matter how many Broadway shows I've done. When I'm standing right in Times Square, there's that feeling of I live in a massive and important place and I'm just a tiny piece of this huge machine that is this city.

Sometimes when I walk across the Brooklyn Bridge, I wonder how did people think to settle here? All these boats that sailed up. I think of the people that emerged and houses and villages that were built. It's kind of mind-blowing.

I didn't grow up here. I had an aunt and uncle here who I used to visit a lot. I remember coming from California to test for *Saturday Night Live*. I can picture myself standing and looking up. In California, everything is so horizontal. And I was standing right by 30 Rock. And I thought, I am surrounded in 100 percent of directions by humanity. Your heart starts to jump into your throat and it's intoxicating.

....

Lillias White, Tony Award–winning actress and singer

When I'm performing on Broadway on a day when there's a matinee and evening performance, sometimes, between shows, I ride the Staten Island Ferry. I love taking the time to head to the ferry terminal to take the boat to Staten Island and back. It's a chance to get some air. I have an opportunity to see beautiful New York City from the water. The views are so gorgeous. You get to pass right by the Statue of Liberty. And being on the ocean and feeling the waves rocking makes me appreciate nature. You know who's in charge. It gives me a reason to love what I do and makes me love New York even more. I'll ride over to Staten Island and come back and do my second show completely refreshed. I've been doing it for many, many years. It's good therapy.

The Staten Island Ferry, Whitehall Terminal, 4 South Street; (718) 876-8441; www.siferry.com

....

Cynthia Rowley, designer, author of the *Swell* series, and guest star on *Project Runway*

The afternoons I have free in New York, which are unfortunately few and far between, are ideally spent jetting around the city to as many art galleries as possible. A good art show is food for my eyes. The exciting thing about the New York art scene now is that it's not just limited to one style or geographic corner; good art is all over the place.

I suppose my dream day—culling from both past experiences and hopeful future visits—would be to kick off an afternoon by revisiting the "50 Years at Pace" exhibition that was up last year, which comprised works in all three of Pace's gallery sites . . . and not just run-of-the-mill curated material, but collections in which every piece was iconic, or just completely extraordinary!

My next stop would have to be the Gagosian Gallery, which always has fantastic work from some of the greatest artists of our era—Richard Prince, Dan Colen, John Currin—and the Gagosian bookstore is completely mesmerizing as well, as it hosts design objects in addition to its impressive collection of art volumes. Another of my favorite contemporary galleries is Gavin Brown, which recently exhibited my friend Rob Pruitt's art work, and Elizabeth Dee's place taps into brilliant talents like Josephine Meckseper and Ryan McNamara.

I like to end my gallery days on Orchard Street and in the spaces that surround my husband's HALF Gallery on Forsyth. It's the responsibility and the pride of these smaller galleries to discover the unsung treasures and new talents of the New York art world. And I'll be waiting to check them out!

The Pace Gallery, 534 West 25th Street: (212) 929-7000; 32 East 57th Street: (212) 421-3292; 545 West 22nd Street: (212) 989-4258; www.thepacegallery.com

Gagosian Gallery, 980 Madison Avenue: (212) 744-2313; 555 West 24th Street: (212) 741-1111; 522 West 21st Street: (212) 741-1717; www.gagosian.com

Gavin Brown's Enterprise, 620 Greenwich Street; (212) 924-5258; www.gavinbrown.biz

Elizabeth Dee, 545 West 20th Street; (212) 627-7545; www.elizabethdeegallery.com

HALF Gallery, 208 Forsyth Street; (212) 260-8797; www.halfgallery.com

....

Yigal Azrouël, fashion designer

My favorite thing to do in New York City is to surf. Surfing is my life. I don't check the weather, I check the wave conditions. And if it's a good wave, it doesn't matter how cold it is, I can go. I have the perfect wetsuit that keeps me warm. I go to Rockaway Beach—yes, even in the wintertime. It's gorgeous there and it gives me so much joy.

....

Amy E. Goodman, contributor to *Today* and author of *Wear This, Toss That!*

When you visit The Big Apple, you tick off the "firsts" straight out of a guidebook: a walk through Times Square, a frozen hot chocolate at Serendipity 3, the view from the Empire State Building. When you live in the city, seasonal must-sees are added. Thus, I set out the winter of 1999 as a journalism student at Columbia University's Graduate School of Journalism (dressed poorly in thin layers as only a native Californian would know how) for my first Christmas tree at Rockefeller Center, having heard of its legendary illumination.

As with all things great in NYC, it required everything short of an arm wrestle to get close enough to see it. Throngs of holiday shoppers poured in from 6th and 5th Avenues that fed into the heart of Rock Center, where the tree stood towering over the ice rink and gilded statue of Prometheus below. Dodging tourists' cameras and the jostling crowd, I started to lose my patience. Channeling my inner boxer, I ducked, swayed, and sprinted until I finally stood under the prodigious boughs of green.

Then I looked up.

Aside from the redwoods of Northern California, I'd never seen a tree so majestic. It is one thing to see a postcard, but quite another to stand beneath the grand specimen, traditionally a Norway spruce. All sounds faded and my vision zoomed as I searched for the top. In an instant, I felt the heart of the tree beating with mine. I realized that no matter what one's religion, the tree is a unifier in this diverse city . . . a symbol of something much bigger than any one person.

Since that first freezing encounter, I've pushed through numerous crowds and seen multiple Rock Center Tannenbaums and the magic is never lost. With my work around the corner and regular appearances on NBC's *Today* show a few steps away, I see the tree through various stages of development: the arrival on a crisp November morning, the scaffolds for light stringing, the Tree Lighting Ceremony broadcast live across the globe. What was once a 20-foot tree erected by construction workers during the Great Depression in 1931 has evolved to 30,000 environmental LED lights and a 550-pound Swarovski star topper. Even a helicopter is used for its initial discovery.

It's those dark December mornings when headed to studio that I cherish the most. At that before-dawn hour as I dash across the plaza, with eyes watering from the cold despite being bundled in a down coat, hat, and scarf, it's usually just me and the tree. And I always stop. And I look up. And I still feel pure, unwavering awe.

Rockefeller Center Christmas Tree, Rockefeller Plaza, between West 48th and West 51st Streets and 5th and 6th Avenues; (212) 632-3975; www.rockefellercenter.com

....

Alex Von Bidder, co-owner, Four Seasons Restaurant

New York is the most exciting place in the world and gives me the diversity of experience that I've never found anywhere else. It has a lot to do with the water and the people visiting. They're coming to us. It seems that nearly anywhere else, you have to go to an exciting place like this. Here you can have all this excitement or within an hour, you can be away in the mountains, in the woods, by the ocean. It's all available.

My favorite thing to do in New York is to sail. I like all boats. I like being on the water, getting some fresh air and a new perspective. And in New York City, you can go on a two-hour cruise like the *Shearwater* and forget all about your land of worries. You can go out for lunch, you can go out for cocktails. They do moonlit cruises by the Statue of Liberty.

All sailboats bring back memories of how it might have been. Instead of getting on a speed boat you get out there and take your chances on whether there's wind or not. But in either case you get away from Manhattan and you look at it from a different perspective. I see the enormity of Manhattan.

My fascination with Manhattan is how it went from this little plot of land that was inhabited by the Indians to this incredible metropolis. And I get the best view from farther away. When you go south from the tip of Manhattan, looking back is just fantastic and makes me feel good living here.

Whenever I go sailing with a group of people it's just magical. In the beginning there's lots of chatter and excitement. By the time you're out there about a half hour, 40 minutes, it turns silent, and everybody just listens to the sound of the water, the waves, and maybe the flapping of the sails, or the breeze. It becomes a meditation.

My favorite sail is the cocktail cruise. It's not about the cocktail, it's about the setting sun. It's the end of the day and usually you're tired or you're just exhausted from work, and it just refreshes everything, all the senses. The air is better. The salt air is better. And there's nothing as peaceful as looking at the water.

Shearwater Sailing, North Cove Marina, World Financial Center and the Hudson River; (212) 619-0885; www .shearwatersailing.com

....

Sarah Jones, Tony Award winning playwright, poet, and actress

I haven't found any place else that feeds me the way New York can, challenges me the way New York does, forces me to keep committed to writing and to discovering new characters. No place else has that connection for me in the same way.

Once a week, even every few days, my life is not complete unless I get on the subway. Actually, my office is next door to my apartment, so I don't even need that transportation to get to work anymore. And I live in the West Village and everything I do is pretty much near here. So, for me, the subway is now largely a research facility. I can't tell you how often my inspiration comes from just jumping on a train line that I would never otherwise discover. I may or may not actually have to go anywhere but on the train itself.

I rode out to Greenpoint the other day just to kind of look around at how the changes are happening with young hipsters mingling with Polish people and Russian people. Just being on the train gives you characters. The interactions people have, the people I bump into are endlessly inspiring. I met a woman the other day who inspired a new character I'm working on. She actually made a little bit of a splash in the music world years ago and now is singing with these incredible pipes underground.

I'll pick a line I'm not used to and usually go right up to people. And if they're street performers, or a guy playing the bucket or selling a CD, I always buy the CD or donate something. When they're taking a break as the train rumbles through and you can't hear them, I'll say, "You might think I'm crazy or you're not going to believe this but I'm doing research." Of course, they think I'm insane. And that's fine. Sometimes, I really do follow up with people. But, at the very least, I've got a music collection of CDs that I've bought.

In a way, the train is the most intimate public space there is because people have to live their lives. They have to interact. It's like being in the backseat of a cab but with 100 other people.

Sometimes the subway and the bus are the sites where stories are sort of weaving themselves right in front of my eyes. I grew up in Queens and used to ride the bus and take the subway there. And I became fascinated by the kind of narrative that I'd see playing out in front of me.

....

Karen Mason, actress and recording artist

When my husband, Paul, and I first moved out to Queens, we discovered a Home Depot right on Northern Boulevard. And of course, we suddenly needed nails and other household repair things and the Home Depot is open 24/7. During our trips there, we found a Stop & Shop almost next door. It's right off the N or R train on the 46th Street stop.

We discovered that the Stop & Shop has open rooftop parking and the view of the skyline of Manhattan is utterly spectacular! A lot of times Paul would just run in and get stuff and I'd be sitting in the car looking at this fantastic view. I love the skyline to begin with. It was always one of my favorite things when I first moved from Chicago. Coming from the airport, taking the taxi home, and seeing the island of buildings was always inspiring. And now to be able to see the skyline from the second floor open lot is so special. It's close enough you can see all the buildings and yet far enough that it just looks like Oz.

I see the height of the buildings, the depth of the city. I can see the Citicorp building, the Chrysler building, which is one of my favorites, and the Empire State—that whole center midtown-ish area that I grew up believing was New York. You're on the edge of this parking lot and there aren't a lot of tall buildings in Queens. So we get a really gorgeous unobstructed view. I could sit and watch and watch for hours.

Working in the theater at night, I don't get there at dawn very much, which I'm sure is spectacular. But I love visiting during dusk when the sun is coming down and the light is so beautiful. The perfect night is when it's kind of that pinky, bluey, gray thing that kind of happens.

During one summer, Paul and I actually made an awful lot more trips to the grocery store. And one night we heard the sound of a saxophone. There was a guy who would practice because nobody would tell him not to. Sometimes we would sit in the car, listen to the saxophone, and watch the skyline. It's so romantic and peaceful.

We used to live on 14th Street and could see the World Trade Center from our apartment. During 9/11, we basically watched it dissolve—which was so surreal. And so the skyline is even more precious to me now. As we get older, we start appreciating the frailty of everything, everyone, and the frailty of time. So I think, enjoy it now. And in fact, there are times when I just say to Paul, "No, no, I'll go to the Stop & Shop. Let me go. This will be my trip."

Super Stop & Shop, 34–51 48th Street, Long Island City; (718) 728-7724; www.stopandshop.com

....

Jenny Lumet, acclaimed screenwriter

I cannot think of a moment when I'm not inspired by New York. There's the diversity and passion of the people here. Stuff matters to people here. They care about art. Even if it's bad art, they care about it. And I'm so down with bad art.

When I need to get away, I like to check into fancy hotels. And we have some of the greatest hotels in the world here. During my last birthday, I checked into the Carlyle hotel and had room service. It was so civilized and quiet. The Carlyle has a great history. It's small, has a fantastic bar, beautiful murals—delicious. The rooms are gorgeous and the beds are like heaven. What's not to love about the hotel? If someone wants to foot the bill, I will go to the Carlyle three times a week. Absolutely.

The Carlyle, A Rosewood Hotel, 35 East 76th Street; (212) 744-1600; www.thecarlyle.com

....

Stone Phillips, Emmy-winning television journalist

I like going to Chelsea Piers and hitting golf balls. I love the challenge of getting the balls over the net and out into the Hudson River and always failing. I'm not a real golf aficionado. I play in a few tournaments here and there and I'm very mediocre. But it's fun to hit a few balls on a nice day. And I get a kick out of the fact that you can hit golf balls in Manhattan.

Chelsea Piers is a playground for boys and girls to have a ton of fun playing soccer, basketball and golf. I think it's one of the gems of New York. Before I was ever inside, I remember passing the place and thinking, that looks like a closet hut. What could possibly be in there? And then when I walked inside there was so much to it. And I go to a lot of dinners and charity functions there.

When I first set foot in the city, I said, "This is it, there is where I want to be." I love the diversity of New York. You can hear any language or see any skin color walking down the street. It's what America is all about. New York is a wonderful collection of all the wonderful things in the world.

Chelsea Piers Sports & Entertainment Complex, 62 Chelsea Piers; (212) 336-6666; www.chelseapiers.com

. . . .

Sally Jessy Raphael, Emmy-winning television host

I've been around the world during Christmastime—to London, Rome, Paris, Africa—but nothing compares to New York. Not even close. You can feel the energy and excitement all over the city. I love the twinkling lights and the crispness in the air.

New Yorkers make the most of the holiday. In other cities, maybe two department stores have windows. In New York, everybody does them. On my block, everyone—I mean everyone—goes caroling. You should see the combination of people—celebrities, politicians. It's just amazing.

My husband and I like to take people on a tour of the different windows of the stores. The biggies are Lord & Taylor, Macys, Saks, and Barneys, which does very hip, creative, and cutting-edge windows. We'll visit all of them in one day or night. Also, the windows are lit so you can do that at any time, which is great. And the store doesn't have to be open so it's not so dangerous for your pocketbook.

It's fun to begin our tour at the Rock Center Cafe next to the skating rink at Rockefeller Center. From the giant windows, you can watch people ice skate while you dine and get a nice view. It really puts you in the mood. Then we take an underground passageway to Saks. A lot of people from out of town don't know about the huge passageway between Rockefeller Center and Saks Fifth Avenue. Then we'll visit the window at Saks. And not only does Saks decorate their windows, they project stars on its entire building above the windows.

A great store to visit at Christmas is the Flight Club, which sells vintage and impossible-to-find sneakers. It's the perfect gift—especially for producers. They tend to wear sneakers. And it's a treasure for nearly any teenager. Many of the sneakers are limited edition and they've only made four or five of them.

And each year, the Metropolitan Museum of Art has the most beautiful tree with an elaborate Neapolitan baroque creche. I love that tree almost as much as the one at the Rockefeller Center. And they play beautiful a cappella Christmas music as part of the exhibit.

I am a veteran collector and model railroader. And when you do layouts for railroads, you always have to bear your gage in mind. You can't suddenly have a large human being standing next to a small railroad track. I've spent a lot of time thinking about the relative size of things and that creche tree is the best example of relative size. People don't realize that the figures in the back are almost double or triple the size of the figures in the front. They're arranged in gradual gradation.

Some figurines are very humorous, very funny, which you don't expect to find in a creche. You don't expect a funny donkey. But every year I see something on the tree that I didn't see before.

Flight Club, 812 Broadway; www.flightclubny.com

Saks Fifth Avenue, 611 5th Avenue; (212) 753-4000; www.saksfifthavenue.com

Rock Center Cafe, 20 East 50th Street; (212) 332-7620; www.patinagroup.com

....

Justin Gimelstob, Grand Slam Doubles tennis champion and broadcaster

What would be my ideal day in New York City? I'd start with a run in Central Park, then visit the Guggenheim Museum, have dinner at Scalinatella, and finish the night at the Boom Boom Room.

First of all, the park is fantastic and I ran in the marathon for the first time in 2010 for the Justin Gimelstob Children's Fund. Andy Roddick bet me $10,000 that I couldn't finish in under 4 hours, 45 minutes. But I hit the finish line by 4:09:58.

As for the Guggenheim, I just love modern art, especially Kandinsky and Picasso. Growing up in New Jersey and having three boys, my mom was quite overwhelmed by sports. One thing she demanded was that we got a little bit of culture. So she brought us to the Guggenheim when we were young and I've been going since.

I've been to the Peggy Guggenheim museum in Venice. And I'm hoping to get to all of their museums throughout the world. At the Guggenheim, the architecture is as appealing and interesting as the art. And so you get a nice combination of art and the building—it's a piece of art too. I grew up in a very modern house designed by a very famous modern architect, Charles Gwathmey. My parents introduced us to modern architecture at a very early age and gave us an appreciation for it. I thought it was cool when I discovered that Gwathmey worked on the Guggenheim.

And I love eating at Scalinatella Restaurant. It's one of those old-school Italian places with great food and a warm atmosphere. You go down the stairs and all of a sudden you are transported to another time. The old-school Italian waiters are dressed up in formal attire. You know that every single thing on the menu is going to be great.

The atmosphere at Scalinatella is formal but it's also inviting. They take great pride in their presentation but the quality of their food is also excellent. It's just one of those places where it's fun to get dressed up and have a night out. You feel it's an occasion when your night is built around having dinner there.

And then I go to the Boom Boom Room, the cool bar on top of the Standard Hotel—on the roof. The architecture is beautiful. Picture floor-to-ceiling windows, the bar is in the middle, and beautiful views high on the rooftop overlooking New York. It's just the place to be. It has a sexy vibe and they serve great martinis and champagne.

Solomon R. Guggenheim Museum, 1071 5th Avenue; (212) 423-3500; www.guggenheim.org

Scalinatella Restaurant, 201 East 61st Street; (212) 207-8280

The Boom Boom Room, 848 Washington Street; (212) 645-4646; www.standardhotels.com

....

Debi Mazar, actress and star of *Extra Virgin* on the Cooking Channel

My perfect day in New York? First, I'd wake up and have a fabulous coffee with my husband. I would go to brunch at Il Posto Accanto. It's a romantic Roman trattoria owned by my girlfriend Beatrice. She's from Rome, a fantastic cook and her dishes change depending on the season. The carbonara, a pasta with egg and bacon sauce is one of my favorites. It's like getting breakfast and dinner. And she does wonderful soups like minestrone.

I would have a fabulous brunch and then I'd walk along the Lower East Side to give my husband a verbal historical tour on Jacob Riis. I love New York history. Riis was a photographer from the mid to late 1800s. He came from Denmark and was so blown away by how the immigrants lived like 20 in an apartment. And he photographed and documented how they lived. You have to get his book, *How the Other Half Lives.*

So I would show my husband what Jacob Riis may have shot. Most of the buildings are gone, but you see the alleyways. And when I pass by I get a sense of how the immigrants lived. It reminds me of what my family went through. I feel like I didn't give up and came from nothing.

I used to live nearby on Bedford Street in a historical building built by the Dutch called Twin Peaks. It's one of the oldest buildings in the city and was all wood with fireplaces and so cool.

And after visiting, we would have some Puerto Rican food at La Taza De Oro on 8th Avenue and 15th Street. It's been there forever. I would probably get some mondongo (tripe soup), mofongo (mashed fried plantains), rice with gonzales beans, flan, and some Puerto Rican coffee. So I'd load up on that and we'd take a taxi and drive all though Harlem. And I'd give my husband a driving tour on the history of jazz to show him where all the music we love together all started between Sugar Hill.

From Harlem we'd go down the West Side Highway and through the tunnel and on to the Belt Parkway out to Brooklyn. The Belt Parkway is my favorite and I always loved it—you wrap around the city and it's right on the water. We used to pass a store called Caesar that sold dumb tacky, tacky stuff and you'd only find it there.

We would wait until it gets dark so we could see how the Verrazano Bridge looks like a string of pearls. We would pop some champagne and sit under the bridge and make out. And afterwards, we would go to L & B Spumoni Gardens in the heart of Bensonhurst for a slice of pizza. It's not my favorite pizza in the world. It's my favorite American Italian pizza. They have the best square pizza. It brings back a memory of a certain part of my life. Then we could go driving through Brooklyn, which is a city of churches. What a perfect day.

Il Posto Accanto, 190 East 2nd Street; (212) 228-3562; www.ilpostoaccanto.com

La Taza De Oro, 96 8th Avenue; (212) 243-9946

L & B Spumoni Gardens, 2725 86th Street; (718) 449-1230; www.spumonigardens.com

....

Lainie Munro, dancer, choreographer, and legendary dance teacher

My favorite New York is romantic New York. My husband and I love to visit all the places that were a part of our story of how we fell in love. We start with Serendipity and a frozen hot chocolate at this restaurant on East 60th Street, where we had our first date. Then we walk through Central Park over the bridge that spans the pond across from the Plaza Hotel, where we first kissed. Then we go to the gazebo on the lake—the spot where after a break, we decided to get back together. We'll walk to Cherry Hill where we had our wedding pictures taken with our families, and of course we like to finish our walk by lighting a candle in the church where we married, Blessed Sacrament on 71st Street. It's a beautiful church; the architecture and stained glass were inspired by the St. Chapelle in Paris.

Serendipity 3, 225 East 60th Street; (212) 838-3531; www.serendipity3.com

The Church of the Blessed Sacrament, 152 West 71st Street; (212) 877-3111; www.blessedsacramentnyc.com

....

David Parsons, artistic director and founder of Parsons Dance

I'm from Kansas City but I've been living on the Upper East Side since I was a very young man, a teenager. And what that does is give me a community. I live on Lexington Avenue between 90th and 91st. And when I have a free afternoon, I love to experience that block. Each side has all these wonderful businesses that I am a patron of and know. There's my laundry, shoe repair, hair place, coffee shop, pizza place, framer, and Turkish, Italian, and Japanese restaurants—all in one block.

Peri Ela is a wonderful Turkish restaurant to have lunch, and the owner knows me very well—since he opened his restaurant. And he's been to many of my productions. The restaurant serves the best Turkish food in New York City. I'm a lamb lover. And they have a lot of lamb dishes which I like.

I'll get a regular slice of pizza at my pizza place, Hana's Pizza. I'll pick up my shoes at the shoe repairman, Alex Shoe Repair. I'll grab my haircut at Giovanni Sacchi. We also have Juliano's coffee shop on the corner, which is a neighborhood haunt. They have the best coffee around. My Pilates studio, Mind Your Body Pilates, is there too. So I can yell out my window at my instructor. And it's all in one block.

The neighborhood is very dear to my heart and I love that it has a slower pace. There's just something about the small businesses that really make it a community. It's kind of a little oasis or a village. And it's nice to see a real quintessential New York block with a lot of businesses that are thriving.

Peri Ela, 1361 Lexington Avenue; (212) 410-4300; http://periela.com

Hana's Pizza, 1376 Lexington Avenue; (212) 987-9130

Alex Shoe Repair, 1364 Lexington Avenue; (212) 369-7211

Juliano Gourmet Coffee, 1378 Lexington Avenue; (212) 987-4540

Mind Your Body Pilates, 1370 Lexington Avenue; (212) 426-7960; http://mindyourbodyfitness.com

Giovanni Sacchi Hair Salon, 1364 Lexington Avenue; (212) 360- 5557; www.giovannisacchi.com

. . . .

J. Elaine Marcos, actress and dancer

I love to do ladies' night with my castmates from whatever Broadway show I'm in. Now I'm in *Priscilla Queen of the Desert*. All the ladies get together. Or sometimes, after a show closes, you don't get to hang out with them anymore. All you want to do is have that dressing room time. Often, we'll go to Spa Castle, which is a giant spa on several floors all the way out by Flushing, Queens.

It's hilarious. I literally go there all day because I just love to sweat. I love bikram yoga and I love the idea of just sweating my a** off. During the summer, there's an outdoor area where you can have massages. And there are all these muscle relaxing places. So it helps me relax and you can literally sleep in the sleeping rooms. It's kind of funny.

There are so many different saunas and Jacuzzis, and it's so removed from the city. I visited Spa Castle with the cast of my ladies from *A Chorus Line* and we were just all exhausted at the end of the day, because we were sweating like crazy. We take the 7 train all the way out, and there's a shuttle that just drives you right there. It's a great place.

Spa Castle, 131-10 11th Avenue; College Point; (718) 939-6300; www.nyspacastle.com

....

Juliette Jeffers, actress and author

I don't even have to think about it. My favorite thing is going to the Fountain of Youth, a small, quaint spa in Queens. I know about Spa Castle, which is great, don't get me wrong. But if I want a place where I can be zen and have some peace and quiet, I go to the Fountain of Youth. I get the scrub and massage combination and it seems as if they do not stop. They scrub, apply oil, work on your face, wash your hair; everything. It's all for like a hundred bucks! Afterward, you feel like you have baby skin. It's crazy. I also get the deep tissue shiatsu massage. The place is nothing fancy, but it gives me my zen moment.

Fountain of Youth Health Spa, 3202 Linden Place; (718) 445-1234

....

Joy Behar, Emmy-winning co-host of *The View,* host of *The Joy Behar Show,* comedian, and best-selling author

New York is the only place where on a Sunday you can run into a parade, a street fair, and ten people that you know by just taking a walk in your neighborhood. There's always something to do and all on the same day. Most of those things in most cities you'd have to wait like six months between them. Here it all happens on one day.

I like to go to the Walter Reade Theater to see foreign movies. It's one of the major things that people don't know about in this city. I mean, some people know, but it's mostly a big secret. They'll have a film festival with all the new French films, and they'll throw in some classics. Or they'll highlight Italian or Japanese cinema. You get to see movies that may or may not have any distribution in the rest of the country anywhere. I found Walter Reade because I like foreign films and I always search for them. Now I'm a regular Walter Reade patron through the Film Society of Lincoln Center. That's as highbrow as I get.

:....................................

Michael Moore, Academy Award–winning filmmaker, director, political commentator, and author

I would go to lots of movies that you can't see anywhere else. Right here. Foreign films, documentaries, independent films. I love the new cinemas at Walter Reade at Lincoln Center.

Walter Reade Theater, Lincoln Center; 165 West 65th Street; (212) 875-5600; www.filmlinc.com

....

Jane Stern, author

My favorite place in New York is the third floor of the Hospital for Special Surgery because it has the greatest view of the East River ever. I grew up on Sutton Place, and when I was a kid my windows looked out over the East River, the tugboats . . . It was an unobstructed view. Now I have to be sick to go and see that view, but it's worth it.

....

Michael Urie, actor

I love performing in shows at the Triad Theater on 72nd Street and Broadway. The Upper West Side neighborhood is great and the theater is adorable and not very big. It's the perfect intimate venue for music, cabaret, or a show like *Celebrity Autobiography*, which is there on a regular basis.

I jump at the chance to perform in *Celebrity Autobiography* because it's so much fun. Actors read from an autobiography of a celebrity. Even if I wasn't in the show, I would still recommend it for anybody coming to town. The audience laughs and laughs. It's truly delightful.

You never know who's going to show up and read—if it's Matthew Broderick, Kristen Wiig, or Ryan Reynolds. It's a real treat and always a little different. I love reading from David Hasselhoff's autobiography. He's a font of inspiration. Also, they do a great mash up where people read from Sylvester Stallone and Tommy Lee's autobiographies. Sylvester Stallone gives diet tips and Tommy Lee gives sex tips. I usually play Tommy Lee.

The first time I came to New York was the summer after I graduated from high school. I was with a community college theater group. I knew immediately, that I belonged and wanted to live here. I felt like a fish in water. We saw 13 plays in 10 days. Back home in Dallas, where my family took me to the theater a lot, I was lucky if I went to 13 plays in a year.

The first show we saw on that trip was *Ragtime* and we sat in the orchestra. I had seen Broadway national tours of big musicals in houses that were enormous. And while Broadway theaters are big, they're not as big. It might have been the first time I was seeing a musical where I could really see the actors' faces and feel part of it. That was before Audra MacDonald [one of the stars of the show] was Audra MacDonald. I felt like I was in on something very special and thrilling.

After the show, I remember coming out of the theater. Everybody was on a cloud because we loved it so much. It was playing on 42nd Street. At 11 p.m. it was still bright because of the lights in Times Square.

What is also profound about Times Square is that at 7:45 and from 10:30 to 11, there are just hordes of people walking around with tickets and Playbills. There are just so many theaters and so many seats that get filled.

Broadway is doing better than ever and had its best year ever last year. Of course, that has a lot to do with the fact that ticket prices are so high. But they're filling the seats. Shows are running.

Celebrity Autobiography, Triad Theater, 158 West 72nd Street; (212) 362-2590; www.celebrityautobiography.com

INDEX

ABOUT THE AUTHOR

Jeryl Brunner is a writer and journalist whose work has appeared in *O* magazine, *People*, *US Weekly*, *National Geographic*, *Traveler*, *Travel + Leisure*, *Delta Sky*, and *In Style*, where she was a staff correspondent for many years. She has interviewed hundreds of celebrities, including Meryl Streep, Julia Roberts, Nicole Kidman, and George Clooney. She lives in Manhattan. Visit her at www.mycitymynewyork.com.

© Karen Schaler